# FALLEN EAGLE

### HAROLD E. WILLS

"The budget should be balanced,
the treasury should be filled,
public debt should be reduced,
the arrogance of officialdom should be tempered and controlled,
and the assistance to foreign lands should be curtailed
lest we become bankrupt."—*Cicero, to the Roman Senate*

Halcyon House, Publishers
Kansas City, Missouri

# FALLEN EAGLE

Copyright © 1989 by Harold E. Wills

All rights reserved. No part of this book may be reproduced in any form or by any electronic or mechanical means, including information storage and retrieval systems, without permission in writing from the publisher.

Halcyon House, Publishers
Box 9547, Kansas City, Missouri 64133

ISBN 0-911311-20-3

Library of Congress Catalog card number 89-080736

# A NOTE FROM THE PUBLISHER

It has always been the role of the novelist to make the final statement for any historical era. Not one scholarly tome has recorded the agony and pathos of the 1930s half as well as did John Steinbeck in *The Grapes of Wrath*. Arthur Koestler's *Darkness at Noon* gave the world its first real insight into the workings of the Soviet political state, and George Orwell made clear for those with the wit to see how Neanderthal perversion ruled the bureaucratic mind.

And so it is with *Fallen Eagle*, in which Harold Wills tells about the likely conclusion to our "rush to convulsion." For it is a fact that men take leave of their senses as a mob. They come to their senses individually, one at a time. They are always too tardy to confer rational behavior on the whole, but in time they benchmark the preservation of reason nevertheless.

We may never know why the abstraction of debt came to sponsor such utter unreason in the era between World War II and the great convulsion described herein. For now it is enough to say that by 1989, the year of publication for *Fallen Eagle*, Americans had borrowed so much money and purchased so much on credit that they owed each other and foreigners well over $11 trillion. The few who could comprehend this awesome fact merely shrugged their shoulders after a while, and recalled that "we had no barbarians." This esoteric quote summarized contemporary history by recalling how taxation during the declining days of ancient Rome—when life became an unequal contest between bureaucrats trying to collect taxes and citizens trying to avoid them—made it necessary to flee Rome and seek refuge among the barbarians. Indeed, during the decline and fall of the United States there were no barbarians to welcome the weary. There was only social implosion amid breathtaking change.

We wonder aloud why the leaders of the Western nations could not deal with the mathematical impossibility of public policy. They seemed never to understand any ecology's requirement for parity—parity of exchange between microbe and food, soil and plant, country and city, city and state, nation and nation. There was a time when the peddler stood under the manor wall, casting a shadow no bigger than the palm of a hand. No one could suspect that this creature of so little consequence would one day mastermind stock and commodity exchanges, and wipe away the trappings of nobility while recasting the scope of political and economic order.

Grammar school students can recite the details that accompanied the birth of the American nation, yet the wisest and most educated of men remain at a loss to explain why the geyser of creative genius was put out. Much as the peddler under the manor wall in an earlier era changed the world, so did a new invention, namely debt money. Under this scheme, each unit of money became a fractional part of a debt. Men educated beyond their intelligence saw this invention as an open sesame to wealth beyond the dreams of avarice.

We can only speculate why governments couldn't comprehend the nature of this debt money, and why they permitted the banking industry to transfer one industry after another to foreign shores. Certainly, the American record has established the parameters for stability. For the one hundred years between 1812 and 1913—in spite of wars, depressions, crop failures and other anomalies too numerous to mention—a market basket of commodities cost about the same at the end of that period as it did at the beginning.

The birth of credit money could never have been invented by a novelist, but it takes the novelist to make its consequences come clear. And so Harold Wills explains how near-confiscatory taxes became the norm, not so much to pay the legitimate expenses of government, but to sustain the unsustainable: a mountain of debt compounding itself well beyond the point where mathematical ambition and physical possibility part company.

The magic of debt money was perceived to free man from the dead hand of the past. Between WWII and the start of the 1980s, public and private debt doubled itself each decade. And then the doubling doubled its speed. And with doubling whole populations became surplus, to be ministered over by so many social programs they could no longer be enumerated. Even the most informed government statisticians lost count of American companies that had been turned into shells, all in homage to free trade based on the international offering of ten cent an hour labor. As international trade rolled on, farms and factories collapsed. Those who remained in business conceptualized debt as a substitute for earnings until they too collapsed, sending employees home and into the streets.

One must arbitrarily select the moment in time from which to proceed forward, or look back—and so preliminary historians have made note of the milestones that brought America to the impasse novelist Harold Wills envisions: a steady rise in judicial tyranny, the one-man-one-vote ploy, official assassinations, *Roe vs. Wade,* and an almost comical raising of the national debt ceiling from time to time.

Then there came the day when new debt money injected into the system delivered less new national income than new debt. And now the programs could no longer be funded without inflation robbing those they were designed to help. By the late 1980s a new phenomenon appeared on the American scene: the homeless. They were few at first, pitiful, dirty, diseased—and they could be ignored. But as the factories continued to close, more earners became unemployed.

Families caught in this trauma seemed unable to understand what was happening because they were too young to remember the 1930s, and so they took shelter in the mores of the times, reaching for divorce as a solution and to government as a safety net. The first sapped the family's strength to stand on its own, and the last failed miserably, for the net was rotten and unraveled. The institutional arrangement called "the law" soon enough deprived the human rejects of homes and apartments, and a new term was born: *shelter people.*

Even in the final stage, more debt seemed to paper over this cancer. And computers continued to accommodate the traffic so well that October 19, 1987—the day the stock market crashed—was seen not as an early warning system, but as a hairline crack that could be ignored.

*Fallen Eagle* is fiction, but it is also fact—and history and economics and sociology rolled into one. More than these things, it is a warning. It seems to tell America's leaders,"Gentlemen, you are mad!" Ortega y Gassett, the great Spanish philosopher, once wrote that history draws its nourishment from the valleys, and not from the heights. Indeed, it does—in time. Those who contemplate the future must absorb the follies of the past, for "multitudes, multitudes in the valley of decision" said Joel in the Bible, have ready their answer.

*Fallen Eagle* sounds out the dimensions of that answer.

—*Charles Walters, Jr.*

# FOREWORD

History, according to an ancient adage, has an unpleasant way of repeating itself as the years and centuries pass. That is the underlying theme of this novel which is a fictional account of a nation and world after well-identified contemporary trends have been allowed to reach their ultimate conclusion.

Simultaneously, this is and is not fiction. It is a novel in which every incident, and every chapter, has already occurred somewhere in the world when these same circumstances existed and, by neglect or innocence, were allowed to run their course to the final breaking point. In this context, *Fallen Eagle* is a novel of the present and past—not of the future.

Desperate and disgruntled mobs led by a self-styled holy man created Cromwellian England and deposed the Shah of Iran. In both cases, a new and unworkable social order was created, one in which all incentives to progress were removed. In each case, the end result was a universal drabness combined with a national lethargy.

Parallels to the society that was overthrown can be found in the Weimar Republic of pre-Nazi Germany and the very brief Kerensky Republic in Russia, both of which were paralyzed by inertia until credibility and currency became worthless.

The establishment of a government-in-exile has occurred many times in recent history, especially during the second World War, when such nations as Holland and Belgium were forced to govern from temporary quarters in one of their former colonial possessions. It happened once to the United States, when the British burned Washington during the War of 1812.

The rescue of specific persons from internment in their native land, using a motor vehicle for escape, has occurred many, many times in recent decades, especially from Hungary following the abortive revolution of 1956 and from China after the fall of Chiang-Kai-Shek's republic. Although it is forgotten today, the fall of republican China triggered a massive truck convoy that threaded its way several hundred miles between battles before reaching safety in French Indochina.

The shocking final chapter in this book also is borrowed from the pages of the turbulent history of this century. It, too, has happened before—at least three times—but not in the manner presented here, because these tools were not available in those earlier years. The circumstances, though, are the same, as is the anguish when the ultimate decision is made by a person whose life, in those earlier parallels, was changed forever.

In this context, this is a novel about the past, not the future. It is an account of the frailty of mankind, for whom the experiences of the past are repeated endlessly as the result of a perennial innocence, combined with an exuberant self-blindness to the pivotal events of the past, especially when they occurred on the opposite side of the world and in a nation with an exotic, strange-sounding name.

Today, in the United States, the same currents are running strongly, as strong as when they contributed to the parallel events that could be duplicated here if these currents are permitted to continue until they reach their ultimate, eventual climax. The United States, a very young nation barely into national adolescence, could at some future point become the latest statistic in this list of precedents.

In this context, this is a novel of the past rather than the future. It does nothing but draw upon precedents, insert the necessary ingredients into them, and then project the result into a future that is frighteningly near, within the lifetime of every young person alive today. It is a novel—but, if history is any barometer, it could become fact!

# PREFACE

Nobody can say the United States did not have ample warning that a fiscal and monetary crisis was taking shape, a crisis that would destroy the value of the dollar to the extent that it would be repudiated by other nations and result in virtual destruction of both commerce and living standards in the United States. All historians in these early years of this new century are agreed upon this point. They're also agreed in their puzzlement about why the United States, at that time the most powerful nation on earth, blindly permitted this crisis to occur.

Old records and photographs prove conclusively that, as recently as the year 1982, the former United States had an extremely high standard of living and its government sponsored social programs that guaranteed an income to almost all inhabitants. However, according to the surviving microfilms of newspapers of that period, much of the prosperity of that time was supported by borrowed money, much of it obtained from governments and individuals elsewhere in the world. By 1986, the microfilms show that many writers and some government officials were warning that runaway inflation, steadily rising taxes and high unemployment were ahead if the government persisted in operating upon nothing but borrowed money.

Why were these warnings ignored until it was too late for remedial steps to be taken? Why did the politicians wait until entire families were sleeping in the streets before they agreed to face this problem? Today's historians are not in agreement about the probable answers to these questions. Some cite the United States electoral system, where officials were chosen upon the basis of emotional appeal rather than reason, as a probable cause for the procrastination. Others offer a more simplistic explanation, placing the blame upon an attitude that apparently was universal in that period, a general belief that the United States was invincible, able to handle any crisis that might occur.

Whatever the reason, the United States blindly continued to buy an artificial form of pseudo-prosperity with borrowed funds until the entire bubble burst almost overnight. Today's historians are puzzled about the reasons for this self-blindness and about the reasons why, apparently, nobody in the upper echelons of government sought or studied earlier parallels in world history and their fate when a wealthy nation suddenly or gradually became poor and unable to sustain itself. As one of today's historians put it very succinctly: "If anybody back then had bothered to read history, they would have found that collective misery always produces a messiah!"

That is exactly what happened in the former United States of America; the historians are all agreed upon this point. When the currency no longer had any value, when prices rose almost hourly, when the nation had become almost a global pariah because of its inability to honor its indebtedness and when almost everything in commerce became unaffordable to most of the population—a messiah did arise and found ready followers among a people desperate for answers to their unanswerable problems. History is very clear about this point because it happened in the more recent past.

In hindsight, it seems very clear this messiah brought only hope and not answers. But, to millions of desperate people within the population, hope apparently was enough to cause them to follow this messiah blindly, even into Washington when he overthrew the incumbent government and proclaimed a new order based upon true equality for all people within the land. Why, asks one of today's historians, did nobody apparently see that true equality among humans exists only in the grave? Humans, he says, are competitive creatures for whom there must be always winners and losers!

Historians have studied very carefully the civil war that followed and resulted in division of this old continental power into separate nations, one based upon the beliefs of this messiah and the other a smaller and weaker version of what had existed previously as a continental giant bounded by two oceans. Of course, the messiah fell when his promises proved to be empty; but by then the division had become permanent and, since then, two separate races have developed, alien to each other but speaking the same basic language.

Today's historians consider this virtual collapse and breakup to have been inevitable once the proper forces were set in motion almost three-quarters of a century ago. Nations, they explain, are living things exactly like man, the animals and birds and plants; and they have a measurable life cycle beginning with birth, followed by youth, maturity, old age or decline and finally death. The only difference between nations and living things is that nations are created by man to fulfill a specific need and, once that need has passed, can be terminated by man. The United States, they say, passed quietly from maturity into the start of old age at some point around the year 1970 and from that point onward it became increasingly vulnerable, leading to its eventual end.

Painstaking research into old records has produced this story of how a few inhabitants of that period, one a high government official, coped with the trials and tragedies during those earlier days. As the reader can see, they were just ordinary people not unlike those of today, trying to survive within an extraordinary, puzzling and sometimes hostile environment. However, the real importance of this record is the view it gives of the adaptability of the human spirit when impossible odds must be faced. This is a rare view of conditions as they existed after the breakup had taken place and during that brief, chaotic period when the messiah was stripped of power, leaving a vacuum that remained unfilled until the ensuing power struggle was resolved.

This extraordinary view of personal life in those earlier days is of great value to the scholars of today who spend their lives interpreting history to help prevent it from repeating itself.

# 1

Moving with caution to avoid making any noise, Allen Davis picked his way down the path through the cleared area along the riverside. His new military uniform, laundered only once, felt stiff and it rustled as he walked. The unfamiliar automatic rifle was carried awkwardly, its barrel pointing ahead of him and swung from side to side. Every few steps the young soldier would halt, listen for a moment, and then resume his patrol.

The time was almost midnight. He had been walking back and forth on this path since ten o'clock and wouldn't be relieved for two more hours. This was his third night on this patrol, guarding against any terror squads who might have paddled across the river in a rubber boat. If they weren't halted here, they would scuttle across the cleared land that extended from the riverbank all the way to the old street of Broadway, and then vanish into the city where they would be impossible to locate.

Because of assassinations and bombings, all of the buildings between Broadway and the river had been razed, leaving wild grass, weeds and occasional foundation stones. Each night, this cleared area was patrolled by a chain of soldiers drafted for this purpose. Each man was assigned to a strip of shoreline five hundred feet wide, where he would walk back and forth until his four-hour duty shift was completed. Whenever he reached the end of his sector, he was expected to wait until the next man in the chain arrived. Only then did he begin his return trip, where the procedure was repeated.

If the next man in line didn't appear, that meant his sector had been penetrated by a terror squad and in most cases he was dead. Whenever this happened, a burst of automatic rifle fire toward the river was used to summon help from the mop-up squads stationed at intervals along the riverside. It served also to alert other watchmen along the perimeter, in case more terrorists were en route across the river.

A soft scrabbling near his feet caused Davis to halt and crouch, his rifle barrel swinging suspiciously from side to side. His attention was drawn to his right, away from the river, by another tiny sound in the grass. A small rabbit hopped from the black shadow of an old foundation stone, bounced timidly across a strip of moonlight and then vanished into the shelter of another stone. Grinning to himself with embarrassment, the young soldier relaxed and resumed his lonely patrol. He had gone a few feet when a small voice called from the direction of the wrecked city.

"Hey, buddy," the voice called. "Help me. I'm hurt."

Halting, Davis turned toward the direction of the voice, his rifle swinging indecisively back and forth as he tried to pinpoint the location of this voice. In silence, an arm closed around his chest, pinning his arms to his sides. The cold chill of a knife touched the side of his throat. His final thought was of the small rabbit he had seen hopping away. *I should have realized the rabbit was running from something in the grass, not hopping from one rock to another.* The knife slipped across his throat and his lifeless body was lowered to the ground. Only then did dark forms arise from where they had lain among the rocks, and scuttle across the cleared land until they vanished among the building shells along the east side of Broadway.

Ten minutes later, a volley of rifle fire brought the mop-up squads running to the site where the young soldier should have been. Less than a hundred feet away they found his body crumpled along the path, his throat cut and his rifle gone. Crouching with his back to the riverbank so he wouldn't provide a target for a sharpshooter across the river, the sergeant flicked a quick flashlight beam into the dead face.

"Poor son-of-a-bitch," the sergeant muttered. "He'd only been in the Army about two months. He didn't even have a chance!"

The body was carried away, another man was assigned to the sector and the patrol was resumed. It would continue until six o'clock, when the sun had appeared in the eastern sky. When dawn was beginning to break, when it was light enough to see but still too dark for sharpshooters, a search party combed the riverside. They found a collapsed rubber boat tucked within some tall weeds along an indentation in the riverbank. This was proof the young soldier had been killed by a terror squad, not by a desperate lone refugee trying to escape by swimming across the Mississippi and hoping to vanish into the freedom of the western bank.

The partition had come because it was the one possible solution to the violent friction that had begun when the American dollar became worthless in world commerce because the annual deficit of the old United States had hit a record $2 trillion per year and was continuing to climb. As the dollar had sagged in value, the cost of the U.S. federal government had climbed until it reached $5.5 trillion per year. One by one over the years, services provided by Washington to the states, counties, cities and citizens had been eliminated in a vain battle by Congress and the White House to halt the financial erosion that was consuming the United States.

The skyrocketing cost of government and the size of the yearly deficit were abstract topics that had little meaning to the average citizen, whose initial exposure to them was the dire warnings broadcast almost daily by the television newscasts. Then, as world confidence in the U.S. dollar began to evaporate, the problem became personal. Prices of almost everything started to rise until the point was reached where merchants found it impossible to keep their stores open unless they hiked prices almost hourly. A loaf of bread cost $5 and gasoline was $4 per gallon.

Caught between continuous price hikes by their suppliers and demands by their employees for wage increases, factories and merchants began a pattern of layoffs that became an avalanche. Within weeks, the jobless rate in the United States soared to almost twenty percent, accompanied by a seventeen percent inflation that included everything needed by the citizens, whether or not they still had a job.

Then, in quick succession, three things happened that caused the mounting citizen unrest to become a torrent. Imported items of all types, including automobiles, vanished from the stores because the nations in which they were produced no longer had any confidence in the ability of the United States to survive. In response to this move, every responsible nation on earth began dumping U.S. dollars, which were considered worthless currency. Congress approved, and the President signed, a bill that imposed taxes averaging $18,000 per year against all American wage-earners. This didn't happen without a battle, though.

Somehow, dissenters in Congress gained possession of a copy of the Grace Commission report, prepared back in 1984 at the request of Ronald Reagan, who had been President at that time. This report was divided into two separate sections, the first devoted to identification of waste within the federal government. This portion was given high visibility by the White House but the second section, a forecast of the probable economic future of the United States, was suppressed and buried because of the dire predictions it made of the future status of the nation.

This report was prepared by the heads of some of the largest corporations in the nation. Now everything it had predicted had occurred almost on the exact schedule foreseen by the panel. Until a copy was resurrected by these dissenting Congressmen, the report had remained hidden, buried, for close to fifteen years. When these lawmakers had copies of the forgotten report distributed to all members of Congress, all state governors and to members of the news media, pandemonium exploded in Washington and across the nation.

President Calhoun, new in the White House as a result of the 1996 election, tried to calm the frightened nation in a special address which, because of its wistful nature and the worried frown of the President, did nothing but produce scorn and anger among the millions of viewers. Riots erupted in every major city, led by homeless, hungry people who had nothing more to lose. These riots were watched on television screens by millions of Americans and also by viewers in other nations, those still willing to trade with the United States despite its worthless currency.

Within weeks, during which riots continued, the U.S. found itself virtually isolated from the rest of the world as one nation after another took formal steps to sever all but basic diplomatic relations with the United States. American products could no longer be sold abroad because they were unaffordable. No more imported products were entering the U.S. except on a barter basis. One by one, American military bases abroad were closed at the request of the host country which no longer considered the United States to be a reliable partner.

At this point Washington began curtailing its transfer payments to state governments—whose yearly budgets all included federal funding for many programs, especially those in the social sectors and involving farmers. With these funds terminated, the state governments had no choice but to kill every program which included federal dollars in its funding. In cutting services, the states were joined by the cities and counties, which also had received federal funding for most of their programs.

Within a matter of weeks, millions of people depending upon Washington were left broke or homeless. This group included the elderly, the jobless, widows, the poor and those with physical or mental disabilities. It included hospitals, schools, mental homes and prisons. It included city buses, airports and subsidized apartment complexes. It also included sewage disposal plants, rural electrification projects and highways, especially the interstate system.

Almost overnight, Washington's crisis had been expanded to include every state, city, county, township and neighborhood in the nation. Unless a messiah appeared somehow, the nation found itself facing a gray death of its familiar society and community structure. Within a month, a fortress mentality became implanted within every family in the nation whose homes, if one was still owned, became their fortress. With the sewers no longer functioning, it became commonplace to see a householder digging a privy hole in his backyard. Bicycles, if a person was lucky enough to own one, were the most reliable form of transportation within a community.

The unavailability and cost of gasoline almost overnight made the use of automobiles a luxury limited to special occasions such as a funeral or by people who, somehow, had managed to amass a stockpile of fuel. With no more new automobiles available, America became gradually a nation of old cars whose numbers dwindled for lack of tires and spare parts. By now, the riots were confined to the major cities. In the small towns, a spirit of bitter resignation had settled like a dark cloud over the occupants. And then the President made another of his futile, pitiful moves, one that was the turning point in replacing urban riots with an organized insurrection. He scheduled another address to the nation, this one delivered from the warm, well lighted luxury of the White House with the family Christmas tree in the background. Worse yet, it showed the President seated in a comfortable chair and wearing a soft, informal sweater.

While people were freezing in cardboard boxes or abandoned buildings and others were surviving by burning the used oil from the crankcases of junked cars, the President was sitting in comfort in a warm room beside a huge Christmas tree decorated with blinking, colored lights. This incident marked the turning point in the dissolution of America. The isolated riots that erupted and then dwindled away were replaced by a loosely organized, formal revolt. In desperation, governors of several eastern states ordered the National Guard to restore peace. Only a fraction of the Guardsmen responded to this order. Within two days half of them had deserted, with several joining the revolutionaries.

When Congress convened in January, it was a sham. Almost three-fourths of its membership had remained at home rather than face the dangers of travel back to Washington. Even if gasoline and automobiles were available, the empty highways were not only in disrepair but were infested with bands of thugs surviving in the one way available. There were no more intercity buses. After several machines were wrecked by roadblocks and then pillaged, the bus lines restricted their operations to short commuter lines. Passenger trains had vanished. Lack of maintenance and the absence of reliable weather reports and traffic control had reduced the number of airliners to a small fraction of the former fleet, and these few operated sporadically, whenever they were able to obtain fuel. So, in this climate, most of Congress simply remained at home when the session convened.

After the second week, Congress didn't even bother to meet; it was pointless to continue sitting in those huge halls that were almost empty. After that time, those members who were in Washington sat in their offices and went through the motions of dictating constituent mail that wouldn't be delivered, writing speeches for absent audiences, and comparing opinions with others who were doing the same pointless things. A month later, in disgust and resignation, the session was adjourned. It would never convene again; the job of Congress had become meaningless.

And then Richard Poynter burst upon the scene, first in New York and then in Boston and other major cities in the industrial northeast. Poynter, a former television evangelist and self-styled messiah, preached a hodgepodge of evangelism and militant socialism. The riches of the land and everything built upon it belonged equally to every person. In the eyes of God, a government able to bestow wealth and comfort to one person while denying it to others was sinful and "should be plucked from our midst and cast away." It was God's duty for every man, woman and child to pluck this abhorrence from America and replace it with God's design that would "put an end to this misery and bring us, all of us, the true wealth of God as He has promised us in His great design of this wonderful world and this wonderful country."

"Let not the heathen stop you," Poynter thundered in every city of the northeast. "He is but clay and there are a hundred and a thousand of us for each of him. Let the banner of the true believer fly above the White House. Let the riches God gave to this land be distributed fairly among its people and by its people, and not by a handful of misguided heathens who led us into this Valley of Tears. Join with me in this Holy Crusade!"

As he travelled from city to city, Poynter's flock mushroomed until it became a ragged army, too large to be controlled by the few local authorities still available. The tone of his bellowed remarks became sharper, no longer confined to generalities but now calling for his followers to seize their rightful places in this "blessed land of God." Somewhere Poynter had acquired a staff who accompanied him wherever he went, a staff he called his "twelve disciples." Somewhere he had acquired a flag, a huge banner with a bright yellow cross bisected by a sword emblazoned upon a royal blue background. Whenever Poynter entered a city, the disciples would be marching ahead of him, one of them carrying the banner proudly.

Gathering recruits en route, his army began marching toward Washington. As they marched, they became a symbol of order in a disorderly world where fear had replaced hope. They sang as they marched, militant old hymns from the forgotten past. At the head of the column marched Poynter and his disciples with the yellow and blue banner carried proudly and defiantly. They marched through New York and New Jersey and then headed south across Maryland, their final obstacle before reaching Washington. In order to arrive in Washington at dawn, they marched all night, a ghostly army that was silent except for the normal sounds of passage.

In one house in the Maryland suburbs of Washington, the sleep of its occupants was disturbed by a continual soft rustling and the unfamiliar sounds of passage made by a moving army. The occupants of the house crept to a window and opened the shades fearfully to peer outside. What they saw was like the waves of an ocean, beating against a shoreline illuminated by the moon. For almost an hour, the unending stream of humanity tramped in virtual silence past their home. Softly, to keep awake and alert, the mass was humming an old, familiar hymn.

The sun had appeared on the eastern horizon when the army, unopposed by any of the local authorities, arrived at the White House and flowed like a sea of oil around the building, across Lafayette Park and into Constitution Avenue, isolating the Treasury Building and the Willard and Washington hotels. Led by his disciples bearing the huge banner, Poynter marched to the White House gates, which were thrown open by two security men who abandoned their posts and joined Poynter's army. As soon as the gates swung open, the army flowed inside, an ocean of humanity that soon filled the White House grounds, overflowed onto the porches and hid the helicopter pad. The White House doors were thrown open; resistance to this overwhelming mass was impossible and pointless.

Poynter and his disciples marched inside. The President, his family and as many Cabinet members as he could locate had fled during the night. Except for the domestic staff and a few disconsolate security guards, the White House was empty. The incinerator was still hot from sensitive documents burned in it during the night. The roar from the mob outside was like that of an angry ocean when the blue and yellow banner was raised on the White House flagpole. Alone, Poynter emerged from the building and dropped to his knees with both arms extended toward the sky. He remained in that position for what seemed an eternity. When he arose and raised one clenched fist toward the sky an exultant roar burst from his army, so loud that pigeons on the roof of the Treasury Building erupted into the sky in panic.

That afternoon, squads led by the disciples neutralized all of the other federal offices in Washington and rounded up the few remaining Congressmen and Senators, escorting them and other high officials to the White House for an audience with Poynter. Afterward they were all placed in the Blair House, guarded by squads from the invading army. By nightfall the former government had ceased to exist, at least in Washington. The next morning, Poynter called a press conference to which reporters were hauled by members of his army. It was a command performance; members of the news media had no choice but to attend.

At the press conference, Poynter was seated behind the familiar desk in the Oval Office; behind him was the new yellow and blue flag, its cross pierced by a sword plainly visible to the viewers. Along one wall sat the twelve disciples, now attired in conservative business suits. Each wore a miniature version of the flag pinned to his lapel.

"Ladies and gentlemen," Poynter began, "you were brought here to witness the birth of a new nation, a nation of the people, for the people and by the people, a nation where every man, woman and child is equal under the true ideals of pure social democracy. It is a nation where everyone creates the rewards equally, and shares equally in these rewards."

He continued for an hour. The excesses of the United States, he stressed repeatedly, had made its downfall inevitable. As proof, he cited the total collapse of the economy and the currency that had become so unstable it was rejected by most nations of the world. The staggering $5.5 trillion debt that had choked the economy was dismissed by Poynter as "the work of the devil" and would be repudiated. A new form of currency would be issued to replace the dollar.

Rigid price controls would be imposed on all items in all stores and factories, based on the value of the planned new currency. To curb possible profiteering, all banks and other financial institutions would be nationalized as soon as possible.

Although elections were planned for the future, the new nation for now would be governed by Poynter and his twelve disciples who, he said, would replace the former Cabinet. Almost as an afterthought and with his voice pitched to its most sonorous level, Poynter named the new nation he had created. It would be called the American Social Republic, or A.S.R. A dead silence followed by a collective gasp filled the Oval Office at this final announcement.

Within days the new government was functioning and peace returned to the eastern states. This, alone, was enough to cause Poynter to be accepted there. But that wasn't the case in the south or west. A new interim capital had been established in Denver, Colorado, where the President and his Cabinet had fled. In a harsh, abrasive voice President Calhoun termed Poynter a rebel and repudiated any claim Poynter might have to Washington or the government of the United States. Unfortunately, this televisionappearance wasn't seen anywhere but in the western states. Elsewhere, it was jammed by orders from the White House.

Nationalization of all land, ordered by Poynter as a means of socializing America, was the spark that converted grumbling into open rebellion. Immediately, the Dixie states joined forces and issued an ultimatum to Washington: either rescind the nationalization order or face a new civil war. Because the A.S.R. couldn't afford to face hostile forces on both south and west, the order was erased for all of the southern states. No immediate effort was made to enforce the order in the western states because of their remoteness from Washington and also because other matters had higher priority.

One of these matters was the arrival in Washington of a peace delegation from Soviet Russia, offering military, industrial and economic assistance to the new nation. The rebellious western states were allowed to simmer until a mutual assistance accord was signed between the A.S.R. and the U.S.S.R. News of this agreement reached President Calhoun and his Cabinet at their interim capital in Denver. Immediately the President summoned his Cabinet and the members of Congress from the western states, and war was declared against the American Social Republic.

That was how it began. The war, with neither side able to defeat the other conclusively, continued for more than two years. Finally, it was resolved in a treaty establishing the borders of the two nations at the Mississippi River and, in the north, at the state line dividing Wisconsin from Minnesota. The war ended with an agreement to end hostilities—not with a peace treaty. This terminated organized combat but did nothing to halt or prevent raids into the opponent's territory. It did nothing to prevent infiltration into an enemy city, followed by sabotage of vital functions or terror attacks on public gatherings.

St. Louis and West Memphis, both located on the Mississippi River, were especially vulnerable to these terror attacks. To reduce the risk, all buildings along the riverbank were razed; in St. Louis, this extended to Broadway. One bridge was left open. The others were disabled to prevent passage on foot or in a vehicle. At all major cities, military units patrolled the riverbanks from dusk to dawn. The military draft became a permanent part of life in the U.S.A.

All of this happened five years ago. Today the same uneasy truce prevails and terror squads continue to try to infiltrate the U.S.A. which, because of massive aid from Japan and the Orient, has settled into a new type of normality. Automobiles remain scarce because too much of the refining capability was located east of the Mississippi. Stores are open but many forms of merchandise remain unavailable. A new capitol building, with a new President, exists in Denver, which became the permanent seat of government of the U.S.A. But there are few young men on the streets of any town; they are all drafted as soon as they pass their eighteenth birthday.

\* \* \* \* \*

Allen Davis, the young soldier who had fallen victim of a terror squad along the bank of the Mississippi River at St. Louis, was given a short military funeral and then was buried at Jefferson Barracks, joining more than a hundred other draftees killed during nighttime patrols along the river. A standard message of praise and condolences was prepared, to be delivered to his parents in a small town in Kansas. Already his place on the patrol squad had been filled by another very young draftee who, if he survived two months, would then be assigned to less hazardous duty for the remainder of his two years spent in uniform.

This was a ritual performed daily somewhere along the river from St. Paul to St. Louis, West Memphis and the suburbs of Baton Rouge. In all instances, the procedure was the same: the body would be buried in the nearest cemetery, the parents of the victim would be notified by members of the Civil Guard and his personal possessions would be sent home. It was an unpleasant job, made no easier because it occurred so often. This, more than anything else, was the reason for the intense hatred that had developed within the U.S.A. for anyone or anything that was a part of the American Social Republic.

By now, reunification of America into a single nation extending from the Atlantic to the Pacific oceans would be impossible and unworkable; two new races of people speaking the same language had developed, with the broad Mississippi River providing a barrier to keep them separated from each other. This young soldier who hadn't yet reached his nineteenth birthday was the latest victim of the uneasy peace between the two nations.

Sighing with weary resignation, Lieutenant Butler prepared and signed the familiar letter of condolences to the young soldier's family and initialled the inventory of possessions that would be shipped back to Kansas as soon as possible. Because it was easier and more efficient, it had become routine practice to wait until a dozen or more men had died and then make a single shipment of all of their personal properties. That way only one vehicle, whether it was a railroad car or a truck, would be needed. Even though peace had returned, vehicles and fuel were both still in short supply.

His unpleasant chore done, Lieutenant Butler didn't turn to other tasks. Instead, he rotated his swivel chair so it faced the window and spent almost fifteen minutes gazing absently at the small tree outside his office, at the birds which fluttered without care through its branches and at the white clouds ponderously making their slow way eastward across the vivid blue sky, while thoughts as bitter as acid slithered through his mind.

*Where will it end? How long can this go on and how long can I continue signing letters to parents waiting for their sons to come home? Will we ever go back to the world I can remember, where this was one country and you weren't afraid all the time?* He had no answers to these questions and couldn't permit himself to dwell on them, or even ask them, in moments like this because that was the way to insanity or despair. It wouldn't change because it couldn't; it was too late for any change, and neither side was strong enough to defeat the other. This was the way things were, and if you hoped to keep your sanity you couldn't afford to ask yourself questions like these.

Cursing, Butler turned back to other unpleasant tasks awaiting a decision. The young soldier was forcibly consigned to a dark crevice in his mind, one with a dark curtain over the entrance. Things were as they were and it was his task to guard this sector of the international boundary. That was his job, and he would do it as long as necessary. But it wasn't pleasant.

# 2

It was a beautiful day, one which made a man glad to be alive and able to sit on the front porch and enjoy it. The weather was warm but not hot and a gentle breeze stirred the leaves on the two trees in the front yard. At peace with himself and the world, Dwight Davis rocked in the folding chair he had placed on the porch of this small house he and Ellen had bought more than twenty years ago.

There were the familiar sounds of a settled residential neighborhood, the voices of children in some nearby yard, the erratic mechanical whir of someone pushing a lawnmower and, in the kitchen, the movements of Ellen as she baked bread. Because there were so few cars in common use today, the sound of an engine had become an interruption rather than a routine element in the day. Lately, as he became older, Dwight had taken to sitting on this porch as much as possible, allowing his thoughts to flit wherever they desired. It was a form of relaxation now that Dwight had passed his fiftieth birthday.

Now that times had improved somewhat, Dwight was a contented man, able to work at least three days each week and, if times continued improving, this would be increased to five full days, almost doubling his paychecks. Even if it did not increase, he and Ellen were better off than most people in these frightening, unsettled times. They had this house which they had bought as soon as he had returned from Vietnam. They had survived that period of raging inflation when prices of everything increased each day. In fact, they had used the almost worthless dollars to pay the remaining balance due on this house, thereby providing them with a secure place to ride out the inflationary storm.

Like most people, they hadn't expected America to disintegrate and become two nations at war with each other. To Dwight and Ellen, the war was a remote event that didn't reach into this small Kansas town. But it had created shortages of everything, and Dwight's old car still stood idle in the garage when it needed repairs that couldn't be made even if they were affordable. Today, like most people, Dwight walked to work and stopped at the grocery store on his way home in the evening.

The one thing that disturbed Dwight nowadays was the absence of young people in the town. Now that the military draft had become permanent, the boys all left as soon as they reached their eighteenth birthday, thereby leaving a town containing nothing but girls. What really bothered Dwight was the way the girls were marrying older men, some as old as Dwight. If this continued, in a few more years the town would be filled with young widows! Dwight chuckled at this thought.

He and Ellen worried about Anne, their daughter, who had married a man two years younger than her father and now lived in Colorado. Anne was seventeen and her husband was pushing fifty. Because of the absence of proper medical facilities today, he likely would not live much past sixty or so, and then what would happen to Anne? In the world of today, how would she raise any children they might produce?

He sighed and his thoughts turned to Allen, his son, who now was in the military after being drafted two months ago. Because of the war and the partition, Allen had been forced to grow up far too fast. He had been denied any memory of the familiar world remembered by his father.

For the Davis family, the past had died more than five years ago when Washington had fallen and the President had vanished temporarily. Dwight had just backed the car out of the garage and, as he did each morning, automatically turned on the car radio while he waited a few moments for the engine to begin running smoothly. Instead of the customary local program, there was the almost hysterical voice of a network reporter trying to keep the nation informed about the chaos underway in Washington. There was a sob in his voice when he described the blue and yellow flag as it was raised over the White House.

At first Dwight thought this was a horror melodrama being aired by the station but, if so, it made no sense to interrupt the normal news and sports that were so popular among the local listeners. Then the local announcer interrupted with a special bulletin from the Governor of Kansas. All citizens were urged to go about their normal affairs but to keep their radios or televisions turned on at all times. All National Guard members were to report immediately to their armories and be prepared to remain on active duty as long as this emergency continued. After this announcement, the program returned to Washington and the agonized voice of the network reporter.

Dwight's first thought was of Ellen and the two children who were preparing to leave for school. Allen had just entered high school and Anne was in the seventh grade, beginning to show the outlines of adulthood and feeling superior because she had escaped from elementary school. Through the opened windows, Dwight could hear them inside the house, competing with each other for Ellen's attention as they did every morning. Obviously, neither the radio nor the television was turned on. The Davis family was proceeding with its usual morning ritual, unaware that history was being made.

Although he still couldn't remember doing it, Dwight turned off the car radio and the engine and returned inside the house where, like an automaton, he had walked through the busy kitchen into the living room, turned on the television and called Ellen and the children to him.

Ellen, he recalled, at first had thought Dwight was ill but, as she watched the TV and heard the reporter, her eyes had grown round and one hand had unconsciously covered her mouth as she listened, staring at the picture of the White House with a monstrous yellow and blue banner flying above it. Dwight hadn't gone to work that day and the children hadn't gone to school. They had spent the day watching the nation collapse. That night Dwight had lain awake until almost morning, re-hearing over and over the hysterical voice of the network anchorman in Washington. He felt Ellen tossing and turning beside him, muttering incoherently in her sleep.

War had erupted as soon as the President had surfaced in Denver and formation of the American Social Republic was announced in Washington. To prevent them from falling into the hands of the A.S.R., all American warships had gone to sea from naval installations along the east coast and the bases had been destroyed with explosive charges. All Air Force bases in the eastern states had been destroyed as soon as the last plane was airborne and headed west. Vehicles on the bases then moved westward in armed convoys and didn't halt until the Mississippi River was behind them.

Initially, Army units in the east were used to try to overcome the A.S.R. mobs and liberate Washington, but this was a dismal failure. Not only were there many desertions by soldiers unwilling to fire on unarmed mobs of fellow Americans, but defeating the A.S.R. was like trying to defeat a sea of oil. An Army unit would charge into one of the mobs, but the unending mass simply folded itself behind the soldiers, leaving them trapped within an ocean of humanity, against which rifles were useless. There was no escape from such a trap so, eventually, either the units surrendered or were smothered into submission. Once disarmed and stripped of their uniforms, the soldiers were freed to fend for themselves, naked in a hostile land.

The same thing happened at military bases not abandoned and destroyed. They would be overrun by a seemingly endless mob of unarmed people who, like a tidal wave, would flow into every building and every inch of the base until, in desperation, the occupants surrendered. It was a new form of warfare for which the military wasn't prepared. Within weeks, the final Army base in the eastern states had been overwhelmed and had ceased to exist as a fighting force. Today, except for a few who had made their way to the Mississippi and those who had turned up in Canada, nobody knew the fate of the occupants of these bases.

The A.S.R., during that period, had somehow created an army and equipped it with weapons seized from existing military bases and those supplied by the Soviets. Rolling forward like a tidal wave, this army had headed west to overwhelm the rest of the former United States, gathering recruits as it moved. It was the Mississippi River, not military force, that stopped them. By that time, most bridges across the Mississippi had been destroyed by the defending troops of the U.S.A. and heavy artillery had been moved into place along the riverbank, aimed to fire at pointblank range. The stalemate that resulted led eventually to peace talks which created two separate nations in this part of North America.

By that time Dwight had been drafted, assigned to the inactive reserve because of his age, and had drilled faithfully one day each week in the local armory. After a year, during which the A.S.R. was recognized as a nation by most of the world, Dwight had been discharged and permitted to return to civilian status. Allen was completing high school and upon his eighteenth birthday would be required to spend two years in uniform, serving in some branch of the military where a need existed. Anne was now in high school and had discovered boys. Overnight, she had blossomed from a child into a young woman.

Rocking idly on his porch, Dwight's thoughts wandered through those earlier, unpleasant days when for a time life consisted of an unending parade of uncertainties. There had been three unpleasant years when the economy was in a shambles and the dollar's value gyrated up or down almost every day. Shelves in most of the stores became almost empty before mercantile and financial assistance was pledged by Japan and other Oriental nations. Most of the new factories built since then had Japanese owners and the bonds they purchased had brought an acceptable strength to the dollar.

The aroma of baking bread drifted out of the opened front door and into Dwight's nostrils. Mentally he could picture Ellen sitting in the kitchen intently watching the clock to be sure she removed the bread from the oven before its crust blackened. Because bread was still difficult to buy, twice each week Ellen baked enough to supply the family. After all this time, she still wasn't comfortable with the chore and was fearful about producing charcoal rather than bread. They were lucky, though; here in southwest Kansas there had been no interruptions of natural gas, as had occurred in so many parts of the nation. Even in the worst period, their home had remained warm throughout the winter months.

Dwight's attention was drawn to a pair of cyclists riding slowly in his direction from the center of town. They were unusual because, until now, the street had remained empty of any form of traffic. In today's world, bicycles were far more common than automobiles even though gasoline was again available. People rode cycles because repair parts for cars were, in most cases, not to be found anywhere, not even from rusting hulks in junkyards. Too many repair parts had been manufactured in or near Detroit and that source of supply was lost now, apparently forever.

Gradually, as they pedalled nearer, Dwight was able to identify the two cyclists. The taller one worked in the feed store and the other was an accountant. Both wore the blue uniform and red armband of the Civil Guard, a volunteer force created during the war of partition to patrol civic facilities such as electrical generating stations to prevent sabotage. Now, with peace returned, their functions primarily consisted of carrying messages or aiding stranded motorists on the virtually empty highways. To wear the blue uniform, they were required to spend at least one day each week on duty in the little room set aside for the Civil Guard in the county courthouse.

Because he had nothing better to do, Dwight watched the approach of the two cyclists as they flickered into and out of shadows cast by the tall elm trees in the yards of each home along this street. One moment, they would be outlined sharply by the bright sunlight and, in the next, their shapes would be softened by shade. It was, Dwight thought idly, like a light that automatically turned on, then off and then on again. He smiled to himself at this silly thought. And then he became suddenly alert and chilled when the cyclists pulled over to the curb in front of his house, alighted and lowered the kickstands on their bicycles. The taller rider removed a small briefcase from a basket on his cycle and the two men walked up the sidewalk toward Dwight. Arising from his chair, Dwight walked to meet them at the porch steps.

"Afternoon Ben, Art," he greeted them. "What can I do for you?"

"Afraid we have some bad news for you, Dwight," the taller Guard replied in a low, pained voice. "We've been ordered to deliver this letter to you. I just wish there was some way to avoid it, but there isn't. It's about your son."

Dwight's hand was shaking as he reached for the envelope. He was opening the envelope when he heard a scream from inside the house. Ellen had seen the two Civil Guards on the porch and immediately feared the worst. She burst out of the screen door and stood at Dwight's elbow as he finished opening the envelope. She stood with one hand covering her mouth and the other clutching Dwight's sleeve. A low moan escaped from Ellen as she read the brief letter over Dwight's shoulder.

"We regret to inform you that your son, Allen Davis, was killed in action while defending his country on the St. Louis front," the letter said. There was more, barely scanned by Dwight and Ellen in that moment, and the letter was signed by Allen's commanding officer. By now Ellen was weeping uncontrollably, sagging within the arm Dwight had kept around her waist. Turning and making a motion as if to push the bad news away from her, Ellen ran into the house. The men on the porch could hear her as her grief erupted in the privacy of her home.

"I'm awfully sorry about this," Art, the taller of the two Guards, said in a low voice. "Whenever we have to deliver one of these letters, I'm never able to sleep for several nights. Dwight, if there's anything I can do, you call me at any time."

"That goes for me, too," Ben added. "You know you can count on me. Suppose I have Leota come over and stay awhile with Ellen? She needs somebody now, of all times. Damn it, I'd rather take a whipping than have to deliver one of these letters!"

Dwight, still in shock, didn't reply immediately. Then, in a low and strained monotone, he began to speak.

"I think that would be fine, Ben," he said. "You have Leota come over any time she wants. I know Ellen would be glad to have her here. Do either of you know how this happened? How did Allen get...killed?" He hesitated before using the word "killed." It seemed so final, so cold.

"We never know," Art replied gently. "These letters just come in on the facsimile machine and we put them in envelopes and then deliver them. I can tell you one thing, though. Allen didn't just die; he was killed in action. If he had just died, the wording would be different."

Dwight stared into space for several moments and then turned back to the Civil Guards.

"Will he be coming home?" he asked. "When do we have to go meet him? We've got to know that so we can make the proper arrangements."

"He won't be coming home," Ben answered in a soft and sympathetic voice. "They never send them home because transportation is so erratic anymore. Everything is done where they fall. In St. Louis, that would be the military cemetery. Please don't take me wrong, Dwight, but the best thing you can do is hold regular services here and then put a stone in your family plot. That's all you can do in these circumstances."

"Thank you, Ben," Dwight replied in a strangled voice. "I appreciate your honesty even if I don't like what you said. But how can I tell Ellen this? It'll break her heart."

"I don't know, Dwight, I just don't know," Ben murmured. "I don't know when it will end, either. Where's the justice in all of this? Sometimes I wish it was me. At least I've had a chance to live a fairly long life!"

Because there was nothing more to be said, the Civil Guards mounted their cycles and pedalled away, back toward the downtown area. For almost a minute, Dwight stood on the porch, absently watching them as their shapes flickered into and out of the shadows of the elm trees. After they had vanished from sight, he turned slowly and entered the house to find Ellen lying on their bed, sobbing quietly.

There was nothing that could be said to lessen her grief so Dwight absently walked through the house and stood for almost half an hour in the doorway to Allen's room, still filled with the juvenile acquisitions he had accumulated during his younger years. The room had always been a warm, welcoming place. Now it felt chill and empty, abandoned.

During the good years when the children were younger, Dwight and Ellen had gradually drifted away from church attendance. The two children went each week to Sunday school but, for their parents, Sunday morning had become a time to rest, to sleep later than on weekdays and then linger in the kitchen reading the Sunday newspaper. It was a time for an extra cup or two of coffee and for slow, meandering conversations, a period when time had no special meaning.

Lately though, beginning with the crisis in Washington when the President fled, they had resumed church attendance, this time at the Lutheran church within easy walking distance of their home. Their first visit had been made by impulse, in reaction to some forgotten dismal news seen on television. Neither Dwight nor Ellen was Lutheran and, at first, Anne had objected because it meant abandoning her familiar class in Sunday School. She relented, though, after she found many of her friends were Lutherans.

What began as impulse had by now become habit; almost every Sunday saw Dwight and Ellen among the Lutheran congregation. Gradually, the church had become a strong cornerstone in their lives, especially so during that period when nobody really knew whether the United States would survive or vanish as a nation. Now, in their grief, Dwight and Ellen turned to this church for comfort and for advice about handling a funeral in these unusual circumstances.

Not only was the pastor sympathetic and helpful, but he also handled the job of placing an obituary in the local newspaper. This was not, he told the Davis family, the first funeral held in his church for a soldier who had fallen and been buried elsewhere. After leaving the church, the next job was to try again to reach Anne in Colorado. Making long-distance telephone calls today, even with the improvements that had occurred, wasn't easy. Because of the dangers and difficulties in travelling, they didn't expect Anne would be able to attend the funeral unless, somehow, she could come by train— and today's train travel was slow, unreliable and extremely uncomfortable.

The railroads, since the partition, had done wonders in giving rail service to the communities along their lines but it had been makeshift because so many of their cars had been lost when bridges across the Mississippi were destroyed. After the highways had become too dangerous to use, the railroads had tried to restore passenger service by converting anything available into passenger cars. This included ancient coaches previously used to move section hands from one rail repair job to another. More and more, passenger coaches built on the undercarriage of unusually long cars built originally to haul new automobiles were appearing in the trains, easily identified by their box-like shape.

Even though more passenger trains had appeared to help meet the demand, they were a slow form of transportation because of the deteriorated roadbeds over which they moved. Until recently, following completion of new steel mills in Colorado and Utah, railroad rails had been impossible to obtain unless they were imported from the Orient. And because of breakdowns, automatic track-laying machines had become scarce and were impossible to replace. The one alternative to these machines was manpower, and most of the younger men had been drafted into military service.

With these obstacles to be faced, it was a miracle the railroads had continued to provide even reduced service. But somehow they had continued to operate, and were safer and more reliable than the highways. Today, except for local travel, most people avoided the highways; they were far too dangerous for anything but organized convoys.

If Dwight and Ellen wanted to visit Anne, who lived a mere one hundred and fifty miles away, they would need to supply themselves with enough gasoline for the round trip, learn the time of the next convoy—which was printed daily in the local newspaper—and then join other vehicles at its starting point on the west edge of town.

One or more National Guard vehicles always led these convoys, another would be in the middle and one or two would follow the final private car. The convoys operated daily, on a scheduled basis, with each National Guard vehicle heavily armed and manned by a squad of uniformed guards to provide protection from attacks by isolated A.S.R. terror squads or gangs of homeless people heading west after managing to cross the Mississippi River. The Guardsmen also were able, usually, to repair most failures in the highway surfaces such as a washout or fallen telephone poles that blocked passage.

The convoy network had been organized almost three years earlier in response to orders by the new President. It had been a way to keep the highways open to prevent isolation of one community from others. Since that time the convoys had become a routine part of life, even though their continued operation made the military draft mandatory to provide guards for the vehicles. Thousands of young men, those not sent to the Mississippi front, spent their entire two-year military term riding back and forth along a specific stretch of highway.

Dwight hoped that if Anne were able to attend Allen's funeral, she wouldn't try to make the trip from Colorado in a convoy; too many things could happen that would cause her car to be left behind at the roadside. Even a flat tire was excuse enough for leaving a car parked on the highway shoulder, its occupants crowded into other vehicles so the convoy could keep moving and maintain its schedule. Cars left by the roadside were seldom recovered. They were commandeered by a roving band of refugees or were stripped of all usable parts and then just sat there, rusting hulks. The highways were littered with these metal cadavers.

Dwight and Ellen were fortunate when they returned home from church; they reached Anne by telephone on their first attempt. Her clear, young voice answered after the second ring. It sounded exactly as it did when she had lived at home and was attending high school. She giggled when she heard Dwight's voice.

"You must have got my letter already," she exclaimed. "Aren't you proud of me? I didn't really expect you would call, though."

"What letter?" Dwight asked, suddenly confused. "That isn't why we've called you. Are you sitting down? I don't know how to tell you except just to say it. Allen was killed on the front. We just got the news today. The funeral is in three days."

At this point Ellen rushed from the bedroom and grabbed the telephone from Dwight, sobbing uncontrollably. Dwight was left standing, uncomfortable and uncertain about what to do next. Whatever Anne said to Ellen appeared to comfort her mother. Ellen stopped sobbing and listened intently for almost a minute. Finally, the conversation ended, she handed the telephone to Dwight but remained near, almost touching him.

"Dad," the voice on the telephone said, "are you there? Like I told Mom, I don't see how Bog and I can come right now. I'm pregnant. I'm going to have a baby, and travel is so dangerous. Oh, Allen, poor Allen, and right at this time.

"Why did it have to happen?" she asked with a sob. "What did he do to deserve this? He was my big brother, nothing could ever happen to him. Why? When will it end? Now he'll never get to see my baby and he won't be anything but a picture and that's all my baby will ever know of him."

There was nothing more to be said so, after a few final words, the telephone call was ended. Dwight's mind was a muddle with a single thought repeating itself, over and over again. *A life has ended and a new life is beginning.* Little Anne! A mother! It was only yesterday when she was in elementary school and spent one entire evening making Valentine cards for her classmates. Or that time she caught a turtle in the yard, brought it into the house and put it in the kitchen sink—where it was found much later by Ellen, who had immediately ordered its removal. A mother! And Allen would never see the baby.

Dwight recalled one year when the family had visited Washington during his vacation, riding in luxury aboard a passenger train and staying in one of the best hotels in the nation's capital. The children had been very small. Anne had tried to be ladylike aboard the train, but Allen soon became bored and had to be amused. Dwight had taken him to the dome car so the child could watch the scenery flowing silently past the speeding train. In Washington, Dwight had taken his family to meet Pat Conway who, back then, had worked as an aide to a Congressman. Pat and Dwight had known each other when both were very young, just beginning their adult lives. Today, Dwight was still in the same old job—or what was left of it—and Pat was a Congressman, one of the lucky ones who had not been in Washington when the city fell.

Somehow, the days passed following the visit of the Civil Guards and the telephone call to Anne, and it was time for Allen's funeral. There had been a constant parade of friends and acquaintances in and out of the house where Dwight and Ellen had lived for so many years. This had been good; Ellen had been kept so busy there was no time for grieving. That would come after the funeral, when Ellen and Dwight were left alone in that empty house.

The final rites were brief but telling, especially the closing words of the Lutheran pastor, added almost as an afterthought.

"Is it God's will that we should live divided like this?" he asked, to himself as much as to the mourners. "Is it right that we should live, brother against brother and father against son, in a divided land where there is no peace? How, oh God, have we sinned to bring your anger down upon us like this? Here lies a young boy, struck down by his brothers just as he became a man, and he didn't even know why! Oh God, give us wisdom, the wisdom to know how we have sinned to bring your wrath down upon us!"

The church was silent during this final emotional passage by the minister. Ellen sat with one hand pressed to her mouth. Dwight stared into a faraway distance visible to nobody but him. And then it was over. Because there was no casket, there was no reason for anyone to remain in the church and there would be no procession to the cemetery. Eventually there would be a gravestone, but with nothing beneath it.

Over and over, like a phonograph record that repeats itself, thepastor's final words scampered like mice through Dwight's mind. Was it God's will that a nation with a proud heritage should live divided with its people virtually at war with each other, or was it a failure by the people themselves that had caused it to happen? Did we live too easy for too long and throw away tomorrow so we could enjoy the passing pleasures of today? Was today's dangerous and divided land the result of God's wrath or did we do it to ourselves?

Dwight had no answers to these questions which, he admitted to himself, he had purposely avoided asking or facing until now. Maybe, he thought, that was what went wrong with the entire nation that had existed and been respected when he was a child. Maybe everyone in the old United States had tried too hard to prevent unavoidable changes from happening, so hard they had blinded themselves to everything but what they wanted to see.

The Lutheran minister in this small Kansas town may have, Dwight felt, hit upon the truth of the troubles that had divided the land and, as he said, pitted "brother against brother and father against son."

Dwight sighed, deeply troubled. Thoughts like these were too deep for him, too unsettling and foreign. But that funeral, the pastor's final remarks and the absence of a casket had forced Dwight to question realities that he had, until now, accepted as part of life. The funeral had been that of his son, but he had no son, not really. Where a casket should have been, there was nothing. There would be nothing in the family cemetery plot, nothing but a headstone standing over an empty spot of grass.

Who was it that killed Allen? This was the second time Dwight had actually used the word "killed" to describe what had happened. Was it a young man like Allen whose one difference was that he had been born east of the Mississippi River? If so, if they were alike, how could Allen have become the enemy? They were both Americans, so how could they have become enemies?

The preacher had been right; it was brother against brother and father against son. Dwight had no answers but each question seemed to generate another which, like the first, led nowhere except to more and more unanswerable questions.

It was almost dawn before Dwight fell asleep that night. With Ellen turning restlessly beside him in the bed they had shared for so long, Dwight remained awake, trying to examine once again the troubling questions with which the preacher had ended Allen's funeral.

It was well after midnight before the most agonizing questions of all forced themselves like sharp, gnawing teeth into Dwight's mind and left him even more disturbed than before. *Am I in some way responsible for Allen's death because I drifted along with a way of life that was easy, and did nothing to change it for the better? Are all of us who did nothing equally to blame? If so, God help us all! We deserve everything that has happened!*

# 3

Carefully brushing against the young female typist in this crowded Congressional office in Denver, Tim squeezed through the narrow space to reach the copy machine. He inserted a single sheet of paper, pushed the counter buttons for fifty copies and hit the starter switch. While the machine was running Tim turned so he faced the girl at the typewriter.

"I'll bet this is the only country in the world with its capitol in a shopping center!" he remarked, smiling. As expected, the girl giggled.

"That's irreverent," she replied. "Everybody knows this is a shopping center and they're building a new capitol south of town. Besides, this isn't so bad. It's easy to get here."

The buzzer on her telephone sounded. She answered, listened for a moment and then turned toward Tim.

"Boss wants you," she told him. "Better take your pad. Oh, and when you come out, he has some work for me. Can you bring it?"

Motioning for her to watch the copy machine and put the copies on his desk, Tim grabbed a yellow pad and headed toward the closed door in the partition dividing this small store into two separate offices, one as a reception and working area and the other to provide some privacy for the Congressman. This office was no better or worse than any of the others in the shopping center that had been commandeered when the government moved from Washington to Denver. In a sense, a shopping center was the perfect place in which to house a government.

The small stores had been converted into offices for the members of Congress and the two large anchors, one on each end of the center, were where the Senate and House of Representatives met. Members of Congress not fortunate enough to be assigned to a store location had cubicle offices in medium-sized stores which had been partitioned for this purpose. During the past two years the capitol had outgrown these quarters, resulting in several barracks being built in the shopping center parking lot. These housed the many support facilities required by Congress even in its present sharply reduced size.

With all of the states east of the Mississippi River lost, Congress had shrunk to less than half the number of members it had enjoyed during its two centuries in Washington. The Senate could have met in a banquet room. The House of Representatives contained barely a hundred members if all were present, which seldom was the case because of the uncertain status of public transportation.

Even after five years, it was a makeshift government that extended to the President and the Cabinet departments. The President lived in a rented mansion surrounded by a chain-link fence in the foothills above Denver and the Cabinet departments functioned in rented quarters scattered here and there around the city. The only common denominator for these various sites was that all were guarded heavily by squads of Marines armed with automatic rifles and bazookas and supported by a military tank stationed at each location. A helicopter was kept manned at all times, day and night, on the lawn of the Presidential mansion, ready to whisk the President and his family away to underground safety near Colorado Springs at the first sign of trouble.

On more than one occasion, fanatical terror squads from the A.S.R. had managed to reach Denver despite its remote location. Each time until now, they had been killed or captured by the Marine guards. But everybody knew they would keep coming until a true peace existed or America was reunited under one flag. Nobody knew when, or if, that time would ever arrive. Until it did arrive, the current uneasy truce that was neither war nor peace could continue. It could persist for a year or a century or even longer.

The current balance of power provided some security for the people of Denver which, because it was now a national capital, was a natural target for enemy forces. The A.S.R., because it contained all of the populous eastern states, had more than enough manpower to launch an invasion; but the U.S.A. had the firepower and was protected by the Mississippi River. Almost all of the jet aircraft of the A.S.R. were old models supplied by its ally, Soviet Russia. They were no match for the planes of the U.S.A., which had been salvaged at the time Washington fell. In addition, the U.S.A. had an operational Navy but the A.S.R. did not.

Intelligence reports reaching Denver indicated that Poynter and his Council were reluctant to attack the U.S.A. until or unless they were able to solve some of their internal problems. Hunger was no longer an issue in the A.S.R., partly because of better harvests but primarily as the result of collective rationing that guaranteed a basic diet to everyone, rich or poor. Seizure of all urban property had provided homes for everyone, with the rich and the suburban residents among the worst losers. But, to retain the unfailing loyalty of the people, the A.S.R. leaders couldn't afford a military adventure that resulted in a disastrous and bloody defeat.

The small terror raids into the U.S.A. brought tiny "victories" to the A.S.R. but, more importantly, perpetuated the enemy status of the U.S.A., thus assuring loyalty within the A.S.R. Whenever a terror squad was killed in the U.S.A. the news was broadcast throughout the A.S.R. and the dead terrorists became martyrs. By now, children who had been small at the time of the partition were young adults indoctrinated in hatred for the U.S.A. and its people.

Without knocking, Tim entered the Congressman's private office and sat down, leaning forward with one arm resting on the corner of the desk. The Congressman was completing a telephone call and motioned for Tim to wait. As usual, he was in shirtsleeves with his necktie loosened and dangling beneath his collar. From the time when he had held Tim's position, as aide to a now-dead Congressman, Pat Conway had always put comfort before style in his personal priorities. Since being elected to Congress four years before the national collapse, Conway had become noted by other lawmakers as a "mechanic," a man able to locate all the pieces of a legislative puzzle, draw them together into a consensus and then translate that into meaningful action.

His call completed, Conway sighed, turned toward Tim and began arranging various piles of paper on his desk. He pushed one of these piles toward Tim.

"When you go, take these out to Julie," Conway said. "I've signed these letters and they're ready to go. Now, let's get on to other things."

He pulled another pile toward him and from it extracted a single sheet upon which he had written his view of action that should be taken. This issue dealt with agricultural marketing problems in today's world of countless uncertainties. The next pile was devoted to military needs and expenditures and, like the first, it contained a summary the Congressman had prepared. As each matter was discussed, Tim made notes of the actions he would need to take to set the stage for passage or rejection of the issues. Finally there were only two tiny piles left, one consisting of three sheets containing lists of names and addresses. It was, Tim knew, that day's casualty count from the Mississippi front. Conway always postponed this topic until a discussion with Tim was almost completed.

"You know what this is," the Congressman said, sighing. "You know what to do with it. Send the usual letter over my signature to all of the families, but there's one I want to call to your attention. It's on the second page and I've marked it so you can find it. I want to talk to him in person so, when we're finished here, get him on the phone for me. I'd rather you did it than Julie because it's personal.

"I knew Dwight Davis back when both of us were young and I still had some hair left. We used to drink beer together and for awhile we both chased the same girls. When you were still a kid, Dwight and his family visited me here in Washington—I mean, when I was in Washington—and I remember his son. He was just a boy then and there was a daughter, too, quite a bit smaller. Damn it, why do things like this happen? Why couldn't I see it coming in time to try to do something? Anyway, I want to talk to Dwight myself. It's the least I can do. Now, let's get on to this last item on today's agenda."

He pulled the final pile toward him and from it extracted the customary summary sheets he had prepared. Before speaking, Conway leafed through the pile, scanning each page and hesitating on several. From experience, Tim knew this was an important topic with the Congressman. Whenever an issue had high priority, Conway always refreshed his memory before discussing it. The duration of the pause indicated the degree of priority. Tim sat forward, alert. This pause was so long the issue must be extremely vital to Conway. Finally, his review completed, the Congressman sat forward and, leaning on his elbows, began to speak.

"For now, this has to remain private, just between the two of us," he began. "I know without asking that you have taps inside the executive agencies; I did too, at your age. You wouldn't be worth a damn as an aide if you didn't! As quietly as possible, without making any waves, I want you to use those taps to find what, if anything, is being done about repatriation of our citizens from the A.S.R., and especially from the area around Washington.

"Also, there are a couple more things I need. I want to know how conditions are around the Washington area, especially living conditions, and I want to know—I need to know—if there is any way, legal or illegal, to get someone out of there. You know, of course, that I am referring to my daughter and her family. As far as I know, they still live in Arlington, but it has been almost a year since I heard from them."

"What if something happened to them?" Tim interrupted.

"Yes, I want to know that, too. By now it's better than not knowing."

A loud bell rang in the hallway outside the office, signalling the start of the day's session in the House of Representatives. Conway sighed, adjusted his clothing and departed, leaving Tim still sitting at his desk. Because he was naturally inquisitive, only one thing about this assignment bothered Tim. What excuse would he use with Julie to explain his absences from Conway's office?

As soon as the Congressman returned from roll call, Tim tried to reach Dwight Davis on the telephone. On his third attempt, he was successful. When a faint male voice answered, Tim pressed the intercom button and, as soon as he heard Conway begin speaking, hung his telephone on its base. With this assignment completed, Tim now had time to plan his strategy for pumping information from normally secretive agencies.

When Conway heard the intercom button buzz, he became apprehensive. Without being told, he knew it would be Dwight Davis he heard when he answered. What could he say that might help? How was Dwight taking the sudden loss of his son? It had been so long since the two men had spoken, he didn't know how to begin. But at least this personal call was a gesture to an old friend.

"Dwight?" he began. "This is Pat Conway in Denver. I just learned this morning about your son and wanted to call you personally to let you know how sorry I am. The only time I saw him was when you visited me in Washington. Is there anything now I can do to make things easier for you and your wife? I'm sorry, but I don't recall her name."

The two men talked for almost fifteen minutes, recalling the days when both were much younger and comparing notes about their lives since those earlier times, trying to fill at least part of the void that developed after Pat had gone to Washington. The call ended with an almost plaintive request from Conway.

"Let's keep in touch this time," he said. "Let's not wait until a tragedy like this happens again. Call me any time and I'll see that you get through to me. I'm so sorry, Dwight, this had to happen. We've got to bring this thing to an end, somehow, so people can live like they're supposed to live and not in permanent fear. We just have to! It can't wait any longer!"

By the time the conversation ended, Tim had left the office without telling Julie where he was headed. Once again, the bell rang in the hallway and Conway headed for the House floor. When he returned three hours later, Tim was still gone and Julie was upset and angry. Conway had to pacify her with the information that Tim was on a special assignment. She smiled when he apologized for his forgetfulness.

It was late afternoon when Tim returned. Instead of stopping at Julie's desk to pick up any telephone messages, he continued across the room and opened the door to Conway's private office, hesitating only long enough to see if Conway was alone. Without waiting for a response, Tim entered the office and shut the door. Conway peered over his glasses but remained silent, waiting for Tim to begin speaking. Without asking, he knew Tim had spent the day digging in the executive departments as he had been asked to do. Obviously, he had discovered something.

Conway was torn between desire and dread. His concern over his daughter and her family had been mounting steadily during the past year, a year in which privileged news available only to the federal government had become worse rather than better. The U.S.A. had intelligence sources in key locations—New York, Chicago, Boston and Washington, among others—and if the information was accurate, living standards in the A.S.R. hadn't improved under the new communal government. If anything, they had become worse after all residential property in the metropolitan centers had been nationalized to guarantee living quarters for every citizen regardless of his or her position in life. As a result, four families had, many times, been crammed into a house initially built for single occupancy.

This had brought unaccustomed luxury to the destitute, the street people, the jobless and also those who previously had never been able to make rental payments because they promptly spent whatever they earned, but it had resulted in the ouster of many families from homes they had purchased so they could enjoy comfortable security. Nobody knew what happened to these people when they were forced to leave their home. They just seemed to vanish into the streets.

Everyone in the A.S.R. seemed to have plenty of money, the intelligence sources reported, but it had no real value and was worthless for anything but a form of barter with the stores which, in turn, used it to pay debts owed to each other or to suppliers. For mathematical convenience, the dollar had been retained as the official currency, with the new bills printed in the federal printing plant in Washington. Like the A.S.R. flag, they were yellow and blue. Instead of the likeness of Washington, Lincoln or Grant, the new currency was emblazoned with the familiar cross and sword.

Virtually free living quarters, plenty of spending money and controlled prices for almost anything needed daily created the glue that so far had assured loyalty to the new A.S.R. regime. The only dissenters were the homeowners, corporations and financial institutions. The homeowners were squelched by nationalization of all land and the masses of free lodgers placed in their homes, and the corporations and financial institutions acquired new management when they were nationalized, thus making them an arm of government.

This left the masses as the controlling factor in the new government and, as long as they received housing, food and plenty of money, they wouldn't rebel or question the source of their economic improvement. As long as they remained passive and silent, the present government would remain in power. But it couldn't last indefinitely. Already, several European nations were beginning to question the stability of the A.S.R. and its ability to perpetuate itself as a major country. Information reaching Denver indicated that continuing aid from Russia was the main ingredient keeping the A.S.R. afloat in the global community of nations.

Recently the A.S.R. central government reportedly had been conducting a purge of malcontents who had defied the land nationalization program. This, of course, included most homeowners, merchants and land investors who distrusted the new currency and the centralized government. Squads of federal police were rounding up these people and placing them in the adjustment centers established in each state. In these centers, the occupants were forced to learn a needed trade—for which they were well paid—and were required to spend part of each day in mental therapy sessions. The only escape from these centers was a vow of unquestioning allegiance to the goals of the A.S.R.

Conway had heard these tales in Congressional gossip and he had heard the testimony of intelligence officials in the privacy of Congressional committee hearings. He had seen films from satellite observations of the A.S.R., films that showed empty factories, farmers working their fields with horses and crews of laborers, and suburban housing areas with armies of people crawling like ants around each residence. He had seen military bases, and other similar installations that apparently were intended as relocation centers for malcontents, with one or more located in almost every state. As the days passed, Conway became more and more disturbed by the knowledge he was acquiring. The course being followed by the A.S.R. reminded him of old movie footage from the time of Josef Stalin in Russia. The A.S.R. appeared to be following the same course as Stalin, but with a better educated population than Russia.

He determined to take whatever steps were necessary to try to remove his daughter from the A.S.R. The death of Allen Davis at the hands of a terror squad was the trigger that spurred him into action. When he asked Tim to explore ways to penetrate the A.S.R., it was more a reflex action than a planned move. If Tim learned something, a plan of action could be developed from this knowledge. If nothing was learned, there would be no bureaucratic risk to Conway. Aides to Congressmen were notorious for their curiosity. Conway leaned forward in his chair, awaiting Tim's report.

"Did you ever run across a man named Geoffrey Henderson?" Tim asked, leaning forward and lowering his voice so the sound couldn't be heard by Julie if she approached the door. Conway shook his head. The name meant nothing to him.

"I picked this up over at one of the sensitive agencies," Tim said. "Don't ask me which one; you're better off if you don't know. Anyway, Geoffrey Henderson, from what I was told, is like a cross between Jesse James and Robin Hood. For a price, he specializes in bootlegging people out of the A.S.R. I guess he has some of their people on his payroll, because his price is high. How's that for a grabber? They've got tons of that yellow crap, but they prefer greenbacks! I guess rugged individualism isn't quite dead yet over there!"

Conway frowned at these comments. When Tim saw the Congressman's annoyance, he became serious again.

"I had to go clear over to Byers, but I found this Henderson and talked with him," he continued. "I was lucky to find him. He's usually gone somewhere. He said it was possible to get anyone out of the A.S.R., if they were still alive and not in one of those concentration camps, but it wouldn't be cheap and there were no guarantees. All he will guarantee is to find out whether your daughter is alive or dead. That's fairly cheap, he said, and once you learn that you can decide whether or not you want to buy the rest of what he has for sale."

Conway leaned back in his swivel chair, absently removed his glasses and rubbed his eyes, staring vacantly into space somewhere above Tim's head. Tim had unearthed the answer he sought, but now did he really want it? This wasn't what he had expected to hear and it left him chilled. *My God in heaven, have we come to this? How have we sunk so far that living persons are bought and sold like loaves of bread? If we condone this practice, and even use it as an extension of official policy, are we really any better than they are? But I don't really have any choice if I expect to see Cynthia again, even if agreement with these terms leaves me feeling dirty and shamed. God help me, I don't have any other choice!* As if it helped to cleanse him, Conway drew a deep breath and turned back to Tim.

"How do I know I can trust this man Henderson?" he asked. "Did your agency tell you anything about that?" There were long pauses between *your* and *agency*.

"They use him," Tim replied softly so Julie couldn't possibly hear his words. "They use him a lot. That's how I found him. According to my sources, he's the best there is."

"How would I meet him?" Conway asked.

"He's hard to get because there's so much demand for his services, so I set up a meeting tomorrow morning at eight o'clock in the Hilton lobby," Tim responded. "He won't meet anywhere but in a public place. If you don't want to do it, he gave me a telephone number where I can leave a message.

"If you want to do it, you're to bring $5,000 in currency and the latest photograph of your daughter that you have. He said you'd have your answer within no more than two weeks and decide then whether to go any further."

*Like cold meat or a can of tomatoes,* Conway thought. So this was how living human bodies were bought and sold! They were nothing but merchandise! He felt like he was on a speeding toboggan rushing downhill on a slide that ended in a sewer. He wanted to escape, somewhere or anywhere, but there was no escape. He had no real choice but to hire this man if he were ever to have any peace of mind. He told Tim to meet him in the Hilton lobby the following morning. After Tim had introduced the Congressman to Henderson, Tim would leave because the resulting discussion would be private and personal.

Conway and Tim had waited less than ten minutes the next morning when Henderson entered the hotel lobby, pausing just inside the door to scan the room, his eyes pausing briefly upon each occupant. Recognizing Tim, he walked to where the two men waited and was introduced to Conway. Then Tim left as planned. This brief pause gave Conway an opportunity to study Henderson and find any traits that could prove useful in the negotiations. He found nothing. Henderson was unreadable, as self-contained as a statue!

He was a slender man, no longer young, and he wore anonymous tan trousers and a tweed sports jacket. His thinning hair was cut short in the style of long-gone years. But it was the face, especially the eyes, that chilled Conway. The features were neat and regular, bisected by the slash of a thin moustache, but it was the eyes that held Conway's attention. They were as sharp as the sheen of lumps of coal and they held a burning intensity that didn't waver. They reminded Conway of the eyes of a hawk or some other bird of prey. They were the eyes of an old-time pitchman to whom other people were nothing but marks to be used in acquiring a profit. Under the scrutiny of these eyes, Conway felt diminished and naked.

"Senator," the man said in a surprisingly soft voice, "why don't we sit down and talk business? I suppose you're ready to do business or you wouldn't be here?"

"Congressman," Conway automatically corrected him. "I understand you can locate my daughter and her family and let me know if they're well or not, if I pay you $5,000. How do I know I can believe what you tell me, or that you won't just tell me what I want to hear?"

"I don't work that way," Henderson responded in that soft, calm voice. "If I did, just once, I'd be out of business. I know your young assistant told you I do a lot of this work for the government. That's the only reason I'm here this morning. Call it an official favor if you want to. I don't care. All I need is the money, a photograph and enough personal data to make a positive identification and I'll get to work. You'll have your answer in about two weeks and then we can go from there."

The man's callous statement left Conway speechless. He knew the country needed men like this, but he had never met one throughout his official career. For some unexplainable reason, he felt both violated and shocked, somehow unclean. Much of his money, he knew, would be used to bribe A.S.R. officials and this would be a flagrant violation of both his oath of office and theirs. If he agreed, he would become no better than the opportunists within the A.S.R. Against his best intentions, he began probing Henderson for his own peace of mind. If he could find what made Henderson tick, perhaps there could be a rationale for his actions.

"Why do you do it?" he asked. "One day the A.S.R. kills the son of a friend of mine and the next I'm about to do business with them, through you. That makes us no better than they are!"

"We aren't," Henderson replied flatly. "It's only a lucky accident that we're here and they're there. I'm just a businessman filling a need that we helped to create, you and me. I didn't always do this but I'm good at it, damned good! I wouldn't be talking to you like this if you weren't a Congressman. I'd just walk away. If we had kept our noses clean, you and me and especially you, this need wouldn't exist and I wouldn't be in this line of work!"

"What in the hell do you mean?" Conway asked angrily, outraged at Henderson's comment. "How can you say that I helped to create this mess? I resent that! I've done everything I could to try to get a good government working here. Damn it, you have no right to make these accusations!"

"Don't I?" Henderson responded in his soft, unruffled voice. "How long have you been a Congressman? Ten or fifteen years? Do you remember back in the early eighties when the country went technically broke because the federal government began spending over a trillion dollars each year? Where did Washington get its money to spend? From the people in the form of taxes! The more taxes people have to pay, the less they have to spend on other things. There comes a point where there just isn't enough money to go around. That's when the trouble really began.

"If you were in Congress then, you know this is true! You can't pump the country dry to support yourselves without having it blow up, sooner or later. I was in the oil business then and I saw it happen in a lot of little tin-pot countries, and it always began the same way. The place got topheavy with a little central government sucking the people dry to support itself. It always ended from the bottom up in mob scenes by people who didn't have anything to lose.

"Sooner or later, some Moses appeared to lead them out of the wilderness and that's when the government fell. That's when I was long gone. I learned to read the signs and I just folded my rigs and left. That's what I did this time, but I didn't have any rigs to fold by then. I didn't read the signs right. I didn't realize the same thing could happen here.

"Now, you see why I say we're both partially responsible for this mess? How can you deny it? Like I said, I wouldn't be talking to you like this if you weren't a Congressman!"

Conway was shocked by the intensity of these words, spoken in the same soft and expressionless voice. Not knowing how to respond, he sat quietly for several moments while Henderson waited, unmoving and with the same unreadable expression on his face. As he analyzed Henderson's comments, a chill more bitter than the Arctic settled over his mind. *God help us, the man could be right! We could have created that revolt by our own blindness! We could have been so intent upon holding onto the past that we forfeited the future.* Even though Conway had been a freshman legislator at that time, he had been a part of the process that led to national disaster. And it took this unfeeling man, little more than a hired thug, to pull this possibility out of the darkness to which it had been consigned, and hold it in a light so brilliant it could no longer be hidden.

"You may be right. I just don't know," he said defensively. "Now let's get back to the reason for my being here. I want to get this matter settled, to know the location of my daughter and how she is. That's why we're here; not to debate who's right and who's wrong. But just tell me one thing. Do you go into the A.S.R. yourself or do you have someone else do it? It makes a difference."

"I go in," Henderson said softly. "And, I use other people. They're no different than we are. Don't ask me anything more. I won't answer you. I can't."

The meeting ended when Conway gave Henderson an envelope containing a photo of his daughter, a page with personal data about her, and $5,000 in currency. After telling Conway to await a telephone call within two weeks, Henderson left as he had arrived, silent and alert with his eyes roving around the hotel lobby. It was several minutes before a shaken Conway arose from the chair and returned to his office in the shopping center that had become a national capitol. He didn't attend Congressional sessions that day. He couldn't because his mind was a confused muddle of conflicting thoughts.

The days passed slowly. While he awaited the expected telephone call from Henderson, the Congressman spent as much time as possible in researching that period between 1980 and the breakup of the nation. Tim and Julie were kept busy locating records and bringing them to the office for Conway to study. He became almost a fixture in the Denver newspaper offices, poring over microfilms of old issues of that earlier period. As the days passed, Conway was absent increasingly from Congressional sessions and missed several important votes. Then the research suddenly ended. Conway had reached a conclusion that had deep personal significance to him.

Henderson, the hired mercenary, had been frighteningly accurate in his analysis of why Washington had fallen and the continent had been splintered into two nations virtually at war with each other. *We sat in Congress, playing our parliamentary games with each other, and were so absorbed with ourselves that we were blinded to what we were doing to the masses of people. We wouldn't or couldn't see* that we were creating a mass of people on the underbelly of America who, because of their declining position in society, were unknowingly just waiting for the right spark to ignite them and form them into a mob so dense that opposition was not possible.

As he groped toward this conclusion, one thought repeated itself over and over in Conway's mind. It was exactly like Henderson described it in places he called tin-pot countries. *Of all of us, from the President on down, this mercenary saw what we could not and acted in a way that, to him, had become familiar. Now what? Where do we go from here?* Conway had no answers but, out of this mass of knowledge, he had reached one conclusion. Regardless of the cost, he had to get Cynthia and her family out of there as quickly as possible. His research of history had told him that a revolution by the masses almost always was followed by a second conflagration when one faction tried to seize control from another.

The telephone call came on the twelfth day. Instinctively, he knew it was from Henderson when Tim entered his private office just as the buzzer on his telephone sounded. The voice on the telephone was just as he remembered it—soft and expressionless.

"Your daughter is safe but she is pregnant," the voice said. "She is still living in that address you gave me but there are three other families in there with her now. Her husband is dead. He was sent away to a camp in Maryland and didn't return. I don't know how he died but I was able to verify that he did. I have proof of all this and a photograph I had taken without your daughter's knowledge. If you want to go any further, we need to meet."

His heart racing but also like ice, Conway agreed to meet Henderson the next morning in the Hilton lobby. He spent the rest of the day converting assets into cash and then, that night, lay sleepless until almost dawn.

# 4

The ride from Denver to St. Louis was no better or worse than any trip aboard a domestic airliner. Geoffrey Henderson sat toward the rear of the plane, gazing out of the window at the banks of puffy white clouds along the northern horizon. His appearance was almost totally anonymous, no different from the millions who depend upon weekly paychecks for survival. He sat quietly throughout the two-hour flight, concentrating on the job ahead, beginning with arrival in St. Louis.

The meeting with Representative Conway had been brief but with a mutual understanding that hadn't existed at their previous appointment. The Congressman had paid his money, giving instructions that regardless of cost his daughter was to be returned safely to Denver; but after that point Conway had seemed reluctant to terminate the session and leave. Since their previous meeting, Conway had done his homework! Painfully he had been forced to admit that when the breakup of the United States had occurred, there was plenty of blame on both sides. The nation, he agreed now, had been simply spent into rebellion. Henderson smiled to himself. In this admission, Conway had seemed as eager to please as a puppy! Putting these thoughts aside, Henderson's mind turned to the immediate future.

Once in St. Louis, he had to make clandestine contacts to buy the necessary papers to permit him to travel to Washington. Then, at the busiest time of day, he would cross to the other side of the Mississippi. Once in East St. Louis, it would be necessary to bribe an A.S.R. official for passage eastward, probably aboard a bus. He would try to find a schedule that didn't take him through Chicago, where inspections were thorough and risks were high. Maybe Evansville—that was usually a safe city. If he could go through Evansville and Dayton, there shouldn't be any problems. At that point in his thoughts, the "fasten seat belts" sign lighted and the plane dived abruptly for landing at Lambert-St. Louis airport.

Once inside the city, Henderson checked into a small, anonymous hotel on Grand Avenue, near the eastern boundary of St. Louis. Between Broadway and the river the city was gone, bulldozed to create a vacant area along the border. Scattered buildings looming starkly like broken teeth were all that remained between Broadway and Jefferson. When he checked into the hotel, Henderson paid rent for two weeks and told the desk clerk he might be gone occasionally but wanted to hold his room. This created a haven where he could leave extra clothing and items not taken into the A.S.R. He had used this hotel before and knew his possessions would be safe.

An hour later, dressed in shabby clothes, Henderson walked two blocks and entered a tiny bar and grill. Seating himself at a rear table, he motioned to the bartender and spoke a few words. The bartender knocked on a door leading into what could be a storeroom and then returned to his post. A short, extremely fat man emerged from this door, peered around the room until his eyes locked upon Henderson and then joined Henderson at his table. Foaming glasses of beer were placed in front of the two men by the bartender. Until now, neither had spoken.

"Here's to a long life and plenty of women," the fat man said, downing almost half of his beer in one long swallow. "Good to see you again, Jeff. What brings you into town?"

"The usual thing," Henderson responded. "I've got to go across, as soon as possible. I need crossing papers and an identity that will work anywhere over there."

"I can get that," the fat man murmured. "Cost you the usual amount. Come back just before midnight and I'll have it."

"Who's on the bridge now?" Henderson asked.

"Oh, the same bunch," the fat man replied. "They change shifts once in a while but they can't be replaced. Everybody is on the take and they all know too much about each other for anybody to take a chance on rotating any of those bridge guards."

"How about inland?" Henderson asked. "What's the situation there? I'll need transportation, too."

"How far are you going this time?" the fat man asked softly.

"All the way," Henderson murmured. "Washington."

The fat man whistled softly, then finished his beer and motioned for another before he replied.

"It won't be cheap. I'd say the bus is your best bet," he said. "You don't want to go through Chicago and Cleveland or Toledo because they're bastards up there. It's the lakes. Too easy to get to Canada from there. Your best bet probably would be Evansville and Dayton or Cincinnati, I'd say. Not much activity down there."

"Can you fix it up?" Henderson asked the fat man. "I'd like to go tomorrow if I could."

"No problem," the fat man said without hesitation. "You can pick up your ticket and papers tonight with the rest. Cost you $1,000, though. A lot of people have to be taken care of. You can pay it, can't you?"

Henderson nodded and finished his beer. The fat man motioned for two more beers and absently made circles on the table with his empty glass while waiting for the bartender to arrive. Until that man left, Henderson sat silent and motionless.

"How are things east of here?" he asked the fat man. "Has it calmed down any?"

The fat man laughed uproariously, shaking like a mass of jelly, until he began to wheeze. He coughed and rubbed his eyes, then turned back toward Henderson.

"Calmed down? Like hell! They've got their hands full over there and they don't know what to do about it. Nothing's working! People are trying to jump ship all over, every day. In the past two weeks, they sent three of those terror squads over here and all three deserted! Just didn't come back! I guess there was hell to pay when that happened. It sure hasn't turned out to be the promised land like everybody was told it would be. I wouldn't be surprised if the whole thing didn't blow sky high any day!"

This was useful information for Henderson, not only because of his trip to Washington, but to be relayed back to federal authorities in Denver. He ordered two more beers to keep the fat man talking.

"You can't complain," he told the fat man. "You've made a bundle because of them. Just from me alone and not counting the others. What do you see ahead?"

"Like I told you," the other replied. "I look for the whole thing to blow up. They're getting too goosy over there and people aren't buying that socialist crap any more. They'd rather go to their own church and live their own lives than just get a little manna now and then from that horse's ass in Washington. He's phony and a lot of people can see it now!"

"When are you coming back?" he asked, switching the topic.

"As soon as I can," Henderson responded. "I won't be alone. I'll have a woman and baby with me."

The fat man whistled softly in alarm and stared fixedly at Henderson for several moments before he spoke.

"That's going to be tough," he murmured. "You can't use the bus because you won't have any photos of them for the travel papers, and you certainly can't fly. You'll be lucky if you even manage to get out of Washington. I can't do a thing for you there, but if you could get to Wheeling I could fix you up. It'll cost a lot of money; about $10,000 at least."

"I'll get to Wheeling," Henderson said in his soft voice. "You just make the arrangements and I'll be there. And, they'll be with me!"

All of the papers were ready when he returned to the bar just before midnight. Included were a chauffeur's license and the name of a trucking company in Wheeling that operated between there and East St. Louis, hauling steel. In Washington, he would have to obtain papers for the Congressman's daughter and her baby or else try to smuggle them across the states between there and Missouri. It was a gamble either way, but the odds were no worse than others he had faced.

The almost endless trip to Washington aboard a shabby old bus was uneventful except for document inspections made at every rest stop, day or night, by uniformed domestic security officers. Henderson wasn't impressed by the quality of these officers. Most would have appeared far more at home in an unemployment or welfare line than as the uniformed representative of their central government. At each inspection, they only glanced at Henderson's papers and then continued down the aisle. Henderson began to understand why the fat man had hooted with laughter when he had asked about conditions inside the A.S.R. Unless they were aroused by a personal insult, these people couldn't catch a rabbit! They might or might not win an argument with a marble statue!

As the hours passed while the aged bus growled down the pitted highway at a steady forty miles per hour, Henderson spent the time studying the rural landscape and conditions within the small towns where the vehicle stopped to discharge passengers or freight. The farm fields didn't appear to be as tidy as when heavy tillage machinery was part of the inventory at every farm and when profit, rather than assigned production, was the goal of the farmers. At one place in Indiana he saw a gang of people of both sexes in a field of corn, chopping halfheartedly at weeds growing between the rows of ripening plants. A uniformed overseer sat on a nearby camp stool reading a book or magazine, ignoring the workers in the field.

The tiny rural towns were more lively than Henderson had seen them for many years, with few vacant stores and with shoppers on the streets. At first, this puzzled Henderson until he realized the small towns were busy because their citizens no longer owned cars and thus were unable to drive to a nearby city to do their shopping. This had caused new stores to open in their own communities. It was a classic case of supply and demand. *At least,* he thought, *something good has come from this mess!*

Henderson slept most of the night, arousing only when another security inspection occurred, conducted by guards who appeared to be only partially awake. At one town, they stood in front of the bus and did nothing but count the number of passengers while the driver, visibly a veteran of many years behind the wheel, sat drinking a cup of coffee.

It was almost dawn when the old bus ground into Washington and sighed wearily to a stop in the Greyhound depot. The streets at this hour were empty, with nothing moving but delivery vehicles and police cars. Henderson had counted only five moving vehicles along the entire stretch of highway between Winchester and Washington and two of them had been official cars. Normally, at this time in the morning, that thoroughfare should have been filled with vehicles hauling people to work in the federal offices in Washington. Now, it was deserted. Why? This question bothered him.

His papers were checked one final time as he emerged from the bus and headed for the coffee shop for a quick breakfast to restore his alertness. Even though he knew the city well and this wasn't his first visit in his present capacity, he couldn't afford to wander around half awake. He spent almost an hour in the restaurant, studying the customers and trying to estimate their attitudes. Then he strolled outside, and was lucky enough to find the old Ebbetts Hotel still open. For decades, this had been the most anonymous place a person could stay in Washington. It was the ideal location for Henderson.

Within minutes after entering his room, Henderson was asleep but planned to arise before noon. He would spend the afternoon checking the city and finding the address in Arlington where Conway's daughter lived. He would try also to arrange some form of transportation for tomorrow morning, beginning with sources he had used before in earlier assignments. If necessary, he would steal some type of vehicle that wouldn't attract too much attention. As a last resort, he had the name of a person that had been given to him by the fat man in St. Louis, but he hesitated to use it because it was an unknown factor. A person in Henderson's business did not last long if he took unnecessary chances!

The timetable Henderson set for himself was to have all pieces in place by nightfall. Tomorrow morning he would remove Conway's daughter and her child from that Arlington house and be out of

Washington no later than noon, on his way to Wheeling. That was another dimension to the problem. He had to find some form of transportation that went to Wheeling. He had a busy afternoon ahead of him.

As soon as he awoke, Henderson spent almost three minutes in the shower before the water quit, grabbed a quick sandwich in the Greyhound coffee shop and headed toward the rabbit warren of small offices that lined the downtown streets east of the White House. He entered a scruffy building with a cheap credit clothing store on the ground floor and offices with unwashed windows on the second and third floors. The aged wooden stairway creaked ominously as Henderson made his way upstairs and entered a suite marked only by a number painted on the door. The two men inside whirled around and leaped to their feet when the door opened, then relaxed when they recognized Henderson.

"You scared the hell out of me," the shorter one exclaimed as he resumed his seat behind a battered old desk. "I thought that damned door was locked!"

"You're slipping up, Jack," Henderson replied with a small, neat smile that caused his moustache to curl upward. "You won't last long that way! Has the fat man contacted you yet?"

"Not a word," the other man replied. "Is he supposed to ?"

"I thought he would have by now," Henderson said. "It doesn't make any difference, though. It would just have made it easier if he did, but I guess nothing's easy today."

"You can say that again!" Jack exclaimed. "What do you need, Jeff?"

These men were in the same business as Henderson, but operated from within the A.S.R. and almost within sight of the White House. Theirs was an extremely dangerous profession and Henderson didn't like to be seen with them. But because they were partially subsidized by the U.S.A., they were useful and could be trusted. Away from Washington, because their specialty was confined primarily to the District of Columbia, they were of little value. But their assistance could make Henderson's job in Washington much easier. Right now, he needed information from them.

"What brings you here?" the man at the other desk asked.

"A Congressman's pregnant daughter and her child," Henderson replied. "Her husband's dead and I need to know how he died. Art, you're a walking encyclopedia. You can find that out a lot easier than I can."

Henderson slid a paper containing the names and address across the desk. Art frowned at it, then shook his head.

"Doesn't mean a thing to me," he said. "I can run the traps on it, though, and have something by evening. What's your schedule? I hope you don't want to go out today!"

"Late afternoon will be fine," Henderson replied. "Right now, I need to know the lay of the land and I need use of a car for an hour or so to make contact with those people. You can fix me up, can't you?"

Art nodded affirmatively, then offered the use of an old van parked in an alley behind their building. The van, he added, was so battered it was almost invisible! Just then the telephone rang. Art answered and listened for a few moments, meanwhile making notes on a yellow pad.

"We'll get them out to you," he said to the caller. "You can count on it this afternoon. And many thanks for the order."

"Still in the same business?" Henderson asked.

"Same old business," Jack replied while Art made notes on his pad. "Just call Acme Oyster Brokers and you can reach us any time. You might remember that."

His order completed, Art made several telephone calls to suppliers of oysters and, finding one that satisfied, ordered that a delivery be made that afternoon to a restaurant in Silver Spring. Henderson waited patiently until Art completed his calls.

"What's the situation around here now?" he asked.

"Not good," Art responded. "A lot of unrest, particularly from the merchants and the people moved out of those big houses. Also, from what I hear, all hell is breaking loose in the White House!"

"What do you mean?"

"The word is that the beagle—Poynter, I mean—doesn't have any more real power. There was a power play among his Council and he was stripped of anything but a figurehead status. The real power lies in a faction inside his Council."

"How straight is this?"

"Pretty straight; I'd bet my shirt on it! I got it from an aide to one of his disciples, when he was ordering oysters. As he told it, all hell may break loose any day when those holy peckerheads choose up sides and go at each other's throats!"

Henderson gave a low whistle. If this rumor contained even a grain of truth, the difficulties in getting a pregnant woman and baby from Washington to Wheeling would be compounded. He had no time to waste! No later than the following afternoon, he had to be on his way toward Wheeling, using any form of transportation available. He decided to drop his final bomb now, rather than waiting until after he had made contact with the woman and child.

"I need transportation to Wheeling," he said. "I have wheels from there on, but nothing between here and there. Can you do anything about it?"

"Jesus, you sure know how to hurt a guy!" Jack exclaimed, whistling softly before he spoke. "I'm not even sure how to get to Wheeling from here!"

Art tilted back in his swivel chair and gazed absently at the grimy ceiling for almost a minute while Henderson waited patiently for any suggestions about solving his problem. He didn't expect miracles from the two oyster brokers, but the chance existed they might have a secure contact somewhere in Washington who was able to provide transportation. Questions didn't cost anything and frequently were a shortcut to the solution of a problem. His deliberations completed, Art rotated his chair toward Henderson.

"How much money do you have?" he asked. "There just might be a way, but we can't cover it out of here. It won't be free and there are no guarantees. You take your chances."

"I've got money," Henderson replied. "Just remember I'll have a pregnant woman and a baby with me. That limits my options."

"I'll be frank with you," Art said. "It isn't good, but it's better than nothing. I heard of a truck with a sleeper cab that has to be ferried west. I don't know how far, but it's out the other side of Silver Spring. It brought a load in and then the trailer broke down and the tractor has just been sitting there. I found this out when I tried to move a truckload of oysters a couple of days ago.

"I might be able to make a deal with its owner and then use it to move a load of oysters out somewhere between here and Wheeling. I'd provide the trailer and you could drive the thing. We could get you the papers but we couldn't do anything about that woman and child. That part would be up to you to handle. No promises, but I'll try and see if it works!"

"That's all I can ask," Henderson said. "Now, where's the keys to that van? I'd better see what I can do over in Arlington. With any luck, I should be back in about an hour or so."

The van was so faded as to be anonymous, blending invisibly with the traffic on the streets leading to Arlington. Henderson had no trouble locating the address, a once-gracious home with a broad lawn now littered with household discards through which more than a dozen children romped and played. Two faded women sat in patched chairs on the porch. To one side of them, the screen door sagged crookedly as the result of a broken hinge. The women ignored Henderson as he approached and mounted the three steps onto the porch.

"I'm looking for a Mrs. Sheldon," Henderson said randomly to whichever of the women would become the spokesperson. "Cynthia Sheldon. She's a widow with a baby."

"Oh, Cindy," one of the women replied after a pause to make a mental connection. "She's in the back of the second floor. I guess she's up there. She don't go no place much now that she's lost her old man!"

Upstairs, her door was easy to find. It was the only one closed and upon it she had tacked a forlorn file card containing her name. The card was old. It had faded almost white. Henderson knocked on the door and waited. He could hear movement inside the room. While he waited, he glanced down this second-floor hallway which once had opened into a series of large bedrooms. The door into a bathroom at the end of the hall was opened wide, giving a clear view into the battered and faded interior.

Once, and not too long ago, Henderson thought, this was a comfortable and gracious home with plenty of room for visitors and a growing family. It was no wonder the Congressman and his daughter had been proud of it! He could visualize dinner parties in this house, parties where Conway and his wife were guests of their son-in-law and daughter and where the baby had been the center of attention. There would have been comfortable furniture in the living room from where the open stairway led to this floor, and there would have been a big dining table with a lacy covering, standing just inside the two large windows opening onto the lawn.

Today, the living room was little more than a combined lobby and play area for the many children quartered in this house, the dining room was no better than those seen in tenements, and Conway's daughter had been banished into a single room on the second floor of the house she had once owned. It was no wonder that Conway had been concerned about his daughter! Lost in thought, Henderson barely heard the door open or saw the young woman framed within it. Recovering, he couldn't help smiling at his stupidity; lapses like this couldn't be tolerated in his type of work.

"You're Cynthia Sheldon?" he asked. "May I come in?" "Well...I don't know," she replied, shifting position so her body blocked the doorway. "It's about your father. We can't talk out here." "What about him? Is this some kind of trap? I've told the others everything I know!"

"It's no trap," Henderson told her gently. "He sent me to find you and bring you home. Now, can we go inside and talk about it?"

Henderson hadn't intended to tell her this much until after he had learned more about her and especially about her loyalties. It was dangerous to tell too much, too fast. Her sympathies might lie with the new regime. But after her comment about a trap, he had decided to take a chance because her question indicated she was in some kind of trouble, probably associated with the death of her husband. Also, he had heard the movements of a child inside the room, the sounds of a small child playing. There would have been silence if a stranger was in the room with the child.

The interior of the room was no better than a tenement, with too much furniture cramped into inadequate space. Originally this had been a large bedroom. Now it held a double bed, an overstuffed chair salvaged from the parlor, a dinette table with two scuffed chairs, and a large dresser whose top was used for a battered microwave and a dishpan. Cautiously, he lowered himself onto one of the dinette chairs while a small child playing with a wooden spoon stared at him from the middle of the faded carpet.

"I've come to take you home," he said, feeling stupid because no other words immediately came to mind.

"Take me home?" she asked, her voice rising in alarm. "Take me home, where? This is the only home I have! I'm not allowed to leave here without permission. What kind of trick is this? How can you expect me to believe you?"

Silently, Henderson reached into a pocket and handed Cynthia a letter of introduction from her father. This wasn't the first time he had met this type of resistance, so he had come prepared. Until they had seen proof, most people resisted because of fear. They had to be allowed to convince themselves. Once that had been accomplished, they usually became eager participants in the escape. Henderson waited patiently while Cynthia read the letter, tears running unnoticed down her cheeks. The wait gave him time to study her and observe the child. The presence of a small child complicated matters but could prove to be an advantage. A couple with a baby could do almost anything without arousing suspicion. But right now it was time to arouse Cynthia from her bitter tears and make a decision about leaving this cramped apartment.

"Now you should be convinced," he said gently. "We have to talk about when and how you leave here. There's nothing left here for you and your father is waiting. But, first, I have to know one thing. What happened to your husband and why were you so scared when you answered the door?"

"My husband! They came one day and took him to one of those mental camps and that's the last I saw of him. They came back again and told me he had died. That's when we got moved up here. We had two nice rooms downstairs until then. And we even had a refrigerator!"

"How did he die?"

"I don't know," she replied. "Instead of Rich, they just brought back his things, even the little things he had in his pockets. They killed him! I know that much, even if they didn't say so!"

"Why was he taken away?" Henderson asked because this was a crucial question that had to be answered.

"They said he was a political subversive," she responded bitterly. "They said he was working against the government, just because Rich was trying to save this house and couldn't adjust to living in just two little rooms. He was so proud of this house! And it killed him!"

So there it was. Richard Sheldon had been a political activist or at least had given the impression of being one. Something he did or said had attracted the attention of the internal security people and they had removed him from society before he could become too much of a problem. If the normal pattern was followed, it wouldn't end there. Periodically, his widow would be checked to see if she possessed any of those subversive tendencies. She had been moved into this little upstairs room partly as an example of the power they possessed and partly because she could be watched more easily.

Henderson's original intent had been to have her prepare to leave the following morning. Now, because of this new knowledge about her husband, he could not afford to wait. When he left here Cynthia and her baby had to be with him. The two oyster brokers could provide a place to keep them overnight.

"We have to go," he told her as gently as possible. "Now! Gather whatever personal possessions you want to take, as long as they can be carried on your person, but nothing else. When we leave here, we'll have to move fast and can't afford to carry anything along that slows us down. Now, one final thing. How far along are you in your pregnancy? Will you need to take anything along?"

"Pregnancy?" she asked, puzzled for a moment. "Oh, that damned

Loretta in the back downstairs! What did she tell you? Did she say I was pregnant? I thought I might be, but that was before Rich left and I mentioned it to her one day. Damn her and her big mouth! Believe me, I'm not! How could I be?"

Henderson breathed a sigh of relief. This was one burden removed from him. He wasn't surprised. The information he had received and given to the Congressman had passed through several hands before reaching him and had been purchased from a source that was quick but not thorough. Obviously, this source had talked with one of the women downstairs and possibly one of those sitting on the porch when he arrived. That person had simply repeated gossip, which had been included as a postscript to the information forwarded to Henderson. These things happened!

So far, the child had been silent, her mind occupied by the big wooden spoon. She had made no effort to attract the attention of her mother and had shown no curiosity about the strange man in the room. Henderson had seen this before. Children in this new nation learned very early to avoid attracting attention to themselves. Or, if their family was one of the conquerors, they tended to be boisterous and aggressive. Henderson waited quietly, allowing Cynthia to get her daughter ready for leaving. The child would speak sooner or later, after she had become more accustomed to Henderson's presence.

They left with Cynthia and her daughter herded in front of Henderson like prisoners. Henderson even pushed Cynthia once, not too gently, for the benefit of the two women on the porch who were watching intently. As soon as they were safely in the van, Henderson took the shortest route possible back from Arlington and parked the van a block away from the oyster brokers' office. If one of those women was an informant and had given the description of the van, the trail would lead no farther than that anonymous parking space at the curb. Art or Jack could retrieve the van at their leisure. The security people would lose interest in it after it was found to be empty.

Walking like a family, Henderson and his charges entered the office of the oyster brokers. Art was gone somewhere but Jack sat with his feet propped on the desk. When the trio entered, he peered over a magazine he was reading and his feet dropped to the floor as he rotated the chair to face Henderson.

"What the hell!" he exploded. "Why did you bring them here? Do you want to blow us right out of the water?"

"Calm down," Henderson retorted. "I didn't really have any choice because time was running out for them. They were marked and were being watched. I'll explain later about that when we're alone, but right now we've got to get them out of sight until tomorrow morning."

"Where did you leave the van?" Jack asked. "It isn't out in the alley, is it?"

"It's parked down the street at the curb," Henderson said, dropping the keys on Jack's desk. "You can get it later after it's sat there a while."

Holding her daughter Susan by one hand, Cynthia had remained standing quietly just inside the door. When Susan began fidgeting, she moved across the room and sat in one of the battered chairs, the child on her lap. She still hadn't spoken but had listened intently to the men. She understood Jack's alarm over her presence in this office. If there had been any choice, she would have taken her daughter and left rather than be the cause of friction. Becoming aware of her discomfort, Jack turned toward her and smiled.

"Don't worry," he said warmly, "we'll take care of you. Come on with me. We have two rooms at the end of the hall that we keep just for this purpose. You'll be comfortable there while we decide how to get you out."

She followed him down the hall, Susan trailing along beside her. A few minutes later, Jack returned and resumed his seat behind the desk, turning the chair so it faced Henderson.

"Art's out right now making the arrangements," he said. "You'll be leaving early in the morning. It'll be in that truck, like he said. Don't try coming back here. That would be too much traffic into this fleatrap. Give me your room number and then go back to your hotel and wait. Art and I will come there this evening and give you the details.

"The girl and her baby will be just fine here and I'll see they get fed. It's just as well they're here. Now, nobody will have to go pick them up. The best thing you can do is to get out of here and go take a nap or something. Just keep out of sight until we get there this evening."

Henderson always enjoyed the satisfaction that came when one of these operations came together smoothly with most of the initial difficulties behind him. The worst part of this one seemed to be over. Now all that remained was to reach Wheeling and get behind the wheel of the truck that could take him back to St. Louis and freedom. He was lying on the bed, sleeping peacefully, when Art arrived that evening.

# 5

Henderson had just emerged from the hotel when Art arrived, driving a large and official looking car that apparently was saved for special occasions. In the dim light of dawn, it could easily be mistaken for one of the vehicles driven by the security forces. Cynthia and her child were in the rear seat. Henderson slipped into the front beside the driver and the car began rolling before the door was closed. Nobody spoke. Art remained silent while they crossed Washington and entered Silver Spring.

"Almost there," he said softly. "Get ready to make a quick switch. Buddy, you owe me a big one for this! I'm going to bill our friends in Denver for what it has cost us, particularly those oysters and rent for that trailer. Don't ever do this to me again, Jeff, even if it's the President's daughter!"

Henderson remained silent, watching the street ahead. As the city dwindled and became suburbs with fewer houses and larger yards, they passed a slow-moving semi-trailer truck. As soon as they had pulled back into the right hand lane, Art began speaking.

"That was him," he said. "Get ready for the switch and get the hell out of here as fast as you can. Don't stop for anything. The word I get is that today is the day when the Council pitch out the beagle and then declare martial law to cover themselves while they round up as many of his followers as they can locate. You don't want to be around when that happens and neither do I!"

Gradually, he had slowed to permit the truck to overtake the big car. He pulled over to the shoulder and stopped, the truck behind him with its lights turned off. Pulling the girl along beside him with Cynthia carrying Susan, Henderson ran back to the truck, passing Jack en route. No words were spoken. While Henderson was boosting Cynthia and the child up into the high truck cab, Jack leaped into the car and it sped off. Henderson swung into the truck, engaged the gears and it too began moving. The entire switch had taken only seconds to complete.

As the miles fell behind, Cynthia sat rigid and silent, staring out of the windshield. Henderson concentrated upon the road ahead and the quirks of this unfamiliar vehicle that had a tendency to drift toward the right. Unaccustomed to rising so early, Susan had become drowsy and Cynthia had helped her crawl into the sleeper compartment where she now slept soundly in the way only a small child can sleep.

"Let Susan sleep as long as she can," Henderson said, turning his eyes toward Cynthia. "She may need it later on. We shouldn't have any trouble unless we come upon an unexpected checkpoint. This is the same highway I came into Washington on, so I'm fairly familiar with it. But if anything does happen, be ready to move when I say so. There won't be time to repeat it."

Cynthia nodded but did not reply. Her rigid expression didn't change and she continued to stare straight ahead as daylight sharpened the details of the cracked pavement. Her eyes followed the yellow line unseeingly. She was, Henderson thought, just now reacting to abandoning her home and all of her familiar possessions. This wasn't unusual. He had encountered it before, so he resumed his silence. This was a problem any person had to work out alone. The miles passed in silence until they approached the state line dividing Maryland from West Virginia, near the small town of Hancock where they would leave the interstate highway and follow secondary roads almost to Wheeling.

"Get in the back," he told Cynthia. "Get as far back as you can and cover yourselves up so it looks like a rumpled bed. Don't make any noise and don't move."

They were the fifth truck in line at the checkpoint. Henderson waited behind the wheel, inching the vehicle forward as the other drivers submitted their papers and waited while the guard inspected their cargo casually and then peered inside the cab before returning the manifest and the driver's permit. The inspection, Henderson decided, was slipshod—as if the guards didn't really care whether or not they found any discrepancies. Then it became his turn at the inspection station.

Instead of handing his papers out of the window to the guard, Henderson climbed down first from the high cab and stood, stretching and scratching the seat of his pants while the guard made his rounds. He left the cab door standing wide open as he strolled a few feet away from the truck. Because the guard could see entirely across the cab through the opened door, he barely glanced inside before returning the papers to Henderson, who apparently was in no hurry to resume his trip. He completed his stretch, made one final pull at his pants and finally climbed into the cab and put the truck into motion. They hadn't gone a dozen yards before he heard a giggle behind him.

"That was the worst performance I ever saw," Cynthia said, trying to contain her mirth. "You did everything but stand on your head!"

"How could you see it?" Henderson asked, smiling and with his eyes flicking briefly back toward the sleeping compartment.

He wasn't surprised by her outburst. This type of reaction was perfectly normal. When people are suddenly removed from surroundings that have become familiar, no matter how unpleasant or hostile, their first emotion is one of gloomy despondency. Then the pendulum swings, and gloom is followed by an almost uncontrollable gaiety. Cynthia was following this familiar pattern.

He kept his eyes on the road as she slid out of the sleeping compartment and into the seat beside him. The child hadn't awakened despite the activity at the checkpoint and the roughness of this two-lane highway that linked the small towns of West Virginia together. There had been an increasing deterioration in the road's surface since they left the interstate at the Maryland state line. This was a mountain road filled with curves and dips into valleys that almost always contained a narrow bridge. Henderson drove cautiously, keeping well below the posted speed limit. Traffic was extremely light and consisted mainly of other trucks.

They had just emerged from a valley and were grinding their way up a steep incline when they were met by a speeding internal security car with five occupants. The red light on one front fender of the vehicle was blinking. Obviously, this car was on some crucial errand and it was headed toward Washington. On impulse and hoping it would work in this aging truck, Henderson turned on the radio and slowly spun the dial until he heard a strong, nearby station. A news bulletin was being read by the announcer.

"We interrupt our regular programming to bring you a special news bulletin," the announcer said. "Chairman Poynter and two Council members were removed from office this morning by the other loyal members of the Council and will be charged with subversion of the national goals and other crimes against the state.

"The Council has instructed all citizens to remain in or near their homes until this crisis has passed. Only emergency and commercial travel will be allowed on the highways in or near Washington. We'll keep you posted as new developments occur. Now, back to our regular programming."

So it had happened exactly as the pair in Washington had said it would! Henderson had seen this pattern in other countries often enough to be able to predict with reasonable accuracy where it would lead. First came seizure of power by a rebellious mob led by a charismatic figure who promised a magical end to all problems and troubles. Inevitably, because this person was essentially an orator and dreamer, he would surround himself with a cadre composed of those with a more practical view of the problems.

They would march into power surrounded by the almost holy halo of their dream and within weeks or months be confronted by the harsh realities of government and its complex problems. For a time, usually no more than a year or so, they would be sustained by their vision and the blind allegiance of the population. They would tinker and make changes and try to adapt the existing bureaucratic structure to their goals. Eventually, when nothing worked as intended, they would turn upon each other and collectively begin searching for a scapegoat who could be sacrificed to keep their dream alive. Inevitably, the scapegoat proved to be their charismatic leader whose halo had become tarnished and pitted.

The final step, Henderson knew from experience, would consist of a division of loyalties and power as each group among the rebels sought to become the sole survivor of the palace rebellion. This, he knew, was what was ahead now that the power structure of the A.S.R. had exploded into splinters. And with a potential civil war brewing all around him, here he was with a woman, a baby, and more than 600 miles to go before they reached the safety of the Mississippi River! In addition, he was saddled with an aging truck and a trailer apparently filled with oysters! At the next opportunity, he would pull into a truck stop and try to pump information from other drivers.

Almost thirty minutes passed with no other traffic met on this rough, narrow highway before the billboards of a truck stop appeared ahead at the outskirts of a small village. As they slowed to pull into its parking lot, Henderson coached Cynthia and her child to be silent in the cafe and not speak about Washington or the crisis underway there. They were, he told them brutally, outlaws and must behave as such. Cynthia nodded, understanding his motives.

Slowly, ponderous as a dinosaur, the truck crept into the cafe's parking lot. Henderson halted where the vehicle's signs weren't visible from the highway. This was a precautionary move in light of the crisis, because for all Henderson knew the truck could be a stolen vehicle. Both Jack and Art were careful men, so Henderson doubted it; but the cargo might not bear close scrutiny.

While Cynthia awakened Susan and lifted the child down from the high cab, Henderson circled the vehicle to check its tires. This gave him a chance to observe the other parked rigs and the occupants of the cafe. He saw nothing suspicious so he rejoined Cynthia and the child and the trio entered the cafe, taking a vacant booth near the front window. News of the coup in Washington blared from a radio behind the counter. The armed forces, it seemed, were divided in their loyalty. Some units had obeyed orders from the Council while others still supported Poynter and had declared a state of emergency, vowing to protect their territory against invasion by rebels. It was rapidly becoming a classic example of a fallen government and a country in national disarray.

Excusing himself, Henderson stepped over to the counter to talk with an aging, potbellied driver who was listening intently to the radio and frowning over the news from Washington. This man bore the stamp of someone who had spent decades behind the wheel and covered millions of miles of highway and thus should be a useful source of information.

"Which way are you headed?" Henderson asked. "I hope it isn't into Washington!"

"It sure as hell is," the man responded. "Now, with that mess, I don't know what to do! I guess I'll just wait a while. At least I'm not pulling any perishables."

"How's the road down the other way?" Henderson asked the question that had led him to make contact with this driver. For all the other man knew, Henderson was just another trucker asking normal, commonplace questions about the condition of the highways.

"Open and normal, but watch yourself around Fairmont. They had the scales set up there yesterday and were really racking a lot of the guys!"

"That's why I'm taking this back road to get to Wheeling," Henderson commented softly as if imparting a secret. "It's a hot cargo and with the wife and baby along I can't afford to get stopped!"

"Cute little thing," the driver remarked. "The baby, I mean, but your wife's pretty, too!"

While he was gone, Cynthia and the child had left for the restroom and the waitress had cleaned the table. Henderson paid with a yellowback and received change in the new coin of the A.S.R., then went outdoors to wait by the truck. He had the engine running to build up air pressure by the time they arrived. The vehicle began rolling as soon as they were aboard. With the A.S.R. apparently crumbling, they had no time to spare. They had to get into Wheeling and be headed west across Ohio as soon as possible.

The scales were gone by the time they crossed the interstate and were approaching Fairmont, but the streets in that community were virtually deserted except for three large trucks headed toward Washington or somewhere in Virginia. Uniformed guards with rifles stood in front of the post office and city hall. As they left Fairmont, a National Guard truck filled with armed soldiers sped eastward. It was followed by a Jeep with a machine gun mounted behind the driver. Henderson cautiously pulled toward the side of the road to give plenty of room to these military vehicles. The news from Washington, according to the radio, was becoming steadily worse.

The Council continued to denounce Poynter for his crimes against the people and they promised peace and prosperity with him gone. Meanwhile, military units loyal to Poynter were reported to be marching toward Washington to restore the rightful government to power. In Pennsylvania and New Jersey, battles between rival military units were reported. Because of the unrest, the U.S.A. was reported to be massing military forces along the Mississippi, ready to launch an invasion at any moment. The whereabouts of Poynter and the two arrested Council members, according to one news bulletin, were not known. "They may be dead," the reporter added as an afterthought.

*That's what we really need,* Henderson said to himself, *a dead martyr on our hands with this truck in the middle of nowhere and with a woman and baby on board!* As long as he remained visibly alive, Poynter could be fed to the sharks and the crisis would pass; but if he were actually dead, he would become a martyr and this nation would find itself split right down the middle. Even though his idealistic policies had failed, the average citizen still saw Poynter as a dedicated man trying to do his best in the face of crippling odds. Henderson had seen this happen before, in other countries much smaller than the A.S.R. and with a less sophisticated population. He didn't want to be caught on this minor highway if the nation exploded. *Two more hours,* he thought. *That's all I need to get into Wheeling and be rid of this truck.* Wheeling was large enough to permit three people to vanish for a week or a month if necessary. He pushed the old truck as fast as he dared on this broken highway, the miles falling behind them.

And then Wheeling was just ahead of them. Henderson pulled into a truck stop to find directions to the terminal where he would leave this vehicle and exchange it for one provided by the fat man in St. Louis. The oysters, as far as he cared, could lie in that trailer and rot! *If they were oysters,* he added to himself, *and not some other cargo that Art and Jack wanted moved to Wheeling.*

The exchange was made quickly and smoothly. All Henderson had to do was surrender the papers to the old truck, give the name that had been chosen for him by the fat man, and be assigned to another vehicle with a cargo for East St. Louis. Within an hour they were out of Wheeling, across the river and were rolling through the foothills of eastern Ohio toward Cambridge and Columbus. Because they now had legal papers, including identifications for Cynthia and Susan, Henderson relaxed more than at any time since leaving Washington. But they still had a long way to go, and anything could happen before the trip ended.

Cynthia had remained silent since they left Wheeling, concentrating on getting Susan settled in the new truck and keeping the child's mind occupied so she wouldn't disturb Henderson. For a while, she had held Susan on her lap but now the child was in the sleeper compartment playing with an old leather glove she had found tucked beside the mattress. The miles rolled past as Henderson crowded the truck to the speed limit to put as much distance as possible between themselves and the crisis in Washington.

Cynthia felt tired and grimy from the dirty leather seats in these trucks and, because they had eaten nothing since leaving that roadside cafe in West Virginia, she was hungry. She knew it was only a matter of time before Susan erupted from hunger or boredom. Her duty, as Cynthia saw it, was to keep the child quiet so Henderson could concentrate upon driving. She felt very vulnerable, completely dependent upon this man she had met only one day earlier. Even if it was only a shabby room where she lived, she would have refused to leave with Henderson if it hadn't been for that long letter from her father.

For several miles, she sat quietly in the leather seat with her hands folded on her lap, allowing her mind to drift wherever it chose. She recalled her younger days when the family first came to Washington, every detail of her marriage to Richard Sheldon and the day they had bought the house in Arlington. With horror, she recalled the time when the mobs had flowed like a liquid mass into Washington, filling the entire area around the White House and Capitol and obliterating Lafayette Park. *And they kept coming and kept coming until they were like flies on a dead carcass.* She forced her mind away from this topic and began concentrating on the highway to allow its images to replace those dredged out of her memory.

"You know, we'll have to stop and get something to eat before long or we'll have a tiny tornado on our hands," she said, turning toward where Henderson sat behind the wheel, his eyes fixed upon the road ahead and the distant horizon. He smiled and glanced briefly at her.

"Cambridge is just ahead," he replied. "Unless something happens, we'll stop there."

They pulled off the interstate at the Cambridge exit and eased into a nearby truck stop, parking between two other vehicles and where an easy departure was possible. Because of the crisis in Washington that had overflowed into the countryside, Henderson had approached this exit with caution. He hadn't seen any abnormal activity around the truck stop or in the direction of the town, so he had decided this would be a safe place to rest awhile, stretch and obtain food. He planned to be underway again within an hour. That would give them time to relax and he might be able to learn something about road conditions ahead, across Ohio and into Indiana.

They were like a family when they climbed down from the cab and crossed the tarmac toward the restaurant. Cynthia held Susan's hand while she and Henderson walked together like man and wife. Entering the cafe, Cynthia and the child headed for the restroom, leaving Henderson to select a table or booth. He stretched, then chose a large round table near a window with a full view of the parking lot and highway. While he waited, Henderson ordered a cup of coffee and listened to the radio by the cash register. He noticed that everyone else in the room was also listening intently, waiting for the news bulletins that interrupted the normal programming every few minutes.

The new regime in Washington had proclaimed martial law to try to end the unrest that had erupted within hours after the Poynter government had fallen. Several states, especially those in Dixie, had remained loyal to Poynter and had activated their National Guard units with orders to prevent any invasion by forces of the new regime in Washington. In response, the Council in Washington had declared a national state of emergency and the entire Council— minus the two removed members—would appear on television that evening to reassure the people that all steps were being taken to return the nation to normalcy.

In this crisis, Henderson didn't know which way Ohio might jump, whether they would support the ousted Poynter or the new interim Council. Because it was a very conservative state, Henderson suspected Indiana would remain loyal to the fallen regime; but Illinois was impossible to predict. For Illinois, there were three possibilities. It could remain loyal to the original government, it could join the rebel Council, or it could just blow wide open with the big cities supporting one faction while the rural areas went in the opposite direction. And they had to cross both Indiana and Illinois to reach safety!

Henderson left Cynthia and Susan eating sandwiches while he strolled outside to talk with the other drivers and see what useful information he could acquire. Of the five vehicles in the lot, all but one were westbound and the lone eastbound truck had been there since yesterday, awaiting repair parts for its air compressor. The absence of any eastbound units bothered the other drivers, who were huddled together beside a red and white tanker, talking and gesticulating. When Henderson joined them, they fell silent for a few moments while they studied him, then resumed their discussion.

"I tell you," said one huge man built like a bear, "there's some kind of a roadblock ahead or there'd be more eastbound traffic. It just ain't normal not to have anybody going east!"

"Aw, you're full of crap," another driver retorted. "You heard the radio telling people to stay off the roads. They're just holed up somewhere drinking beer and taking it easy."

"All of them?" the huge man wondered. "What about the scheduled boys? They have to keep going. And what about the CB? You heard my CB, that there are a lotta bears ahead. What's happened to him since then? He hasn't said one damned word since then. Nothing! Not one damned word!"

"Maybe he got out of range," one of the other drivers suggested.

"Bull!" the huge man snorted. "That was Coyote and you know Coyote's illegal! He just cranks up his CB and lets it blast! He may have been forty or fifty miles away."

Quickly, before this disagreement could continue, Henderson broke into the conversation. If the interstate highway was blocked anywhere west of Cambridge, he needed to know. He didn't want to get trapped between exits, which almost obviously had been the case with Coyote.

"Did he say where he was when he called?" he asked. "What would be the most likely spot for a roadblock, if that's what it was?"

"Zanesville," one driver replied and the others nodded agreement. "If there's a roadblock, that's where it is; and it's within CB range!"

"Is there any way around it?" Henderson asked.

One man older than the rest and badly weathered by many years behind a windshield stepped forward. Until now, he had only listened.

"There's an old road beginning near Byesville that winds down through Lancaster and Washington Court House that'll take you clear around Zanesville and Columbus and then you can take 68 or 72 into Springfield and you're back on the interstate," he mused. "That misses all of it."

"Why don't we form a convoy and take it?" Henderson suggested and then turned toward the older man. "You know the way. You lead it!"

This offer was made deliberately to recruit the old driver as an ally who now would be forced to defend his suggestion in the debate that would follow. Each of the other drivers, Henderson was sure, would feel compelled to voice some objection to this plan, or suggest an alternate way to solve the problem, before deciding to join the proposed convoy. Meanwhile, time was being wasted and Henderson was becoming increasingly worried by the lack of any traffic on the interstate highway. To try to force a decision, he started the engine of his truck and beckoned to Cynthia and Susan to join him. Until now, they had been watching absently from the cafe doorway.

As Henderson hoped, the engine noise helped to decide the debate. He climbed out of the cab when the old driver beckoned to him and then walked over to the group who were now jockeying for position in the convoy. The old man was smiling broadly, proud to become the leader of this movement.

"I'm taking the front door," he announced. "And Turkey there will have the back door because he's got a good CB." He motioned toward the huge man. "Where do you want to be?"

As they drove out of the truck stop, Henderson maneuvered into third place, two vehicles behind the leader. This would give him the option of turning suddenly onto a farm road if the convoy was threatened by any of the security forces, leaving the front and rear vehicles as buffers. By the time they had rolled past, he could be well on his way down the farm road. If he was followed, he could drop his trailer in the roadway to halt any pursuit. This type of radical strategy was normal for Henderson. He always prepared for the worst possible contingency and, more than once, this had saved him from disaster.

The convoy rolled through Cambridge like a herd of behemoths, then down an ancient brick highway to Byesville, and turned west on an old pavement that must have been the original highway into Cambridge. It was rough and pitted, its edges ragged and lacy from age and hard use. Periodically, there were old iron bridges that shook beneath the weight of these monster trucks. The only traffic they saw was one farm truck and it turned harmlessly onto a dirt crossroad.

Henderson kept the radio turned on and tuned to a Columbus station. Cynthia sat quietly in the passenger seat and Susan was in the sleeper section playing with the old leather glove. For the first several miles, neither Cynthia nor Henderson had spoken after the vehicle began rolling. This permitted Henderson's mind to remain on the road and the distant horizon to try to spot anything ahead before the convoy reached it. For the moment, the radio was playing country music. Then, this was interrupted by another news bulletin.

"Forces loyal to the central government have been putting down the disloyal rebellion of mobs in some sections of Ohio," the announcer read without inflection. "Order is expected to be restored by nightfall. In Washington, the Council has called upon all citizens to remain in their homes. There is no cause for alarm. Stay tuned to this station for further developments."

The convoy rolled on through the early afternoon hours and didn't slacken speed when it crossed the north-and-south highway leading into Zanesville. The choppy hills of eastern Ohio were being replaced gradually by farmland. So far, there was no cause for alarm and other than a few farm vehicles, no traffic had been met. Henderson had to keep shifting his eyes to remain awake. Cynthia had remained silent, dozing in the other seat, and Susan was apparently asleep back in her compartment. The old man leading the convoy was maintaining a relentless pace despite the rough pavement, not slowing for either curves or bridges.

Henderson almost missed the bright brake light on the rear of the truck ahead of him and the space between vehicles narrowed dangerously before his foot swung onto the brake pedal and pushed almost violently. The sudden loss of speed awakened Cynthia with a start. Unconsciously, her hand closed tightly on Henderson's shoulder as the rear of the trailer ahead came closer and closer. Henderson kept one eye on his rearview mirror, afraid that his rapid deceleration would cause the truck behind him to smash into his vehicle.

Gradually the old man ahead reduced his speed and pulled off the pavement, then stopped in front of an abandoned service station and repair shop with a dilapidated sign hanging from one hinge. Before the last truck had sighed to a stop behind him, the old man hopped like an aged rabbit from his vehicle and trotted back to where the other drivers had begun gathering.

"Gotta go water my dog," he announced. "This appeared to be the best place this road had to offer!" He vanished behind the wrecked building and was gone for several minutes, leaving the other drivers standing by the convoy.

"I suppose you've all had your radios on," Henderson commented to the group. "It doesn't sound too good. What do you make of it?"

This triggered a confusion of opinions as each driver tried to interpret the news he had heard from whatever station was on his radio. Henderson tried to absorb and analyze each of their comments to produce a composite picture of the military and political climate through which they were rolling in these monstrous vehicles. The drivers were badly worried, that much was certain. But they were also confident of being able to handle any trouble encountered on this forgotten highway.

Susan had awakened and Cynthia approached, holding the child by one hand. She beckoned to Henderson and he strolled to where she had halted.

"I've never done this before, but I guess there's a first time for everything," she said softly. "Will you keep the rest of them out here while we go behind the building?"

Smiling, Henderson nodded and returned to the group of drivers who, by now, were trying to estimate the distance left before this road ended and they would return to the interstate. They became silent when the old man warned that if any danger appeared, it would happen when they crossed the main highway between Dayton and Columbus, and that would occur fewer than twenty miles ahead. This was one of the reasons why he had stopped here. He wanted to warn the drivers about that intersection so they wouldn't be caught by surprise.

Cynthia reappeared from behind the building, trying to adjust her clothing as inconspicuously as possible. *Now*, she thought, *I know how it was to be a pioneer in a covered wagon! What am I doing here, out on a strange road with a bunch of truck drivers and doing a thing like this almost right in front of them? It didn't seem to bother Susie, but it made me feel like I was naked!* She forced herself to smile at Henderson when she rejoined the group, who now were ready to return to their trucks and continue the flight across rural Ohio.

The brief stop had refreshed Henderson and he was more alert as the convoy rushed across the increasingly flat Ohio farmlands. There was no traffic on the Dayton-Columbus highway. The trucks shot through that intersection without reducing speed and soon were out of sight of anyone on that major artery. They were just entering a tiny village when the old man sounded three sharp blasts from his airhorns and immediately began braking to reduce speed. The convoy halted at the edge of town and Henderson, pausing only long enough to tell Cynthia to remain in the truck, ran to the lead vehicle. By now, he had become familiar enough with the old man's behavior to recognize this as a panic stop.

"What's wrong?" he asked while the old man was still climbing down from the cab.

"Plane up ahead that could be a spotter," the old man replied. "I've been getting some strange traffic on my CB that's so faint it's garbled; must be twenty miles or so away."

"What was the plane doing?"

"It was so low I didn't see it at first, but it appeared to be moving back and forth like it was looking for something. Must be somewhere around Lancaster; that'd be my guess. I figured I'd better cut 'er down right here so we could decide what to do."

"You did exactly right," Henderson responded, praising the old man for his good judgment. By now, the other drivers had clustered around them and were muttering to each other, alarmed by this new development. Turkey, the huge man, said he also had heard unfamiliar voices on his CB radio. It seemed almost certain that some form of trouble was ahead and if the convoy continued racing across southern Ohio they would become part of it with escape not possible.

"Did you see any signs of life in this town?" he asked the old man. "It looks like it's almost deserted."

"There's life here," the other retorted. "It's just staying out of sight. They probably think these rigs are filled with militia!"

That thought hadn't hit Henderson. It put an entirely new coloration on their dilemma. If the people in this village were remaining indoors because they feared the truckers, they were probably harmless and could become allies. At least it was worth a chance in light of the danger that was almost certainly ahead.

"Scatter!" he shouted to the other drivers. "Park your rigs in front of houses or in a service station or just parked along the curb downtown, and stay in them. Don't get out for anything! Keep your engines running and your air up. We'll give you a blast on the horn when we're ready to go again."

He pointed toward an abandoned repair shop less than a block away and told the old man to follow him and park beside the building to make the truck appear from the air as if it were being repaired. He stopped his vehicle in front of the shop and opened its hood. By then, the other rigs had vanished into other parts of the little town. The convoy had simply ceased to exist—and not a minute too soon. Flying low, a small olive-green airplane bearing the A.S.R. insignia passed overhead, obviously following the highway. As soon as it was out of sight, Henderson trotted over to the other vehicle and climbed inside, into the passenger seat.

"What do you make of it?" the old man asked. "It looked like they were looking for us! When do you think we can go on?"

"I think we're probably here for the night," Henderson replied softly. "Something's going on up ahead and I don't think we dare to move until we know what it is!"

# 6

The coup had been accomplished quickly and efficiently by the Secretary of Internal Affairs, who was the Chairman's most trusted member of the Council. More and more, Poynter had taken to secreting himself in the Oval Office and spending hours writing speeches that might never be delivered, or outlining grandiose plans for complicated schemes that would be impossible to implement. Increasingly, he had been absent from the twice-weekly sessions of the Council and, when present, had been aloof and detached, interrupting debate often to submit outlandish proposals that irritated most of the Council.

There were two members, though, who always agreed with the Chairman whenever these schemes were suggested. By their stubbornness, they would stall debate over important issues for hours and often days. These were the members invited often to join Poynter at a private dinner in the White House or in theoretical discussions in his private study. Like the Chairman, they were dreamers but until now had been tolerated because they were among his original followers and had been with him throughout the long march to Washington.

The final straw came when another Council member discovered a long, rambling proposal written by the Chairman and co-signed by these two Council members, a proposal calling for normalization of relations with the U.S.A. and free movement across the border between these two nations. This paper was brought to the Secretary of Internal Affairs, who immediately circulated it to other members of the Council as a way to judge their reactions. As he had hoped, like him they were outraged that the Chairman should go around them, his own Council, with a scheme of this nature. Didn't he know that, to remain in power, this government always had to have an enemy who could be blamed for any failures or shortcomings? Didn't he know that the U.S.A. was just waiting like a coiled snake for the proper time to strike and destroy the A.S.R.?

If this new form of government was to succeed, it had to have time—time to allow old memories of the United States to vanish and time that would allow this new generation to reach adulthood with no memories of anything but this new social order. Things weren't perfect yet because there were so many changes still underway and not quite completed and this new country was still being viewed with suspicion by some parts of the world, but there had been far more successes than failures. An entirely new social order based upon true equality from the bottom up, with no more dependence upon bones thrown by greedy and wealthy corporations, was being established.

The Secretary recalled his earlier days when he had been pink-slipped by one corporation after another, each time a reduction in the factory workforce occurred. Maybe it was only coincidence, but it seemed that inflation soared each time a job was lost. He had become poorer and poorer while the corporate officers got richer and richer! He had seen them in television interviews, sitting smugly in their panelled offices, and he had heard the reports of profits on radio business programs. When he met Poynter, he had sunk so low he was living in a slum with no hot water, cockroaches in the bed and heat that was so erratic as to be almost worthless. It was the promise of equality that had attracted him to Poynter, equality and the possibility of revenge upon a system that had thrown him away.

Now the Chairman wanted to forfeit all of these gains by opening the door to the greedy system he had overthrown! The Secretary almost vomited at the insanity of this scheme. The Chairman and his two cronies had to go!

Very early in life, Mike Gorcey had learned to play his cards with extreme caution and to wait until he had an advantage before attacking any opponents. Born the son of paycheck parents, his earliest memories of his mother were of her leaving the flat every morning as soon as the sitter arrived. Until he was old enough to attend daycare school, his life had been guided almost entirely by a succession of sitters more interested in themselves than in this small child. He learned to be cautious because he was never quite certain of their reactions.

In day-care school he became aware that society was divided into various groupings, with the prize going to the group with the most strength combined with the ability to maneuver others into joining them, then discarding these allies once the prize had been won. He watched and he learned. By the time he completed high school at the insistence of his parents, he had become a veteran of the streets where he survived by selecting allies carefully and then pitting one group against another. When they were at each other's throats, he had taken what he wanted and walked away to begin the process all over again with new allies.

Mike Gorcey was proud of his first real job in a large corporation where he earned as much as either of his parents. He dressed well, spent money as he chose and was seen often with a girl on his arm. His utopia was shattered when cracks appeared in the nation's economy and he was left jobless as the result of a massive layoff. He returned to the streets and survived by using the knowledge he had been acquiring.

Two later jobs ended much the same as the first. Both were victims of a crumbling, debt-ridden national economy in which the wealth was being wrung out of society like water from a sponge. By this time, Mike's parents, in desperation from what appeared to be a permanent loss of jobs and income, had given up their flat to avoid eviction and gone to live with an elderly relative in New England who had a large house and needed caretaker help. Once again, Mike returned to the streets and used his knowledge to try to survive. He became wary and alert, watching for any opportunity that might appear. Meanwhile, the crumbling of the city's economic base became almost an avalanche and the streets became too dangerous for survival alone.

At this point Mike Gorcey became aware of the movement that was taking shape around Poynter in response to his evangelistic promises of equality and wealth for anyone who would follow him. Within days, Gorcey was a recruit and faithful follower—willing to handle any assignment but always remaining alert to opportunity and, along the way, gathering his own group of followers kept dependent by the favors and prestige he bestowed upon them. It wasn't long before he became part of Poynter's inner circle and he carried the banner when Poynter's army entered Washington. When the new government was formed it was logical that Gorcey should become part of the ruling Council.

But there was a part of him that Poynter never knew and wasn't permitted to see. Despite his high office, Gorcey remained unchanged from the days when the streets were his kingdom and he survived by playing the odds, pitting one faction against another to keep them occupied while he grabbed the prize. In the Council, he watched and waited, meanwhile creating his own private power structure within the overall scheme of government. At the first sign of weakness or dissent, he would pounce. This was one job where he wouldn't permit a layoff to occur!

The time arrived when members of the Council began bickering with each other over almost anything on the agenda and when the Chairman appeared to lose interest in the government he had created. Gorcey knew it was time to make his move when Poynter went into virtual seclusion and began sending aimless, meandering proposals to the Council, measures that did nothing but intensify the already developing split among its membership.

The takeover was almost too easy! Entry into the White House grounds was made with passes issued by Gorcey. His specially selected militia squad simply walked into the Oval Office and bundled the Chairman outdoors and into an unmarked van. Simultaneously, other squads were seizing the two marked Council members. All three were being held in a windowless room inside an empty warehouse in Baltimore. They would remain there, alive, as long as they had potential value to Gorcey. After their usefulness ended, they would vanish.

Once you apply leverage to do away with an opponent, you never remove it until every risk of counterforce has been eliminated. This was one of the earliest lessons Gorcey had learned on the streets. First, and using someone else if possible, you stamp out the strongest opponent. When he has been made into an example of defeat, you give the other opponents the choice of joining you or facing the same fate. These were the tactics Gorcey used with the other members of the Council, emphasizing the utter disappearance of the Chairman and hinting that he was no longer alive. He did this with the Council chambers surrounded by squads from his own personal militia units.

Within two hours the Council was reorganized with Gorcey as its new Chairman. His first official act was to hold a press conference and announce the overthrow of Poynter and two Council members charged with crimes against the people. Drawing upon his own background on the streets where all possible sources of resistance had to be neutralized quickly to create absolute power, his second act was to suspend all civil laws and place the nation under military authority. This was when he overstepped the limitations of his victory.

Almost immediately, riots erupted in most of the major cities, led by people for whom Poynter was almost an idol. Gorcey had failed to take into account the fact that, in the uncertain world of today, much of the population feared change because change generally resulted in the onset of difficult and unpleasant times. It had been only about five years since the new nation was founded by a militant minority and now, apparently, it was falling apart. For anyone with a grudge against the present regime, this was an opportunity to settle old scores by direct and drastic methods.

Placing the nation under martial law before there was time to notify all militia units resulted in almost immediate chaos, especially since the move was ordered by someone other than Poynter. Some units obeyed the order and immediately seized state capitols, courthouses and city halls; but other units, especially those in the larger cities, remained loyal to Poynter and refused to honor the order. Minor battles erupted where two units were stationed a few miles from each other but obeying different masters. By nightfall, the original dream of a new society based upon total equality for all citizens had become a disorganized shambles. Gorcey's street strategy had backfired. Instead of creating order, he had destroyed it!

Once Poynter had been removed from the Oval Office, Gorcey had ordered that all of Poynter's personal effects be hauled away and the big desk cleared of everything not directly associated with governing the nation. His next act was to issue an ultimatum to the civil service personnel in the building: Accept me as your new boss or face the same fate as your former chief! With his power consolidated inside the building, he had ordered that a memorandum be circulated immediately to all federal agencies scattered around the city. This was delivered by armed messengers from his own personal staff. Finally, he ordered that all members of the White House security force be replaced by men from his own militia.

He slept that night in the White House and even wore pajamas left behind by Poynter. This was the culmination of his dream. His power play had been successful. He, a kid from the streets whose parents had lived from paycheck to paycheck, was now the undisputed leader of the nation! His years of watching, listening and learning were over. From now on, the entire world would be watching him and learning from him! He fell asleep that night a very satisfied man.

The news the next morning was grim; it ruined the breakfast he was served in the formal dining room. Pockets of revolution had erupted throughout the nation and especially in the more conservative states such as Indiana, Ohio and Kentucky. Governors of some of the southern states had ignored their oath of allegiance to the Council by placing their National Guard units on active duty, charged with defending their state against any outsiders. And the Russian ambassador was demanding an immediate audience with Poynter, still recognized as Chairman by the U.S.S.R., which had invested heavily in this new nation that now had apparently fallen apart.

That wasn't the end of it! Railroad lines had been blocked in quite a few locations and the U.S.A. was reported to be massing an army along the Mississippi River, ready to launch an invasion at any moment. Gorcey was chilled to the bone by the time he finished reading these reports. Then he became furious at these challenges to his power.

"Fools!" he shouted, hurling a coffee cup across the room. "What's the matter with them? Do they want to destroy everything? If they want force, I'll give them force they won't forget tomorrow! I want an order cut right now and distributed to the proper people with a warning that if they don't obey, they'll join Poynter. Here's what I want to say in it:

"I want all of those rebel militia units put out of action at once even if it means a battle. I want all of those southern Governors arrested and held until this is over. Those redneck bastards! I want all traffic halted on all of the major highways, especially those in the states mentioned in the memos, and I want any truck stopped and held that might be carrying supplies to those damned military units that won't accept this government. Let the bastards starve!

"Put this out in strong words over my signature and see that plenty of copies get circulated. Put in that this order goes into effect at once, immediately, and I want a report every day from anybody who is involved. Let them know they can be replaced if they don't get results!"

Response to this order by military forces stationed in Columbus was the cause for the small airplane seen by Henderson and the convoy while they were stopped at the tiny Ohio village. A few miles beyond the town, the plane circled and returned to make a lazy pass over the village, then departed toward the east. Henderson relaxed and glanced toward Cynthia, who was sitting rigidly with one hand covering her mouth. Her eyes were opened wide, staring at nothing. Her fear musthave been transmitted to Susan because the child was crouched, immobile and silent, in the sleeper compartment.

"It's all over for now," Henderson said softly, smiling at Cynthia. "I doubt if they'll be back."

Whether the spotter plane returned or not made no difference. Its presence indicated that a crisis existed and included some form of turmoil in this part of Ohio. Even though it would drain the battery, he had kept the truck radio playing while they waited adjacent to this old building. From where he sat, he could watch the old man slouching in his vehicle a few yards away and he was able to see another member of the convoy, probably Turkey from the appearance of his rig, parked next to the curb in the tiny downtown area.

Suddenly an awful thought hit him. Were any of these truckers using their CB radios to talk with each other? If they were, this could have been what attracted the spotter plane, which probably was equipped with a CB unit to permit the pilot to monitor truckers on the highway. He decided to take a chance and go talk with the old man, who obviously used his CB unit as a rolling party line. After telling Cynthia to remain in the truck, Henderson dashed a few yards to the other vehicle and climbed inside.

"Have you been using your CB?" Henderson asked the other driver. "Has Turkey or any of the others been using theirs? If they have, don't answer them. We can't afford to be heard and located!"

"What do you think I am?" the old man replied in annoyance. "Of course I haven't used it! I have more sense than that! Somebody else is, though, but he's so faint I can't hardly hear him. I'd guess he's over near Lancaster someplace or maybe on another highway. I guess all hell's breaking loose up around Columbus and down near Dayton or Cincinnati, one or the other."

"What did he say?"

"Like I said, he was so faint I couldn't hardly hear him but he said something about explosions and a lot of Army traffic on the road. He faded out so bad I couldn't make it all out."

"Do you have any idea where he was?"

"Can't tell exactly but I'd say he was somewhere around Columbus or maybe this side of Dayton, but that's awful far for a CB to carry unless he was illegal like a lot of the boys are today. It kind of spooks me because we'll go awful close to Dayton. I'm not much worried any about Columbus."

"What do you mean?"

"If we stay on this road, we'll thread the needle just north of Dayton and you can almost see the city to the south. I want to get home but from what I've heard on the radio and that CB, I don't know whether I want to take that chance or not."

Henderson frowned. Initially this old road had seemed to be a good way to avoid the interstate across most of central Ohio and they had taken it because, at that time, their only motive was to miss roadblocks on the major highways. They thought they could slip through this gap and be out of Ohio before nightfall. Now there seemed to be a very good likelihood this old highway would become a noose around their necks before they had gone many more miles.

"What would you suggest?" Henderson asked.

"If we go on, there's a state road that goes northwest through Mt. Sterling and Newport and you can go on through Urbana and Piqua and miss Dayton entirely, but you'd still have to cross the interstate between Columbus and Springfield and that old state road goes to hell as soon as you enter Indiana. I just don't know. We might be able to make it."

"And there are military bases in both Dayton and Columbus, and Columbus is the state capital," Henderson commented, musing aloud to himself as he tried to organize his thoughts.

"There sure are!" the old man exclaimed. "With the hell that's going on, I sure wouldn't want to be caught there!"

"What if we stayed right here until we knew what's going on?" Henderson asked. "You've been around a long time. Do you think the other boys would agree to that and really stay, or would they just say to hell with it and then go ahead and leave?"

"What if I went and talked to them? This burg is so little it couldn't be more than four or five blocks long!"

"You do that," Henderson said firmly. "Talk to each of them and while you're at it, try and see if anybody lives here. They could have been moved to a collective co-op."

Cynthia was having trouble with Susan. When Henderson returned to his vehicle the child was sitting on Cynthia's lap and crying bitterly. She had been confined too long in the sleeper compartment and had become fretful and restless. Also, she was hungry because she hadn't eaten since morning and it was now the middle of the afternoon, almost four o'clock. This was another problem Henderson had to try to solve, but any action would have to wait until the old man returned from the other trucks.

Radio programming now constituted almost nothing but news bulletins. Scattered riots by dissident groups had caused the entire nation to be placed under martial law, with orders given to restore the peace at any cost. Battles between National Guard units loyal to their state, and federal forces, were continuing in parts of Ohio and Indiana and in most southern states. To halt the movement of supplies and manpower to the rebels, all intercity traffic was being stopped and roadblocks had been erected along the major highways. Military forces along the Mississippi River border were being strengthened in preparation for the expected invasion by U.S.A. troops.

This was worse than he had expected, but if they were to survive this trap they had to keep informed; so Henderson, fearing for the truck's battery, started the engine and let it idle until the old man returned. His thoughts were confused. Either they were in a tiny island of safety or they were caught between battles in Dayton and Columbus. In a sense, they were in the eye of the storm but with almost five hundred miles to go before reaching safety across the Mississippi. But was it really safe there? If they managed to reach East St. Louis, would they be walking into a battle? And if they didn't make it, what would happen to Cynthia and her baby? He had no answers to these questions. Really, there were no answers.

Henderson hated inaction. He would rather force an issue than become the victim of it. Rather than continue sitting idly in the truck, he decided to explore the old building they were parked beside. If they had to remain here for any length of time, it could provide shelter where Susan could move about instead of remaining confined to the truck. Warning Cynthia to stay in the cab, he climbed to the ground and tried the front door of the building. It was locked, but a sliding doorway on one side opened when he pushed against it.

Inside, the building consisted of three rooms—a grimy office, an even dirtier restroom and a large shop area with tools and bits of metal scattered across the floor, all of it covered with dust that told Henderson the place hadn't been used for at least a year and possibly longer. He tried the lights. They didn't work. However, water flowed from a faucet in the restroom and the toilet flushed. Not only did this indicate the place was served with water from the town's system, but someone had kept it heated the previous winter. Probably, he speculated, machinery was stored in here during the coldest months. He was just finishing his inspection when he felt rather than saw the presence of another person in the room. It was the old driver. Cynthia had told him where Henderson could be found.

"Talked with the other boys," the man said. "We won't have any trouble from them. They have the hell scared out of them by those radio reports. I don't think you could get them to leave here if you wanted to! Couple of them are worried about their families but there isn't a damned thing they can do about it and they know it. Hell, I'm worried about my family too, but I've been stranded before.

"Bill—he's that curly-haired one in that red truck—he's parked in front of a house and he talked to the people living there. It's an old man and woman. There's only about three houses in this town that are occupied. The rest were moved out to a collective this spring.

I saw a little store downtown, but there's not much left in it."

Henderson wasn't greatly surprised by this report. The drivers weren't fools. They knew when to take a chance and when to back away and wait for better odds. By using one or more of the empty houses, they would have shelter and probably some form of food supplies. It would be a tight fit, but they could squeeze three of the trucks inside this building and if necessary put the other two in driveways beside vacant houses. First, though, they would need to neutralize the store and place all of its foodstuffs in one location. They could, he decided, be much worse off.

Within an hour, they had moved their personal possessions into a pair of vacant houses that still contained furniture, and the trucks had been secreted in the machine shop and an abandoned downtown garage. The storekeeper had proven to be sympathetic and cooperative, especially after he had met Cynthia and Susan. Like the drivers, he was frightened about the reports bombarding him from his television set that was able to pick up only the Dayton stations—which had to be watched through a cloud of electronic snow.

There had been no further sign of the spotter plane after its one flight over the community. And there had been absolutely no traffic on the highway. Just before sunset, while the drivers sat on the porch of one of the houses, Cynthia prepared a meal of potatoes and canned meat that had been found in the kitchen. There was also a loaf of somewhat stale bread obtained from the store. Freed from her prison in the truck, Susan ran and played from room to room inside the house. There could be, Henderson thought, worse places to be stranded.

After eating, the drivers and Henderson returned to the porch and sat listening idly to the song of the evening insects. At first the men were almost silent, each absorbed in his own private thoughts. It was Turkey who put these thoughts into words.

"How long do you suppose we'll be stuck here?" he asked. "We may be here for days or even weeks! Does anybody have any ideas?"

"I'll give it two days," a sandy-haired driver commented. "And then I'm gone if the whole damned country isn't gone by that time. My wife's got a baby coming and I can't spend the rest of my life here!"

"Where would you go?" Henderson asked quietly. "You know all of the highways are blocked. Where were you headed?"

"Belleville," the driver replied. "At least, you've got your family with you! You don't have to sit and worry."

The talk continued until dusk began to creep across the village, leaving long shadows on the porch. One by one, the drivers headed for the rooms they had chosen, each carrying a flashlight brought from his truck. They had agreed that, for safety, no lights should be used in these supposedly vacant houses. Sighing heavily, Henderson went inside to where Cynthia was preparing Susan for bed. The child had just emerged from the bathroom where, to Cynthia's delight, she had found not only a clean tub but also towels, a washcloth and soap.

After Susan was asleep, Cynthia and Henderson returned to the porch where they sat rocking silently in the swing, each absorbed in his or her personal thoughts. The night in this village was so silent that individual insects could be heard as they fluttered through nearby foliage. And then, far away, the roar of gunfire destroyed the silence. They weren't individual explosions, but only low and sharp rumbles that made an unpleasant ripple in the night silence.

"Oh God, what was that?" Cynthia murmured, clutching Henderson's arm so tightly her nails bit through his sleeve.

Before Henderson could reply the screen door creaked open and Cassidy, the old man, stepped quietly onto the porch and stood for a moment, listening intently to the distant rumbles that had disturbed his sleep in the upstairs bedroom he had chosen to occupy.

"We aren't going anywhere now," he murmured. "Not now and maybe not for quite a while. I've heard that sound before! Those are cannons!"

Henderson had reached the same conclusion and was listening intently to try to determine the direction from which the rumbles came. They were so faint they could have come from anywhere. The many tall trees in this village erased any opportunity to watch the horizon and perhaps spot the flashes of distant explosions whose origin could be either a battle or a burning munitions dump, a possibility he felt was unlikely. They were too erratic to be an exploding dump, which generally went off in one monstrous blast.

"You know this country pretty well," he said, turning toward Cassidy. "What's your best guess? Dayton, Columbus or where?"

"There's no wind, so it's hard to tell," Cassidy replied. "But if I had to choose, I'd say it's at Dayton. They've got a lot more military stuff there than Columbus, and a big National Guard battalion. I don't want to say but if I had to guess, that's the way I'd see it."

Hearing a faint wail from inside the house, Cynthia arose and went indoors to try to comfort Susan, who obviously had been awakened by the rumbles or just the strangeness of this unfamiliar house. Cassidy remained standing, his head tilted toward the probable direction of the battle. He turned slightly so he faced Henderson in the porch swing.

"What are you going to do about them?" he asked, obviously referring to Cynthia and the child. "If that is a battle, you can't take them out of here if we have to leave and you can't leave them here with that going on just a few miles away. I'm old enough to learn caution so I'll stay here until hell freezes over before I go out into a war, but we can't hold the rest of the boys much longer. Most of them have got families and they want to get home."

These were some of the questions bothering Henderson. If this was actually a battle it could be part of a general rebellion. For the moment they were safe in this house but it was located midway between two large cities, both containing military installations. Their only way out of here was by highway and it would be like threading a needle to avoid the military traffic moving on the interstates. The only way they could leave here without crossing an interstate was south, and that led directly into Dayton.

How long could he hold the other drivers here? Most of them had families somewhere and wanted to be home. He might be able to hold them for about two days before they became impatient and decided to try their luck on the highways. And their departure would jeopardize anyone left behind in this village, because sooner or later they would be stopped, seized and questioned. If that didn't happen, they were bound to be seen on this old roadway, somewhere between the village and the interstate. By one means or another, he had to keep them here as long as possible.

"We'll stay here as long as we can," he answered Cassidy. "I don't see any other option. I'd appreciate it if you'd help me try to keep the other drivers from leaving until it's safer on the roads than it is now. And I'll appreciate it if you'll stay out here awhile and listen while I listen to the radio and try to learn something about what's going on."

Leaving Cassidy sitting in the swing, Henderson went inside and turned on a radio they had found on a table in the dining room. Turning the volume low so it would block out distant stations, he spun the dial until a strong signal was received. Judging from local references made by the announcer, it was a Columbus station which had abandoned any pretense of normal programming to devote its time to an endless string of news bulletins, many of local interest.

The National Guard, at the orders of the Governor, had seized a military installation near Columbus and military airfields at Dayton but were being opposed by Army units loyal to Washington. The Governor had taken this unusual action in reaction to a similar, earlier move by the Governor of Kentucky, who had resisted the order nationalizing all state and local governments. State and local politicians were reported to have denounced this order throughout the nation, calling loudly for active resistance against it.

Until now, the lower levels of government had remained passive because they had been left alone and allowed to pursue their own policies within the loose guidelines of Washington. Their methods of operation had remained unchanged since the days when only one nation existed on the continent. When war erupted with the breakaway West they had supported Washington because it was their historical duty to do so. After the war ended and when peace had been restored, they had been kept pacified and cooperative by the virtually unlimited number of the new yellow dollars allocated to them for projects they wanted to pursue.

Gradually, though, there had been encroachment by Washington upon the traditional functions of state and local governments as, one by one, their historical duties were annexed to Washington, leaving the elected state and local officials as little more than figureheads handling only localized functions that varied from state to state but with all important decisions made in Washington. This power shift planted the seeds of resentment but, as long as things went smoothly, there was no choice but to bow to the will of Washington and cooperate. Now it was Washington that was in turmoil, while the states and cities remained intact with their governments untouched and in close proximity to the people.

It was Mississippi that moved first after the coup in Washington and the order nationalizing virtually everything in the nation. The National Guard was placed on active duty and ordered to seize and hold every federal installation in the state. This action by Mississippi gave courage to the other southern states and within hours they had taken similar action. Kentucky, on the doorstep of Ohio and less than forty miles from Dayton, was included. The Governor of Ohio quickly joined his neighboring states by taking similar action and ordering the seizure of federal installations.

What he didn't take into account was the importance of Ohio to Washington and the ease of movement from Washington to almost anywhere in Ohio. Almost all railroads and interstate highways in

Ohio led either to Washington or New York, in contrast to the situation in the south where a state of partial isolation existed. Troops could be moved to Ohio in a matter of hours, but several days were required for a move to Mississippi. The new government in Washington had to pacify Ohio or risk losing the entire nation.

This explained the distant battle heard by Henderson and his party. By the time Cynthia returned to the porch after Susan was back asleep, another driver had joined Henderson and Cassidy. The sounds of the distant gunfire had, if anything, intensified while she was gone. Everyone on the porch watched and listened but remained silent, as if there were no words to fit this occasion. Cassidy rose to allow Cynthia to sit beside Henderson in the swing. To Cynthia the air on the porch felt electric, as if it were waiting for something to happen. Even the insects had become quiet, also just waiting.

*We're in the middle of a war,* Cynthia thought. *Will we come out of it alive or dead?* She shivered despite the warm night. Maybe one of them would survive and nobody would ever know what had happened to them. She felt desolated and alone and was afraid to learn the answers to these questions.

# 7

Henderson woke with a start, his heart leaping, when he felt a hand shaking his shoulder gently. It was the young driver with the wavy hair, one of those standing watch on two-hour shifts during the night. Dawn wouldn't arrive for at least two more hours. Henderson felt groggy.

Less than four hours had passed since he had stretched out on the sofa in the living room, forcing himself to relax despite the continuing bombardment that rumbled distantly in the background. Somehow he had fallen asleep. Now, with the shape of the young driver outlined faintly in the hooded beam of a flashlight, Henderson sat up quickly.

"We've got company," the driver said softly. "Convoy going through town. Thought I'd better wake you."

They slipped out of the house and onto the front porch. The soft sounds of heavy vehicles on the move could be heard coming from the direction of the highway. There was no mistaking the growl of large engines or the baritone note of exhaust pipes. After telling the young driver to wait on the porch, Henderson trotted across the yard and through shrubbery until he could get a limited view of the highway, the town's main street. After watching for several minutes, he returned to the porch.

"It's Army," he whispered to the other man. "They're going on through and not stopping, but there must be thirty or forty of them. I counted six trucks filled with soldiers and at least two or three others have big guns of some sort mounted on them.

"Don't wake the others. They need their sleep and there's nothing we can do about it anyway!"

Unless it was bound for Springfield or somewhere in Indiana, why was a military convoy using this secondary road that missed both Columbus and Dayton? If it wasn't a flanking movement to get behind somebody, probably at Dayton, this convoy made no sense to Henderson. He had learned one thing, though. It would be virtual suicide to leave the safety of this village until the distant battle was ended and peace returned to this countryside. Any large truck capable of hauling military supplies wouldn't last ten miles before it was destroyed by one side or the other! And there was Cynthia and the baby to worry about.

Henderson went inside and into the dining room, turning the radio on softly. There was nothing but an electronic hum. The station wasn't broadcasting. To Henderson, this was an ominous sign even though he knew it was so early the station's daily programming hadn't yet started. He sighed and returned to the living room, where he sat waiting for the first signs of sunrise to become visible. There was no point in waking any of the others. There was absolutely nothing they could do and they were much better off sleeping. He waited and dozed until the first ray of sunshine crept like a long finger across the carpet.

The creak of the door opening caused Henderson to leap from the sofa, suddenly wide awake. He relaxed and smiled when he saw it was only Turkey, moving slowly and carefully while he balanced a cup of steaming coffee in one hand. He smiled and stopped when he saw Henderson leap to his feet.

"We found some coffee over there and made a pot," he said. "Thought you'd like a cup."

Gratefully, Henderson accepted the coffee. After last night, he needed something to keep him awake. As he grew more alert he became aware the bombardment had stopped. The morning was clear and quiet, its silence broken only by the songs of birds and the faraway barking of a dog. Whatever its cause, the distant battle had ended. It might be possible for the convoy to leave here today but, until more knowledge was acquired, it would be foolish to abandon this temporarily safe haven.

"What do you think?" Turkey asked. "When do you think we can leave? Those explosions quit about an hour ago. I hope you got more sleep last night than I did!"

"I don't know what that was, but I don't see how we can leave here until we find out," Henderson replied. "I can't take Cynthia and the baby out into a war!"

Once again, he tried the radio. This time, the voice of an announcer filled the room and Henderson quickly reduced the volume so the radio wouldn't awaken Susan. The child needed as much sleep as possible while it was quiet. There might not be another opportunity like this. Turkey moved closer and the two men stood, listening intently to the news bulletins.

The sounds heard last night were those of an Army ammunition depot being destroyed after a member of the National Guard allegedly placed a grenade in one of the bunkers. According to the announcer, this was only one in a series of similar events as Guard units in these central states sought to cripple the striking power of the Army. Several military bases had been encircled by units of the National Guard loyal to the state governors, who did not recognize the new regime in Washington. This led, the announcer reported, to mass desertions by Army enlisted personnel who joined the Guard troops.

Washington was taken by surprise by the sudden military resistance led by governors who opposed nationalization of their offices. The Chairman had remained unavailable and members of the Council had met most of the night, but weren't making any statements. No major battles had been reported along the Mississippi River even though hostile U.S.A. forces were reported to be massed along most of the river's length.

*They bit off more than they can chew,* Henderson thought as he listened to the broadcast. *All it took was one governor to use his powers and call out his National Guard and, with a precedent established, the rest would follow.* There was no way that isolated Army units could win against the massive numbers of National Guardsmen in these states. And how many munitions dumps had been blown up? This one near them almost certainly was not the only one. He would have bet that every federal dump in all of these rebellious states had gone up in smoke the previous night.

He had seen this pattern before, in smaller nations whose rulers had pushed the population into open revolt. The supplies of ammunition had always been early targets because their loss weakened the regime being ousted from power. This led, almost always, to a conciliatory offer from the entrenched central government to buy enough time to re-arm itself. For the rebels, this was the most crucial period in their struggle. If they accepted the offer, considered it a victory and then relaxed, they were invariably smashed later after the central government had the time to rebuild its military power.

But there was always a window of time with an illusion of peace; it might continue for several days, or possibly two or three weeks, before the smashing blows were struck. If the pattern were followed now, it could give them enough time to reach their destinations before the next blow fell. The drivers had to remain nearby, ready to leave at any time. If and when the conciliatory bone was thrown to the rebels, they had to take advantage of it. Henderson decided to remain beside the radio to monitor events as they occurred.

The sound of faint voices followed by a giggle came from the bedroom. Obviously, Cynthia and Susan were awake. He heard one of them scuttle down the hall and into the bathroom. An embarrassed Turkey began backing toward the door leading onto the porch. Before he could leave, Cassidy came clumping down the stairs from the upper floor, his thin hair tangled from a restless sleep. Hearing water running in the bathroom, he halted in confusion and then headed for the rear yard. Turkey laughed loudly as Cassidy vanished outdoors.

All of them sat around the dining room table for almost an hour, finishing two pots of coffee and eating bacon found in the refrigerator of the house occupied by the other drivers. Until she began to fidget and then went into the other room to play, Turkey held Susan on his lap and pretended to be a horse she was riding. Henderson remained glued to the radio, hearing and assessing each bulletin given. It was almost noon before the expected conciliatory bone was thrown to the rebellious governors. All Army personnel were being ordered back to their barracks and the highways were being reopened to the movement of essential and commercial supplies. To assure safety, trucks and buses would be required to move in convoys led by National Guard troops. The governors had been notified and had pledged their support and assistance.

*The fox!* Henderson thought. *If he can pin down about half of the National Guard escorting trucks across the states, they won't be available for military action. That will give him time to get his forces in order and then attack when the Guard is scattered to the four winds and at its weakest!* For Henderson, though, this was the window of time he had been waiting for. The escorted convoys were scheduled to begin rolling tomorrow morning and by that time these five trucks had to be on the interstate and ready to head west. If they left early enough, they could be in Springfield well before the 9:00 a.m. starting time and within no more than about thirty hours they would reach the Mississippi. Today could be spent monitoring more broadcasts.

For Cynthia and Susan, it was a day when the crumbling world outside could be forgotten, a day when Cynthia could live as she once had when her husband was alive and they had no cares beyond the normal ones associated with civilized life. She enjoyed utter and complete relaxation and even rediscovered thoughts and attitudes she had all but forgotten. Because they weren't competing for space she occupied and did not represent a threat, the presence of the drivers didn't lessen her enjoyment of this peaceful day.

Henderson remained near the radio. By noon, the tone of the news broadcasts had become less urgent. The Chairman had welcomed the cooperation of the governors in helping to return normalcy to the nation but he neglected to promise that no retaliatory action would be taken in response to their rebellion. Henderson was sure this omission was deliberate. As soon as the governors relaxed, Washington would pounce. Based upon past experience, he estimated they had no more than three to five days to reach St. Louis and cross the river to safety. He planned to leave this village at daybreak and be in Springfield before time for the escorted convoy to leave the next morning.

It wasn't light yet when they left the houses and walked the short distance to where the trucks had been secreted. Within ten minutes all of the engines were idling to build up air pressure for the brakes, and before thirty minutes had passed the huge rigs were in a line along the village's main street, ready to depart. Once again, Cassidy was in the lead truck and Turkey was in the rear "back door" position. The drivers sat with one hand on the steering wheel and the other on the gearshift, waiting for Cassidy to begin rolling.

The road was silent and deserted all the way to Springfield, past farms that were dark and showed no signs of life; only the presence of livestock indicated these farms were occupied and operating. Before Springfield appeared, Cynthia clutched Henderson's arm and turned toward him, her eyes huge and worried.

"It's like being in a dead world," she murmured tonelessly. "It's like being on the moon!"

"It is a dead land," Henderson replied without looking toward her. "Where it isn't dead, it's dying."

Except for an aged woman raking leaves in her yard, and a cluster of people around a restaurant, Springfield had the appearance of having been abandoned. With no traffic to impede its passage, the convoy rolled freely through the city and to the junction with the interstate highway where the escorted convoy was being formed. About two dozen trucks had already arrived and were being divided into separate groups on the basis of their destinations. Henderson, Cassidy and the young driver from Belleville were assigned to a long-haul caravan whose destination was East St. Louis.

Precisely on schedule the convoys left Springfield, each with one National Guard vehicle in front and two following, one containing fuel for the trucks if it should be needed. Within three hours they crossed the border into Indiana with only a brief stop where Indiana

National Guard vehicles replaced those from Ohio. By mid-afternoon they were in Illinois, continuing to roll westward. Their only break had been thirty minutes during the noon hour at a restaurant along the highway. If they remained on schedule, the convoy should reach Belleville and East St. Louis shortly after nightfall.

Bored by the long and uneventful trip, Susan had gradually become restless, tiring of the imaginary games she tried to play back in the sleeper compartment. To keep her occupied, Cynthia finally had crawled back into the compartment and now both of them were asleep.

That left Henderson's mind free to try to plan the actions they would need to take upon arrival at the truck terminal in East St. Louis. With luck, it would be located in the heart of the city and within walking distance of the one remaining bridge. If not, some form of transportation would need to be located to take them to the bridge. Susan could not be expected to walk any great distance.

Once at the bridge, he would need to park Cynthia and the child somewhere in a safe location long enough for him to survey the bridge and learn, if possible, whether the familiar guards were operating the crossing gate. Also, he wanted to try to learn whether or not the papers provided by the fat man in St. Louis were still being accepted, now that a new administration was in power in Washington. He could not afford to place Cynthia and Susan in unnecessary danger. If the papers he carried were no longer valid, he would have to find some other way to cross the river without becoming the target for marksmen on the western bank.

Night had fallen before they were surrounded by the winking lights of East St. Louis and the convoy was escorted down the exit ramp leading into the city. The National Guard vehicles pulled onto the shoulder to allow the trucks in the convoy to scatter to their individual destinations. As soon as they were off the ramp, Cassidy pulled to the side of the road and halted, motioning for Henderson and the young driver to stop.

"Well, we made it!" a grinning Cassidy said as soon as all of them were together beside one of the trailers. "I thought we ought to shake hands, at least, because we may not cross paths again. I'll tell you, I didn't think for a while we'd make it—but we did!"

The old man stared suspiciously when Henderson asked for directions to the terminal and hesitated before offering to lead Henderson to the place, which was across town and near the river.

"Either you're new on this route or you're not a trucker," Cassidy commented. "Either way, I think I owe you one for saving our hides back in Ohio, so just follow me and I'll take you there!"

Henderson grinned, understanding Cassidy perfectly. This was a man who paid his debts and for whom loyalty could not be compromised. Slapping Cassidy lightly on the shoulder, Henderson returned to his rig and waited for the other vehicle to begin moving. With Cassidy in the lead, they cut across East St. Louis to Missouri Avenue and, near the waterfront, onto a narrow street leading to the terminal. Without slackening speed or giving any sign of recognition, Cassidy vanished around a corner as Henderson pulled into the huge lot partially filled with trucks.

Henderson backed carefully to the dock, waved on by a worker waiting to unload the cargo. Leaving Susan and Cynthia in the cab, he strolled unhurriedly into the terminal office with his manifest and other papers. A man with a head so bald it glistened in the overhead light was seated at one of the desks, reading a newspaper while he gnawed on a sandwich that appeared to be nothing but bread and some type of cheese. Whatever it was, the sandwich was as dry as sawdust. The man gulped to force down a bite when he saw Henderson enter and place his trip papers on the counter. Dropping the sandwich carefully on his newspaper, the man slouched across the room to the counter and studied Henderson's papers for several minutes before speaking.

"Where in hell have you been?" he asked. "We've been waiting for you. Solly wants to see you. In there, in that office." He pointed toward a side door.

Henderson walked over and entered the office without knocking. A tall man so thin he appeared skeletal was lounging in a leather chair in one corner, watching television intently. A partially emptied bottle of beer stood on the floor beside the chair. A pair of large, muddy brown eyes rolled in Henderson's direction as he entered and halted just inside the door.

"I guess you must be Jeff," the man remarked hollowly without rising from the chair. "About time you got here! They've been concerned about you and your cargo over there on the other side. That cargo's valuable! Got something for you. They sent it over a couple of days ago to hold for whenever you got here."

Using his arms for leverage, the man lifted himself from the chair and moved across the office to a small, old safe standing behind the desk. It wasn't locked. Crouching effortlessly, Solly pulled a large brown envelope from the safe and, rising like a stork, handed it to

Henderson. It was a standard trip ticket envelope used by truckers everywhere and, as such, was completely anonymous.

"I need your papers," the cadaverous man said. "They're no good any more. You have new papers for you and your passengers in there. They'll get you across with no trouble. Don't go tonight. It's too dangerous at night. Go in the morning when the other shift's working. That's the best time."

While he was talking in that hollow voice, Solly was moving back toward the leather chair. His final words were spoken while he was lowering himself back into the position he had occupied when Henderson entered. He returned his attention to the television, leaving Henderson standing, uncertain about what to do next.

"Many thanks," he said as he left the office. The thin man, he noted, didn't even turn his head when Henderson left.

An exhausted and bored Susan was asleep by the time Henderson returned to the truck. When he entered, he saw Cynthia watching him intently from the sleeper compartment, an unspoken question in her eyes. He slid into the driver's seat and shut the door to permit the child to remain asleep and undisturbed for the moment.

"We'll be all right," he told Cynthia gently. "I've got new papers and we'll cross the bridge in the morning. Now all we have to do is find a place to spend the night."

The fat man in St. Louis hadn't foreseen this need when he made his preparations for their return, but Henderson knew of a small, old hotel within walking distance of the bridge. It was almost a hovel but it might be satisfactory for just one night. The problem was to get from here to there. The streets in this part of the city weren't safe at night and were no place to take a small child.

The problem was solved with almost laughable ease when the dispatcher told Henderson it was common practice, now that taxis had ceased to operate, to haul drivers to their homes or a hotel upon their arrival in the city. An old station wagon was kept at the terminal for this purpose. Within minutes, Henderson and his two passengers were checked into a hotel near the bridge, a much better one than the place Henderson had chosen. They occupied rooms kept reserved by the terminal for incoming drivers.

Cynthia was restless, unable to adjust to the spacious, quiet room that was a shocking contrast to her previous cramped quarters in the rear of the house she and Rich had once owned. Her mind was a tangled cobweb of erratic thoughts, most of them involving this trip and the drastic changes that were ahead once a safe passage across the bridge was completed. Because of Susan, she couldn't permit herself to think about the possible consequences if they failed to reach safety across the river. She would probably be sent to a work camp and Susan would be placed in one of the many children's homes that had been opened in the past few years, places where political indoctrination began as soon as a child was able to talk.

On impulse, she knocked on the connecting door between her room and the one occupied by Henderson. She couldn't face being alone tonight and it would be cruel to awaken Susan, who was sleeping soundly for the first time since they had left Arlington. Let her rest tonight, because it might be her last opportunity until they reached Denver—or some official camp if they failed to get across the bridge. Henderson gave Cynthia a feeling of security. She had to talk with him and try to untangle her thoughts.

When the door opened and she saw him standing there, solid and quiet, she ran to him and put her head on his shoulder. She felt his arms wrap around her and hold her. He still hadn't spoken a word, but to her it wasn't necessary. He was there and she felt secure in his arms. When she felt him stir, she raised her head to look into his eyes.

"I'm sorry," she whispered. "Just hold me. I'm so scared! I couldn't stand to be alone tonight with that bridge ahead of us in the morning. What if we don't make it? What will happen to Susie then, with me gone? What will become of her in one of those camps?"

"We'll make it," Henderson told her gently, his arms around her. "You know, this isn't the first crossing I've had to make. Just keep thinking of Susan, and your father waiting for you, and we'll make it all right. When we get across, we'll all celebrate because it will be all behind us then."

"How can I let my father see me like this?" she asked anxiously. "I'm a mess, inside and out. I wasn't like this the last time he saw me, and Susie's too quiet. What will he think about that? Kids are supposed to laugh and play, not just hide in a corner somewhere and hope nobody notices them. You've seen how she is. She wasn't always like that. She's learned to be afraid. She's learned to stay in a corner out of sight and be quiet so nobody will notice she's there. Will she do the same thing with him when she sees him? It's ugly! That whole life was ugly!"

Holding her to try to reassure her, Henderson spoke softly to her for almost half an hour. He told her about her father's concern and about how Conway didn't expect everything to be the same as when he had seen her before the breakup. And he was looking forward to getting acquainted with the grandchild he had never seen. Wasn't that incentive enough to face the changes that were ahead? When he finally felt Cynthia relax, he leaned forward and kissed her on her forehead, then waited for her to return to the room she shared with Susan. The door shut softly and he was alone.

Crossing the bridge wouldn't be as easy as he had told Cynthia. It was a challenge and there was always the possibility of a surprise inspection by higher officials, or that an expected guard would be gone at that particular moment. New regulations could have been issued overnight, making the inspection procedures more thorough. This was why he always tried to cross in the middle of a mob of workmen who, each day, went west in the morning and returned home late in the afternoon. Guards always relaxed their inspections at those times to expedite the movement of these workmen.

The presence of a small child was an added complication but it could be used to advantage if Cynthia could control her fear of failure. He would need to watch her closely and be prepared to intercede quickly if she showed any signs of panic. This was the last and most crucial obstacle they would face and they couldn't afford failure. With these thoughts circling in his mind like errant mice, he forced himself to sleep; he had to be reasonably fresh the next morning, when they would cross the bridge to safety and freedom.

He was awakened by Susan in the next room, laughing and teasing her mother. This, Henderson thought, was a good omen. Susan was beginning to act more like children in the familiar U.S.A. She was beginning to lose her unnatural silence, air of secrecy and suspicion of anything strange and unfamiliar. A truly communal society where the roughest always ruled, he knew, invariably managed to create these habits of silence, secrecy and suspicious. *Damn them!* he told himself. Somehow, Cynthia and the child had to cross that bridge and reach the safety and freedom that would permit Susan to be a child.

A light drizzle was in the air as they left the hotel to walk the three short blocks to the bridge. Before they had gone halfway, they were surrounded by others commuting to jobs across the Mississippi. Ahead of them the curving deck of the bridge loomed like a huge ramp, glistening coldly in the morning drizzle, the red light at the inspection station glowing faintly, a malevolent beacon that meant freedom or imprisonment. They were passed by several vehicles, mostly trucks, also headed for St. Louis.

By the time they reached the bridge and continued toward the inspection station located midway across the span, they were wet and chilled from the drizzle. Cynthia's hair hung limply around her head and Susan clung to her mother's skirt, trying to shelter herself from the cold rain. Henderson hunched forward when he felt a few icy droplets trickle down his back, inside his jacket and shirt. They joined the queue working its way gradually forward to the inspection gate, where each person displayed his or her papers and then was permitted to move onward when the gate was raised. Three people had been rejected. They stood to one side guarded by soldiers wearing glistening raincoats and carrying automatic rifles. When the morning rush was over, these three and any others denied passage would be taken to detention camps for interrogation. Later, they might or might not be released.

And then it was Cynthia's turn at the gate, where a border guard stood inside a tiny building, away from the rain. Henderson lagged back, holding his breath. If Cynthia and the child were turned back, he would follow and release them; but that would not be possible if he, too, were seized because of them.

He saw Cynthia hold out her papers, trying to cup them with her hand to keep them dry, meanwhile holding Susan tightly with her other hand. He saw the border guard lean out of his booth, then wave them onward. And, finally, he watched as Cynthia and Susan scuttled through the raised gate to safety on the other end of the bridge. Then it was his turn. Because he was being pushed forward by a crowd of workmen with lunch buckets, the guard only glanced at his papers. When the gate shut behind him, Henderson felt limp and exhausted. Once more, he had managed to penetrate the A.S.R. and return safely to the West. Sighing deeply to get himself back under control, he joined Cynthia and Susan and they walked quietly toward the end of the bridge where two city buses waited, their exhausts rumbling.

No matter how many times he crossed this bridge, Henderson was always shocked by this initial view of St. Louis from the river, once dominated by tall buildings and the spectacular memorial arch soaring into the sky over the riverfront park. Today, the arch still stood like a lonely and somewhat ragged sentinel watching over a wasteland. Jagged frameworks that were the remnants of high-rise buildings jutted like broken teeth over the weed-grown expanse of bare land extending from the river to Broadway, whose west side was dotted by a straggle of faded stores catering primarily to the needs of the workmen who crossed the river twice each day. Beyond Broadway, the former central business district was a forest of mostly vacant stores where broken windows on their upper floors glared like black holes at anyone emerging from the direction of the bridge.

This morning the desolation was broken by a row of Army tents and the presence of a long convoy of military vehicles, including several equipped with rocket launchers. This was, Henderson was sure, a reaction to the crisis underway within the A.S.R. It was a token show of force intended to discourage any military excursions across the river by units of the A.S.R. or rebel bands taking advantage of the crisis.

The three of them walked past the buses and continued to Broadway where Henderson was sure they could hail a taxi. If they had to wait, there would be shelter beneath a metal awning or inside a recessed doorway. They were no longer in a hurry and time had ceased to have any pressing significance. From here, there was nowhere to go but to the hotel where he would leave Cynthia and the child while he reported to the fat man and then, later today or early tomorrow, to the air terminal for a flight to Denver.

Then his work would be finished, and Conway would be reunited with his daughter and the grandchild he had never seen. Of course, there would be a period of debriefing by some official of the government; but after that was completed Henderson could return to his home near Byers and relax a while to permit the unpleasant images of this assignment to fade within his mind. Then, a week or possibly a month later, there would be another call for the special services he was able to provide and, as always, he would respond. This was, for Henderson, a way of life that had been thrust upon him. It wasn't pleasant, but somebody had to do it if this fragile freedom was to be preserved.

# 8

*You're getting old and fat,* President Michael Knowlton said to himself as he inspected his image in the mirror that covered one wall of the private bathroom on the second floor of the executive mansion; *old and fat and tired, so tired of trying to guide a country that has no history and no precedents to provide some sense of direction. How did I get into this mess?* he asked himself as he poked a finger into the double chin that was developing and giving him, he felt, a pudgy appearance.

Every morning he followed the same routine. He would be awake by five o'clock, spend thirty minutes in the downstairs kitchen drinking coffee and then head back upstairs to the bathroom for his morning shave and shower. He was always careful not to wake Lucy, his wife, because he felt she needed her sleep. Lucy had never accepted this official mansion and did not like it because of its lack of privacy. She had never been able to accept the fact that other people were always moving about somewhere in the building. So, to let her rest, the President never woke her until he was ready to go downstairs to his office.

This morning, ignoring the rules of official protocol, he decided to wear his brown suit and a tan shirt. He wore these because he liked them. They were among his favorites and were comfortable. Besides, what difference did protocol make in only half a country? Because of that tragic default of the trillions of dollars' indebtedness by the old United States, about half of the world didn't recognize this new upstart republic anyway, so what difference did it make? Let them accept him as he was or not at all. He straightened his chocolate brown necktie and headed downstairs, pausing only long enough to wake Lucy.

The Presidential office was in a large room added along one side of the house and opening into what originally had been either a sitting room or a guest bedroom. The President was never quite sure which had been the initial arrangement. Absently, his mind already on the day's agenda, he returned the salute of the downstairs guard stationed at the foot of the stairway and armed with an automatic rifle and a grenade launcher. This man was expected to sacrifice his life if necessary to prevent any invaders from reaching the Presidential family upstairs.

Reaching the office where a steaming pot of coffee bubbled on a small table in one less-visible corner of the large room, the President settled himself behind the huge oak desk and, as he did each morning, gazed out of the long picture window at the distant skyline of Denver visible on the eastern horizon. Unfortunately, part of it was obscured by the barracks that had been built recently on the lawn of the mansion. Even though this was a permanent brick building, the President always thought of it as a barracks because it reminded him of a barracks! It housed the executive staff and was always dark and deserted at this early hour of the morning.

As he did every morning, the President read the day's communications from Congress and the military and intelligence sources, and studied the day's agenda. Then, carefully identifying each item by its name, he dictated responses or actions he wanted to see taken. Once this was completed, he turned his attention to the day's political and intelligence analysis that had been prepared for him during the night. As usual, this summary today devoted most of its text to events within the A.S.R. and possible hostile actions the A.S.R. might take against the U.S.A. Frowning with deep concentration, the President studied each item carefully, searching for hidden meanings or anything that might give him guidance.

The power struggle inside the Council in Washington appeared to be ending, with Gorcey firmly installed as Chairman. That item didn't surprise the President. Even after they had been pacified, a certain amount of rebellion still existed within the A.S.R. among the various state governments who violently opposed nationalization. *Now that,* the President thought, *is a matter that might be exploited.* He placed this brief in a separate pile for further study and discussion. More impoverished Mexicans were streaming across the border into the U.S.A. *What in hell are we to do with all those Mexicans? At least ten thousand of them must have crossed the border just in the past week!* He placed this item into the separate pile.

After this was completed the President turned his attention to the day's agenda of visitors to his office and appearances he might need to make at public gatherings. There were the usual pep talks with leaders of Congress, and protocol visits by two new ambassadors now stationed in Denver. One other entry caught his attention and he paused, once again staring out of the huge picture window. This was an appointment with a former fellow Congressman, Pat Conway.

Prior to election as President, he had served in Congress with Conway from the time when the U.S.A. was founded from the wreckage of the former continental power that had fallen before the turn of the century.

Conway had telephoned his secretary yesterday afternoon and requested an appointment today. The President had personally approved squeezing Conway into the busy schedule, partly for sentimental reasons and partly because he knew Conway wouldn't make this request unless he considered it to be important. Now, according to the daily calendar, Conway was due in this office at ten o'clock during a half-hour gap between two boring ambassadors making their initial protocol visits to the head of state.

The first ambassador was barely out of sight when Conway arrived and was escorted into the President's office by his personal secretary, who had been at her desk since eight o'clock. Because the President had brought her with him when he left Congress to become the first elected President of the new U.S.A. following the breakup, she was acquainted with Conway and they were both smiling when they entered the President's office. The President met them just inside the door, his hand held out to Conway.

"Good to see you again, Pat," the President said. "It's been far too long. How can I help you?" He motioned Conway to a seat in an area of the office containing a sofa and chair.

"It's about my daughter. You might recall her," Conway began. "I don't know whether you were aware of it or not, but she was trapped in Washington when that city fell. She just got out and got back yesterday, after coming through the nearest thing there is to a revolution. I know you have your intelligence sources, a lot better than mine, but I felt you might want a first-hand report on conditions inside the A.S.R."

"You bet I do!" Knowlton replied. "That kind of report is a lot better than those stale and homogenized things I'm given each morning!"

While the President listened intently, Conway talked for twenty minutes, omitting nothing that Cynthia and Henderson had told him. The view he gave of the A.S.R. was one of a nation divided and in deep disarray, where suspicion and distrust were commonplace. Such a nation could launch an attack at any time to try to preserve itself through the patriotic loyalty that always becomes dominant during a time of national military crisis.

By the time Conway was finished, he felt both exhausted and

refreshed. From the time of her arrival, he had been upset about Cynthia's behavior and appearance and by the silent, suspicious and watchful attitude of Susan. The changes in his daughter had been so great he hadn't even recognized her when she followed Henderson into the lobby of Stapleton International Airport.

Conway had spotted Henderson as soon as the man emerged from the doorway at the boarding ramp but he wasn't prepared for the somewhat frowzy and shuffling woman who followed him, leading a small child by the hand. Somehow, both the woman and child seemed to project a gray-colored image to the Congressman. Then the image of Cynthia as he had known her throughout her younger years overrode the features of this woman and he recognized her as his daughter. He rushed forward and threw both arms around her. Instantly, the child retreated silently behind her mother, pulling away to keep as much distance as possible between herself and this strange man.

Cynthia was crying softly when they left the airport and Susan sat, still silent and watchful, on the edge of the rear seat in the car. Her tiny hand was never far away from the door latch, ready to open the door to let her escape at the first sign of danger. Conway drove slowly and carefully, saying little, until they reached his home where Cynthia's mother waited. He had purposely not taken her along to the air terminal because he was afraid of her reaction if Cynthia had been harmed in some way during the period prior to her escape. In his brief telephone call from St. Louis, Henderson had given no details, only the time when they would arrive in Denver.

Upon their arrival at the house, with Henderson following in another car, Bea had rushed out tearfully and tried to throw her arms around her first grandchild. When this strange woman approached, Susan had pulled away from her mother's hand and fled to the opposite side of the car where she crouched suspiciously, like a small animal at bay and hiding from predators. As Bea approached, Susan backed away. She wouldn't return until Cynthia went to her and scooped Susan into her arms.

While Conway remained downstairs, listening intently as Henderson reported every detail of the escape, Bea took Cynthia and the child upstairs to a large, airy bedroom that would be theirs as long as they remained in this house. By the time she returned, Henderson had left. Cynthia and Susan remained upstairs to relax and use the shower. Bea descended the stairs like an old, old woman.

"My God, what's happened to them?" she groaned when she

reached her husband. "They must have lived in hell! That child! She isn't even as old as Cynthia was when we bought our new house and she acts like some kind of wild thing. She wouldn't let me near her. She just backs away. Did that man tell you anything about what has happened?"

That night, after Cynthia and the child had returned to their room and shut the door as an automatic gesture of security, Conway gave his wife the full details of Henderson's oral report. Uncharacteristically, she remained silent until he was finished. Conway noticed that Bea was crying softly, a stricken look on her face. Matters hadn't improved the next morning. Hearing her parents moving about in the dining room, Cynthia had come downstairs, leading Susan by one hand. Both looked refreshed and Cynthia had lost her gray appearance, but they still wore the same clothing. The child hadn't spoken, with the exception of a few soft words to her mother.

Bea was at the range, fixing scrambled eggs and bacon, which she placed on the table. Beginning to adjust to these new and, to her, opulent surroundings, Cynthia helped herself and then filled Susan's plate. Conway and Bea chattered like youngsters, trying to make their guests feel at home. Susan didn't touch any of her food until she saw her mother begin eating. Then she quickly gobbled everything on her plate, rose and silently returned to her upstairs room. They heard the door shut and they remained silent for several moments, uncertain what to say or how to act to break down the protective barrier this child had erected around herself.

The next morning, Conway had neglected his normal duties because he was both worried and angry about his daughter and grandchild—worried over their inability to adjust to this unaccustomed privacy and freedom, and angry about a society that made suspicious wild animals out of small children. On impulse, he called the mansion and requested an appointment with the President. Because he had no other avenue for retribution, this was his way of striking out at an unseen enemy. Now, after making a full report to the President, he felt better; but somehow, some way, he had to break through the protective shields surrounding Cynthia and Susan.

That afternoon, even though he missed voting on a minor bill before Congress, Conway left his office early. Bea planned to take Cynthia and Susan shopping to buy, as she said, "some decent clothes to wear." Conway wanted to be home by the time they arrived. He had plans of his own he wanted to pursue on the way to the house. As a way to try to break through Susan's protective shell, he intended to buy her a shiny new tricycle and watch her eyes and reaction when he unloaded it from the car.

Assembling the thing in the store took longer than Conway had anticipated so it was late afternoon before he drove into the driveway, halting beside Bea's compact car. Its presence indicated the shopping trip was over and the entire family was home. To attract their attention, Conway sounded the horn on his car several times before beginning to unload the tricycle. Bea's head appeared out of the side doorway and she laughed, then vanished back indoors. By the time she reappeared, followed by Cynthia and Susan, the Congressman had finished his job and the new cycle was standing in the driveway, its chrome glittering in the afternoon sunlight.

Conway stepped away from the toy and waited, smiling. Bea, still chuckling, stood to one side and watched all of them, especially the child. Cynthia gasped, then gave Susan a gentle push toward the cycle. At first Susan resisted, unaccustomed to receiving anything as big and shiny as this tricycle. The toys she had received up to now had been mostly items found in the hallway outside her room, or make-believe creatures fashioned from pillows or discarded boxes. She took one step forward, then halted and waited for a hostile reaction. When none came, she rushed forward suddenly and her fingers closed around the handlebar. She still hadn't said anything or made a sound.

Gently, in a series of disconnected movements, she pushed the cycle down the driveway and back as far as the sidewalk leading to the side door. The others waited, watching quietly to see what Susan would do next and how she would react once she accepted it as her own personal possession. Reaching the doorway, the child pulled it open and, bracing it with her body, hauled the tricycle inside. The door slammed behind her as she vanished into the house.

Led by Bea, the adults went silently indoors and watched while Susan dragged the cycle, step by step, upstairs and then wheeled it into the room she shared with Cynthia. After waiting a few moments, the adults followed, walking silently to avoid being noticed. Conway felt a chill run through his body when he saw Susan with her new toy carefully placed behind the bed, between it and the wall. She was covering it with the bedspread, which she had partially pulled from the bed. With the cycle hidden and made invisible, nobody could steal it.

*God in heaven,* he thought, *is this what little children are like over there in that other country that should have been part of ours? Is this how Cynthia and her baby had to live over there? It's no wonder they're having a tough time adapting to us. We didn't raise her to have to live like they had to do and she hasn't even mentioned Rich since they got here! He's dead and buried God-knows-where and she hasn't even mentioned him. God help us all for letting this happen.*

Trapped within their helplessness, Conway and Bea went quietly back down the stairway, not stopping until they reached the patio. Conway's face felt stiff, as if it had been frozen. Tears slid unnoticed down Bea's face. Neither spoke until they were safely back outdoors, in the privacy of the concrete patio. Then, unable to hold it back any longer, Bea started sobbing uncontrollably, her entire body shaking. Conway felt helpless while he stood there unable to do anything to comfort her. There were no words to describe the bitter chill he felt throughout his body and there was nothing that could remove the cause of Bea's sobs, nothing but the passage of time—and even that might not remove it entirely.

Gradually, over the next few weeks, minor cracks began to appear in the armor of suspicion Susan wore. Realizing that she was welcome downstairs and wasn't invading someone else's apartment, she no longer spent all her time in that upstairs bedroom with the door closed. Her tricycle was no longer hidden behind the bed. Now it stood along one wall in the garage and she rode it daily, up and down the driveway and along the sidewalk. Even though she didn't trust her completely yet, Susan had accepted Bea as a friend and, lately, had started appearing in the kitchen when Bea was preparing a meal. But whenever a man appeared, Susan would retreat behind her protective shell of suspicion and remain there until he left. This attitude included Conway, and it bothered him.

His experience with Cynthia and Susan had caused Conway to take a deep interest in learning everything he could about that nation on the other bank of the Mississippi River. He read everything he could find and had become almost a fixture in those agencies which had some type of contact with the A.S.R. He used his Congressional privilege unmercifully to obtain information not available to the public or to routine agencies. He was driven by a hatred so intense it colored every action of his life.

In Washington, Gorcey had consolidated his power over the Council and the A.S.R. As Henderson had predicted, Gorcey had used the temporary truce with the state governors to wait until the state National Guard units were scattered along the highways and then had struck, using loyal Army forces to seize all of the armories, occupy the state capitol buildings and take possession of the larger city halls. One by one, the scattered National Guard troops then had been subdued or destroyed. The entire action required only three days to finalize and when it was completed, the A.S.R. was a federal nation with the power of state and local governments broken and destroyed.

Within days, after two members had vanished unexpectedly, the Council in Washington had become little more than a figurehead committee to ratify actions ordered by Gorcey and his personal followers. The national assembly, which had earlier replaced the Congress, suddenly was adjourned and its members sent home, where they were expected to remain until or if they should be called back into session. Once these lawmakers were gone, their staff people were fired or transferred into some other position within government. Finally, the heads of the Army, Air Force and Navy were summoned to Gorcey's office in the White House and were given the choice between immediate resignation or imprisonment for crimes against the state. They were replaced the same day by Gorcey appointees and, with seizure of the military, the coup was complete.

Then Gorcey paused and waited, probing and testing the machine he had built to try to locate any weaknesses that might exist. Whenever he found one he eliminated it, using an elite squad of uniformed men he had organized for this purpose. As the days passed, the size of this elite unit expanded steadily from recruits available in every city and large town, young men who found glamor or satisfaction in wearing the royal blue uniform and in having absolute authority whenever they spoke.

From a distance, Conway watched these developments with an icy detachment. Each day, he read the intelligence reports and spoke with anyone who might be able to add to his storehouse of knowledge about the internal workings of the A.S.R. His routine Congressional obligations became secondary to this quest for knowledge, until his neglect reached a point where it became visible to the other members of Congress. Then, within a matter of days, Conway virtually ended his search and returned his attention to his legislative duties, taking the lead in debates over several major issues.

He had stopped flaying himself to try to find the cause for actions of the A.S.R. that might, in turn, give him insight into the disturbing behavior of Cynthia and Susan because the child, over a period of several days, noticeably relaxed and abandoned her air of deep distrust and suspicion. Instead of being a frightened little animal,

Susan was once again a child, laughing and playing like any other young girl and, occasionally, requiring delicate discipline as a part of the learning process. When Conway returned home one evening and found Cynthia with a new hairdo and wearing makeup as she fixed hamburgers on the patio grill, he knew the battle had been won. His daughter and grandchild were home at last.

Within Congress, Conway had by now become a recognized expert in issues involving the A.S.R. and his prophecies about actions the A.S.R. would take had been alarmingly accurate. He was the first to call Gorcey a dictator and to predict the formation of an elite strike force as soon as Gorcey had consolidated his power within the Council. Conway's new posture in Congress did not escape notice by President Knowlton, who was impressed by the accuracy of his predictions. The President envied Conway. All Conway had to do was debate Congressional bills, allocate funds to the many federal programs and attend committee meetings. A Congressman didn't have to face the daily dilemma of trying to interpret those endless intelligence reports and then make decisions that could lead to war and the possible destruction of the U.S.A.

Michael Knowlton felt insecure in the job of the Presidency. Each day, he wondered if he was adequate for this thankless job. Because he was the first President to be elected after the capital had been moved from Washington to Denver, he had no precedents to provide guidance when an especially touchy decision had to be made. Simultaneously, he had to move with extreme caution and a degree of boldness bordering upon recklessness. It was a bitter tightrope to walk! Members of his Cabinet had been chosen with care but, in the end, the final decision on any critical matter was his to make. Right now, the President was more concerned about the warlike actions of the A.S.R. than anything else because it would leave the southwestern flank of the U.S.A. vulnerable if all available military power had to be moved to the Mississippi front.

At best, the Presidency was a juggling act, especially where the military was involved. Even with the universal draft, there weren't enough young men available to provide the protection needed by this new nation. One army in a constant state of readiness had to be maintained along the Mississippi River front, with special emphasis on the Wisconsin border where a water barrier did not exist. A small army composed primarily of older men spent their time patrolling the highways to intercept enemy terror units who had managed to creep into the U.S.A. A third force was needed in the southwestern states to try vainly to stem the peaceful invasion of Mexicans searching for a better life in the U.S.A.

If too many military units were moved from the Mississippi front to Arizona, New Mexico or Texas, it would leave the U.S.A. unprotected against invasion by the A.S.R.—which now, under its new leadership, seemed to be spoiling for a fight. On the other hand, if too many troops were removed from the southwestern states, the peaceful invasion from Mexico would become a deluge. That left the internal convoy forces as the only available military manpower able to be reassigned; but if they were moved elsewhere, it would leave the highways and farms unprotected.

This dilemma was complicated even further by the emergency powers delegated to the Presidency at the time the new capital was established in Denver. These powers were voted by a Congress which, in that earlier time, consisted of fewer than fifty members. Because of the continuing hostile attitude of the A.S.R., the powers remained in force even though the original President had retired, transferring the office thankfully to Knowlton. These powers permitted the Chief Executive to override almost all actions of Congress if a question of national security was involved. Knowlton was uneasy about invoking these powers because, in his mind, it would be too simple to use them to create a dictatorship in the U.S.A.

For this reason, Knowlton had proceeded very cautiously from the time when he and Lucy had become residents in the executive mansion, using his acquired Congressional knowledge as a substitute for the written records lost when the government moved from Washington to Denver. He had been extremely careful in his selection of people to fill the Cabinet seats, leaving some of them vacant for nearly a year after he became President. Beginning almost as soon as he was sworn into office, Knowlton had started forming his own private informational network to help fill the gaps in the knowledge he was acquiring. The fate of the nation, he knew, rested in his hands and the absence of knowledge could lead to disaster.

He was walking a tightrope and he knew it. Somehow, he had to maintain domestic prosperity within the U.S.A. if the nation was to enjoy the respect of other nations, many of them still suffering from the collapse of the old U.S. dollar. Simultaneously and using his emergency powers, he had to create a show of force along the Mississippi, one strong enough to blunt the territorial ambitions of the new rulers of the A.S.R. To do this, he had to know precisely how many troops he could withdraw from the southwestern states for a period of four or five weeks, just long enough to impress Gorcey and the A.S.R. And he had to have this knowledge in his possession immediately, so he could make a decision. Unwittingly, Conway could have given President Knowlton the answer to this puzzle.

Throughout his recital, Conway had repeatedly stressed the actions taken by Henderson during the escape of Cynthia and Susan from the A.S.R. This man thought on his feet and didn't avoid making decisions. And he was no stranger to serving the central government! Knowlton decided it was time for another visit with Conway, followed by a meeting with Henderson.

When Conway entered his Congressional office the next morning, he found a note asking that he call the Presidential office immediately. An hour later, he was being escorted into Knowlton's private quarters in the residential wing of the mansion. As soon as coffee was served and the aide had departed, the President became serious and businesslike.

"Pat, I've asked you here because of your report to me the other day," he began. "You can't know how valuable it was! It isn't every day you can get a first-hand report from inside a revolution, right while it's happening. I'd like to take that situation a little further and get your opinions and cooperation but, before I begin, I need your word that none of this will be repeated outside of these walls."

"You've got it!" Conway retorted without hesitation. "None of it will go any further without your permission. I appreciate your confidence."

"All right then," Knowlton said. "I have strong reason to believe Gorcey and the A.S.R. plan to try to invade the U.S.A. any day. It could begin within a week or so. I just don't know, but it will be very soon. If we put enough men and weapons along the Mississippi, we can prevent them from succeeding. I'm sure of that. We have the weapons to turn them back even if they do manage to create a beachhead on this side of the river.

"But, and this is why I asked you to come in here this morning, we could win the war and lose our nation. I know you're aware of the hordes of Mexican illegals that are streaming across the border to try to find a new life up here in the north. But I doubt if you really know how many there are. They number in the millions! One entire army of ours is trapped down there along the border, in Texas, Arizona and New Mexico, doing nothing but patrolling the border and rounding up illegals to send home and, of course, they're back again in a week or two. They're like locusts, the way they keep coming.

"Now here's the problem. If we make an adequate show of force along the Mississippi, we'll have to pull most of those troops out of the southwest, but still leave enough to keep the lid on things. But how many is too many? How many can we safely withdraw for a few weeks, and still leave enough to hold back this invasion? Damn it, Pat, I just don't know and I'm getting conflicting stories out of that area, from the Army and from the local authorities!"

"My God!" Conway breathed. "We weren't aware of all of this over in Congress. We knew it was bad, but we didn't know it was this bad! What can I do?"

"Can you reach that man Henderson?" Knowlton asked, changing the subject suddenly. "Do you think you can get him in here so I can talk with him?"

"Unless he's on an assignment somewhere, I'm sure I can get him," Conway replied. "He's a good man. He proved himself to me by the way he got my kids out of that mess back east! When do you want to see him?"

"Now!" the President responded without hesitation. "Now! The sooner the better! We don't have any time to waste. An invasion by the A.S.R. may be only a few days away. Do you think you can get him in here tomorrow morning?"

"I'll try," Conway answered. "I'll begin right now."

As soon as Conway had departed, the President returned to the office wing of the mansion and a gathering of the Defense Council, which met each day to discuss the deteriorating relations between the U.S.A. and the A.S.R. The chiefs of the Army, Navy, Air Force and intelligence agencies had by now grown accustomed to these daily sessions, to the point where they occupied the same chairs each morning. A monstrous map of the A.S.R. hung on the wall opposite the one containing a huge picture window. As usual, the President arrived exactly on time, carrying several file folders.

"Gentlemen," he greeted them. "Let's get this meeting started. You know the procedures by now!"

One by one, the officials reported the status of affairs along the Mississippi and the readiness of their manpower. A common thread wove through all of their reports. An invasion attempt by the A.S.R. seemed to be imminent and it could occur any day. Last to speak was the head of the intelligence forces. His report and impressions always dictated the types of decisions made by the Council.

"I don't really have anything to add that you don't already know," he began. "That petty gangster, Gorcey, is just spoiling for a war with somebody. He's savvy enough to know he can't remain in complete power unless he has a crisis that never ends. Everything my people have gathered has this as a common theme. He's not dumb, by any means, but he doesn't have any scruples, none at all. A lot of people over there aren't really behind him, but they follow him because they don't have any choice.

"My reports from the field indicate the A.S.R. may invade next week or next month, but not much longer away than that."

"Have you picked up anything new about this Gorcey?" the President asked. "Who is he? What does he want? If we can learn how he thinks and what he wants, we may be able to anticipate his actions and prevent them from happening."

"Don't count on it!" the intelligence chief replied promptly. "He grew up on the fringes of the mobs and what he wants is power, absolute power. That governs every action he takes, like it does any dictator. Look how he stamped out poor old Poynter! Nobody even knows what happened to him or where he's buried. He may have gone into an incinerator for all anybody really knows.

"When Gorcey decides to invade us it will be when he decides the time is right and he can win. When it does happen, he'll throw everything he has against us, all at once. That's how he thinks and he learned it from the mobs. It's the tactics they've always used!"

"Make a guess," Knowlton suggested. "When do you think it will happen?"

"About three or four weeks, no more than that. We've got only about that much time left!"

This reply from the head of the intelligence forces caused heads to nod affirmatively on all sides of the table. It didn't surprise the President because it agreed with conclusions he had reached privately, based upon his personal assessment of the crisis. The session adjourned with no decision made on a new strategy that might cause Gorcey to abandon his invasion plans. Knowlton hadn't pushed these experts because, in the final analysis, this decision was his to make. He was the Commander-in-Chief.

When he returned to his office, Knowlton found a message from Conway, who had already contacted Henderson and scheduled an appointment with the President for the same afternoon. Knowlton rang his secretary in the outer office and asked her to cancel or reschedule all other appointments later than 3:00 p.m. A plan for checkmating Gorcey was beginning to take shape in Knowlton's head and he wanted adequate time to explore it with Henderson.

*This man,* the President said to himself, *could be the key to making it work. He knows his way around and he thinks on his feet and is able to improvise if that's what is needed for success. And the government has used him before. His file didn't show any failures at all, absolutely none. Best of all, he knows how they think in the A.S.R. and how they react. He really called the shots on how Gorcey would consolidate his power. Now, if he can perform for me like he did for Pat Conway, we're in business.*

# 9

The rotor blades of the big military helicopter beat the air like paddles, creating a rhythmic undertone of sound. Within the comfortable cabin of the machine Henderson sat slouched beside a window, watching the traffic intently as it crawled painfully along a major highway leading northward, away from western Texas. The situation here was no different from any of the other localities inspected in west Texas and eastern New Mexico.

They had left Denver early in the morning following Henderson's discussion the previous afternoon with the President. At first, Knowlton had wanted Henderson to use the executive jet and visit the major cities, pausing briefly in El Paso, Albuquerque, Tucson and Phoenix and then continuing to San Diego and Los Angeles. Henderson had considered this to be a virtual waste of time and eventually was able to persuade Knowlton to let him make a thorough inspection of this entire region, using a military jet helicopter able to hover above a specific locality, such as a stretch of freeway or the heart of a small community. Also, a chopper could land anywhere. It didn't require a long runway at a major airport.

Western Texas and eastern New Mexico were familiar territory to Henderson because of his experience in the oil fields, but he hadn't expected such drastic changes as those he had seen on this inspection trip. The chopper had zigzagged south from Colorado, following the major highways leading north from the Mexican border. Every highway was filled with vehicles headed north and each large community contained an area where rude shacks huddled shoulder to shoulder, each shack filled with migrant Mexican families whose children played in the dust of walkways separating the shacks.

In one county seat town, a squad of soldiers was seen rounding up the migrants and loading them aboard military trucks for transport back to Mexico. Every larger city had a military installation in a public park or an empty field near the city limits, its tents standing in neat rows along an informal thoroughfare that led to post headquarters, located in a larger tent. Henderson was glad he had insisted on this type of inspection. It provided a better view of the overall problem than just a series of visits to major cities.

While the chopper paddled on toward El Paso, Henderson continued staring out of the window while his mind examined his discussion with the President. Knowlton had been very specific in his instructions. He wanted a thorough inspection of the southwestern states to try to answer three crucial questions. How extensive was the peaceful invasion by migrant Mexicans? Were the military controlling this invasion? And how many military units could be withdrawn temporarily without making their absence too obvious?

"I absolutely must have the answers to these questions, and as quickly as possible," Knowlton had emphasized. "I can't use the regular channels because they're too slow and too public. That's why I'm using you!"

"I don't know whether I can get the information you want," Henderson replied. "I'm not a military man and all I can do is give you my opinion. What if I think you can't afford to withdraw any troops at all?"

"That's one of the things I want to know. I don't want to have to depend totally upon those official military reports. They tend to lean toward statistics and omit the human factors."

"In other words," Henderson said, "you want me to tell you what I'd do if I had to keep order in those states, but needed some of the manpower somewhere else."

"That's exactly it," the President responded firmly. "That's exactly what I want. And you only have a few days to do it. We're facing an invasion by the A.S.R., as I told you, but we also have to be able to protect our backside. What is the minimum it will take to protect it? That's what I want to know!"

The entire conversation with President Knowlton bothered Henderson. He was sure it contained some ingredient kept secret by Knowlton. The more Henderson examined this discussion, the more convinced he became that Knowlton hadn't been entirely frank with him. From what he had seen already, Henderson was convinced of the impossibility of removing any of the troops from the southwestern states. They were the only thing preventing a wholesale migration from poverty-stricken Mexico into the U.S.A. A military invasion could be stopped in a pivotal battle, but the migration of millions of hungry people defied military logic. They were like a swarm of locusts. Swat one and a dozen flew past while you were swatting.

The President must have known this to be the case. This was the key question that bothered Henderson. It continued to bother him as the helicopter meandered over the southwest, landing briefly at each major city in the region. Everywhere, the situation was the same. Municipal services and finances were stretched to the breaking point by the flood of migrants huddling in makeshift shacks while they tried to make a new life in the U.S.A. Commanders at each military base reported they needed more, not fewer, men if this invasion was to be controlled. This view was echoed by elected officials in every city throughout the region.

By the end of the third day, Henderson felt it would be useless to continue this junket. By now, he had stopped in all major cities and had reached Los Angeles which, like the other cities, was experiencing a major invasion by illegal immigrants from Mexico. The recommendation Henderson would make to the President would be to look elsewhere for additional troops for the Mississippi front. Every military base in the southwest was already strained to its limit in an effort to maintain control of the area in which it operated.

He dictated his final report over the telephone from his hotel room in Los Angeles. Tomorrow morning he would return the helicopter to Denver.

Henderson's report didn't surprise Knowlton. In fact, it agreed with his own personal summation of the situation in the southwestern states. Now he knew the type of action he would need to take if the A.S.R. launched a massive invasion along the Mississippi front. He knew what decision he must make when the time arrived. Now all he could do was wait. That night, President Knowlton didn't sleep well. He tossed and turned until almost dawn.

At the time when Knowlton was elected to the Presidency of this new nation groping to adjust itself to a diminished size and role in the power politics of the world, there was no sign of instability within the A.S.R. In fact, the A.S.R. had appeared to be functioning smoothly almost from the day the peace accord had been signed with the U.S.A. Quick recognition of the A.S.R. by Soviet Russia, followed by endless shiploads of needed supplies, had removed most of the worst pressures from the new Poynter government, permitting it to concentrate on solidifying its new political doctrine on the federal, state and local levels.

On the day following his election, Knowlton was embarrassed badly when a news commentator referred to him as "the new George Washington, the first President elected by this new republic." He was not only embarrassed but also upset. The comparison with Washington worried him. Washington had been elected when everything was shining and new. This new republic was tattered and torn, only a fragment of its former self and with more than half of its continental population lost to a hostile new power. Also lost along with the people east of the Mississippi were all of the records left behind when the government was evacuated from Washington, D.C.

With all of the records and most of its personnel lost, the new government in Denver had initially functioned more from memory and intuition than from any formal policy. One of its first actions was to requisition all available copies of the Congressional Record from the Denver public library. This provided at least a written record of the actions of Congress in the final years before the breakup. Next came legitimizing the actions of the new, shrunken Congress that met in a hotel until the new shopping center capitol was completed. A bill was passed unanimously shrinking the size of both houses of Congress, and removing the names of members left behind when the breakup occurred. This new, smaller Congress promptly repudiated all debts of the former United States, and authorized issuance of new currency with an eagle as its official symbol. Then came an audit of all financial relationships with state and local governments and an immediate reduction in taxation to reflect removal of the federal debt.

No permanent Cabinet appointments were made while these actions were underway. There were two reasons for this inaction. First, an existing Cabinet member might turn up any day after escape from the A.S.R., and rightfully demand his job. Also, this new nation might not need the entire Cabinet structure that had previously existed. Until the new government became more formalized, it could function satisfactorily with only hired caretakers in management positions. A retired career diplomat from Tucson was hired as a *de facto* Secretary of State to permit the new nation to court diplomatic recognition by the rest of the world. A former C.I.A. station chief in various European posts became the acting head of the intelligence forces. He was brought back from retirement in Los Angeles.

This was the government Knowlton had inherited with his electoral victory, which caused him to surrender his seat in Congress. His decision to seek the Presidency was made because he felt the U.S.A. had existed as long as it dared in its informal status. If it were ever to gain respect from the rest of the world, the U.S.A. needed to forget its former status and build a new nation within the land area it now occupied. There was very little chance the U.S.A. could regain its lost territory east of the Mississippi River, either diplomatically or militarily. How could it? Diplomatic negotiations cannot occur unless the two nations recognize each other, and that was an impossibility as long as the current form of government existed in the A.S.R. And military invasion of the A.S.R. was unthinkable. Not only would it destroy any semblance of democracy in the U.S.A., but the population of the A.S.R. was so monstrous it would simply absorb any invading force like a sponge.

Knowlton's electoral campaign was built around a theme of creating a better and stronger nation with the tools at hand. He wanted to build a new industrial base using the resources available, with an eye toward making the U.S.A. self-sufficient. As part of this self-sufficiency, he planned to expand agricultural production enough to permit some export sales to be made. These sales would be used as a wedge to gain diplomatic recognition. And he wanted to rebuild the surface transportation system to permit reliable movement of people and goods from one place to another within the U.S.A. It was a shining dream that had captured the emotions of the voters and Knowlton became President by an overwhelming margin.

At first, things had gone well. He had created a streamlined Cabinet in which several seats were combined or eliminated. The Departments of Agriculture, Interior and Labor were merged to eliminate overlapping functions and now operated as a Department of Interior Affairs. The Department of State became the Department of Foreign Affairs and absorbed the intelligence forces as part of its overall responsibilities. New taxing policies for industry had caused factory production to climb sharply throughout the new nation and the rising demand for foodstuffs resulted in a large expansion of agricultural output, especially in the southwestern states. And conversion of the Denver shopping center into a capitol building had been completed and was functioning adequately.

There was nothing President Knowlton could do, though, to prevent the U.S.A. from continuing to be a nation operated by senior citizens. Because of the perennial threat of invasion by the A.S.R. and infiltration of terror squads from across the Mississippi, the universal military draft had to be continued even though it effectively removed all young men from society. Although he hated it, the draft was one curse Knowlton had to bear if his country was to be protected against invasion. During his first months in office, he had sent repeated peace feelers to Washington, but all had been rejected scornfully.

When he had sought the Presidency, Knowlton had seen the job as a challenge. He had high hopes of creating a better, more prosperous nation that could live at peace with its neighbors. Until recently, this dream had seemed to be almost within his grasp. Then two things happened that jerked him back to the reality that humankind doesn't always follow a predictable course.

First came the peaceful invasion of the southwestern states by millions of destitute Mexicans in search of a better life, attracted to the U.S.A. by its expanding agricultural production. They streamed northward like a flowing river of humanity, overwhelming the permanent population by sheer numbers. In desperation, Knowlton ordered military units into the area to seal the border and return the migrants to Mexico. It didn't work. The desperate refugees from poverty began using the dark of night to slip across the international boundary or, as an alternative, they would march across in a horde so large the isolated military units were unable to capture enough to make a dent in the migration.

Once across the border, they fanned out to the irrigated farming areas and into the cities and towns. When no housing was available, they created their own by using old cardboard boxes and building materials salvaged from municipal dumps. At first, residents of the southwestern states pitied these ragged newcomers, feeding them in volunteer soup kitchens and permitting them to erect makeshift housing on vacant land near the municipal limits. This charity backfired, causing more and more migrants to arrive. Eventually, in all major cities, pity was replaced by anger and desperation.

The howls of anguish were heard first from the farmers, who demanded police protection for their growing crops. According to these farmers, the migrants ate everything in sight, leaving barren fields in their wake. Several migrants found in vegetable fields were shot by irate farmers, who then were upheld by local law enforcement agencies. Eventually this problem wound up on the desk of President Knowlton, dumped there by a vexed Congress unable to produce any solution. Like Congress, the President had no magic answer, so he did the only thing possible. He expanded the military presence throughout the southwestern states—and then hoped for a miracle.

To obtain the additional manpower, he was forced to withdraw some troops from the Mississippi front, leaving several rural areas in Arkansas only partially protected. This, of course, led to loud outcries from the residents of that part of Arkansas. Knowlton recalled with distaste the day when an irate delegation from Arkansas met with him and referred to him as a madman and murderer. Their town had recently been the victim of a terror raid from across the Mississippi. They blamed Knowlton for permitting this assault to occur. Privately, he agreed with them. He had ordered the military transfer reluctantly, with full knowledge that such a raid might take place once the military presence was reduced.

Basically, Michael Knowlton was an optimistic man who hated disorder. He distrusted what he could not see or understand. His years in Congress before being elected to this top office had taught him that lack of knowledge usually led to defeat. Obviously, he hadn't known all of the facts about the situation along the Arkansas border and, as a result, this small massacre had occurred. In comparison with his other problems, though, this one was insignificant.

After the delegation had departed, Knowlton admitted to himself that he felt like a raw egg placed in a vise with someone turning the handle gradually tighter until the point was reached when the egg exploded. Despite the gravity of the dilemma he faced daily, Knowlton laughed to himself at this simile. It was this ability to laugh at himself that made Knowlton a good leader.

As the pressures mounted following the peaceful invasion of the southwest, and the overthrow of the Poynter regime in the A.S.R., Knowlton wondered why he had become a candidate for the Presidency, and why the people had elected him. Before the fall of Washington, he and Lucy had been perfectly content in the Congressional life they led. They occupied a rented townhouse in rural Virginia and, at each election, he had faced no real opposition. Obviously, the voters in his home district remained satisfied with his performance in Congress. He and Lucy had led a good life together and had planned to retire on the Congressional pension which now was lost as another result of the fall of Washington. Fortunately, they were home when it happened, trying to find transportation back to the nation's capital. All they had lost were the personal possessions in their townhouse.

He was one of the first lawmakers to arrive at the new capitol in Denver, when the only desks in the shopping center building were banquet tables. For several weeks during the early stages of the war with the A.S.R., he had used a folding chair in a tiny office enclosed by removable partitions. He had been a part of the creation of a new nation from the wreckage left by partition. His optimistic nature caused him to view this more as an opportunity than a disaster. The old continental nation was lost, but a new country without the problems of the past could be created from the territory left after partition.

Gradually, as the time for election approached, he had drifted toward becoming a candidate for the office of Chief Executive. At first Lucy opposed this proposition, but in time she relented—provided she could have her own furniture in the Presidential mansion if he won. The campaign permitted Knowlton to share his dream of a better nation with the voters. Nobody was more surprised than Knowlton by the size of his victory in November. The only jarring note was when that news commentator had called him "the new George Washington."

The first period of his Presidency had brought great improvement to the new nation, both domestically and on a global basis. The new government was functioning smoothly, even though it was housed in a former shopping center. More and more embassies were being opened in Denver by other nations which recognized the U.S.A. as a nation separate from the A.S.R. Industrial and agricultural production were climbing, and jobs were plentiful for anyone who wanted to work. The rosy job picture, Knowlton was first to admit, was because all of the young men were drafted as soon as they became adults.

Lucy had resigned herself to life in the executive mansion, which she disliked because of its public nature. Not only were other people always in the building, and armed guards were stationed at all strategic locations, but the mansion was, to Lucy, like living in a fishbowl always surrounded by tourists. Because she was always followed by an armed guard, Lucy no longer ventured into the massive yard. She sat on the patio only when her husband was present. And, lately, that was very seldom.

After reading Henderson's final report on conditions throughout the southwestern states, and once again reading the latest intelligence summary on activities in Washington, Knowlton shut himself into his office and gave orders to his secretary that he didn't want to be disturbed. Then, for most of the afternoon the President sat at his huge oak desk and stared almost absently out of the picture window that framed the row of peaceful mountains above Denver. He was still there when the peaks assumed a rosy glow from the setting sun.

If this nation was to be preserved, the President knew what action he had to take. The responsibility was his alone and he must be able to live with the consequences. Knowlton walked slowly, like a very old man, when he emerged from the office shortly after dusk.

# 10

The Chairman was furious, so furious that he threw a china coffee cup from the White House pantry across the Oval Office, smashing it against the opposite wall. His wiry hair had tumbled down over his forehead and his black eyes fairly snapped with rage. He swore viciously, pounded twice on the desk with a clenched fist and then pointed, scowling, at the heavy man in the royal blue uniform who sat on the opposite side of the desk.

At that moment, Mike Gorcey forgot he was now head of state of a major nation. His anger was so overwhelming that temporarily he reverted back to the period when his kingdom was the streets, his palace was a tenement and he lived by his wits on the fringes of the mobs found in all major cities. He glared at the man sitting opposite him and then spoke in a soft, clipped voice almost stifled by his anger.

"Bastards! Those miserable bastards!" he said. "I want them found and I want to make examples of them. I don't care how you do it, but you do it. Find them and bring them here to me. I want them, not an alibi."

Julius Floyd, commander of the elite guard who now held the rank of general, seemed to shrink in his chair despite his ample girth. Rings of nervous sweat gradually widened across his armpits. His hesitation before answering became obvious to both men in this large office.

"They're gone," he said hesitantly. "They're gone, where I can't reach them. They slipped over the border during the night, up there in Wisconsin where there isn't any river to stop them. I tracked them that far before I brought it to you. They may be in Canada now!"

"You waited this long?" Gorcey fairly screamed. "Three whole units! That's eighteen men! And, their commanders with them! Don't you know what this does to discipline, you fat fool? That blue uniform you wear is supposed to be special and now we have eighteen men wearing it who have deserted and gone somewhere, but you don't know where. Get out of here and find, at least, where they've gone. Get out! Go do what you're paid to do!"

Gorcey remained angry after Floyd had departed. He'd appointed that man to head the special force because he thought Floyd was capable of providing the leadership he wanted, and instead the fool had been filling his fat gut while three of his top units were deserting, either to the U.S.A. or into neutral Canada. He slammed the desk again with one fist and then consciously held his breath for almost a minute, forcing himself to become calm. There were other matters more important than Floyd and his missing guardsmen.

Painfully, he was beginning to understand why Poynter had made so little progress in rebuilding the nation he had captured. In theory, placing everything under a central control and allocating resources to meet needs should have resulted in a well fed and prosperous country that could exist forever. But it hadn't worked that way and wasn't working properly today, even with the harsh management of the Gorcey regime. It seemed like more pressure produced fewer, rather than greater, results. Nowhere was this more true than in agriculture, which had been given top priority because it was the cornerstone of food production. Unfortunately, agriculture didn't lend itself to assembly line output and it existed at the mercy of weather, insects and the willingness of farmers to spend countless hours in their fields, day or night, whenever a need arose.

Gorcey, like Poynter before him, had tried to wring bigger harvests from the land by assigning more workers to the farms. The result had been less, not more, production because the workers spent only eight hours in the fields and then went home to their barracks, leaving urgent jobs not completed. Neither they nor their foremen were farmers. They were only government employees assigned to duty on a farm. But they were able to put more acres into cultivation. As a result, agricultural production didn't decline, but neither did it rise despite the additional planted acreage.

In the cities, the guaranteed annual wage had caused factory output to sag alarmingly. Because they were paid whether or not they worked, more and more people remained home, went fishing or whiled away their days at pursuits more attractive than work. The guaranteed annual wage had been Poynter's idea and it was one of the dreams that caused him to attract followers. It was the reason why Gorcey had joined Poynter before Washington fell. At the time, the idea was irresistible. Today, to Gorcey, it seemed insane, an invitation to everyone to avoid work. In the brief time he had occupied the White House, he had tried almost everything to get workers back on the job, but the results had been dismal. One-half of the country was supporting the other half!

Today had been one of Gorcey's bad days—in fact, one of his worst since becoming the head of state. It began with a warning from the treasury against issuing any more of the yellow dollars unless they were backed by currency from some other nation that supported its money with gold. The treasury, in its memo, warned that unlimited printing of the yellow dollars would make the currency worthless throughout the world.

That damned guaranteed annual wage! It created this particular mess, for which there was no immediate answer.

As soon as Gorcey had disposed of this problem, it was time for an appointment with the Russian ambassador, who had been insistent about meeting with Gorcey. At all of his visits with Poynter, and in the initial talks with Gorcey, the ambassador had been overly cordial, almost fawning in his efforts to cement a friendly relationship between the two countries. Gorcey had no reason to expect this appointment to be any different. Instead, when the ambassador arrived, he had been coldly cordial to the point of being patronizing.

His message had been very brief and almost an ultimatum. Either Gorcey must take appropriate steps to reduce this country's dependence upon Russian financial aid or, if this were not done, the Soviets would be forced to review the relationship between the two nations. "If we must support your country," the ambassador had told Gorcey, "we would gain more if we annexed it to the Soviet Union." By the time the ambassador left, Gorcey was seething with anger that exploded during the interview with Floyd, who had been a faithful follower since the days of the march upon Washington.

And now it was time for a session with the military leaders where he would be forced to listen to their whining complaints about the morale of their troops, about ammunition shortages and bragging accounts of minor terror raids across the Mississippi—raids that made good headlines in the newspapers but accomplished very little. He was scowling with his head lowered like a cornered bull when they entered the Oval Office. He was in no mood for the meaningless bureaucratic chatter that generally marked these official meetings.

Sensing his mood, the three generals lowered themselves uneasily into the leather chairs and waited silently for Gorcey to make the first move. He continued to scowl at them for almost a minute.

"Well?" he began. "What kind of complaints do you have today? I might as well tell you I'm not in the mood for any more of that whining crap I've heard since morning. If you don't have anything new to report, we might as well adjourn. So, begin. Let's have it."

The generals, representing the southern, central and northern armies along the Mississippi front, restored Gorcey's good humor. According to them, border incidents along the Mississippi had declined sharply and there were definite signs of the U.S.A. withdrawing its troops from the border zone. In anticipation of a possible incursion into the U.S.A., the generals had moved as many troops as possible to sites along the border. While we are strengthening our border forces they are weakening theirs, the generals told Gorcey. He was smiling when they left.

Sitting later with his feet crossed on the big Presidential desk, his head tilted back and resting on his locked hands, Gorcey examined the position of the A.S.R. and the possibility of annexing the U.S.A. by a sudden invasion along the entire length of the international boundary, using so many people they would roll like a tidal wave over the defending units of the U.S.A. Once across the border, they could continue moving until they had seized and occupied an entire tier of states ranging from Mexico to the Canadian line. These states would increase immensely the industrial and agricultural production of the A.S.R. and their loss would further weaken the damned U.S.A.

Dropping his feet to the floor, Gorcey rotated the big chair and fished in a desk drawer until he produced a large roadmap of the United States as it had existed before partition. Staring intently at the map, he ran a finger across the outlines of each state immediately west of the Mississippi—the rest of Louisiana and possibly a piece of Texas, Arkansas, Missouri, Iowa and maybe part of Nebraska, and finally most if not all of Minnesota. If he placed his heaviest concentration of forces in Illinois and southern Wisconsin, he should be able to sweep entirely across Missouri and seize at least the eastern part of Nebraska.

Another vulnerable area was Louisiana, which was flat and narrow, easy to cross with an army. Crossing the Mississippi would be the worst problem but that could be accomplished if he hit Missouri first as a feint to cause the U.S.A. to withdraw troops, moving them north to defend Missouri. Let them go, unmolested. Then, once they were gone, head west across Louisiana and keep moving until all of eastern Texas was seized and occupied. It was possible. In fact, it was very possible. Unless, of course, those fatheaded generals were afraid to do it. On the streets, where you seized every opportunity without hesitation, they wouldn't have lasted two weeks.

But Gorcey had learned very young that you don't attack a

dangerous enemy unless you have adequate firepower and enough willing men to permit you to lose as many as half your soldiers and still emerge as the victor. When things reached a critical point and you spotted an advantage that could give you victory, you threw everything you had at your enemy in one big battle fought on your terms. You chose the time and the place and then you smashed him like stamping your foot on a spider. Yes, it was possible. Seizing those states and then relocating the surplus population into them would solve almost every troubling problem Gorcey faced. Then a few years later he could grab the rest of Texas and gain access to its endless supply of oil, which he could sell for cash on the world market, silencing that damned Russian ambassador.

Without hesitation now that a decision had been reached, he pushed a button on the telephone, one that led to his secretary in the outer office. When she answered, his message was brief and clipped.

"Find those generals and get them back in here. I don't care how you do it, but find them. I've got work for them to do."

While he waited for the generals to be located, Gorcey turned his attention to other matters. According to reports from the various governmental agencies, one of the worst problems facing the A.S.R. was idleness combined with a shocking rise in the birth rate. The only factories reporting capacity production were those in which squads of his elite force had been stationed with orders to keep every machine operating by whatever means were needed. Jails had been emptied, with prisoners assigned to factories. Chronic drunks had been given the cold water cure and then were placed on assembly lines, doing simple jobs.

These tactics didn't work in hospitals or with members of the medical profession. Before being deposed, Poynter had solved the problem of free, universal medical care, which included childbirth, by converting vacated store buildings into neighborhood hospitals staffed primarily by graduate medical students and volunteers. Existing hospitals and medical centers were reserved for the critically ill and those requiring special treatment. Most childbirths occurred in the neighborhood facilities under the care of midwives licensed by the state. Because it worked, Gorcey had seen no need to tinker with this format. He pitched the report on health care and childbirth into the "out" basket on his desk and dismissed the topic from his mind.

He was starting to read the diplomatic report outlining conditions in the A.S.R. embassies abroad when the intercom button on his telephone lighted and rang. The generals, his secretary said, had been found and were now headed back to the White House. With his mind already busy on details of the proposed invasion of the U.S.A., Gorcey only grunted and returned the telephone to its cradle. Already he was visualizing what he could do with the extra land gained in this sudden strike, and how it would build the stature of this nation he headed. Leaning back and propping his feet once more on the desk, Gorcey visualized the time when this new territory had been assimilated into the A.S.R. and he could begin acquiring more land and wealth until the A.S.R. extended all the way to California and the Pacific Ocean. He was still musing about this pleasant dream when the door opened and the three generals entered, standing at attention until they were recognized.

Doors into the Oval Office remained shut and guarded for almost three hours. The session was interrupted only once, when three military aides carrying heavy attache cases were admitted. Afternoon shadows were lengthening on the White House lawn when the military delegation emerged and departed quietly with no smiles visible to the White House clerical staff in the outer offices. In contrast, Gorcey was in excellent spirits each time he left the private office for one reason or another. He looked, one clerk whispered to another, like the cat that just ate the canary.

He had good reason to be in high spirits. His military advisors, after their initial reservations had been scuttled, not only had told Gorcey that such an invasion was possible but also that, if mounted quickly, it had an excellent chance for success. Statistics on troop placements, brought by the aides, had proved this to be the case. Not only did the U.S.A. appear to have only token forces along the international boundary, but there was also an absence of aircraft within easy range of the proposed combat area. For some reason, the U.S.A. had concentrated most of its planes in western Texas and near the Pacific coast, a flight of at least two hours before they could provide aerial support for combat along the Mississippi front.

In contrast, as his advisors told Gorcey, the A.S.R. could move its fleet of one hundred helicopter gunships to sites along the front and have them already in position when the fighting began. These aircraft were a gift from Soviet Russia and were old but serviceable, equipped with both cannons and rocket launchers. In addition, there were several dozen fighter planes seized from National Guard units when the states were federalized. Within no more than a month, everything could be in place along the border and the invasion could be launched. Their final act before adjourning the meeting had been selection of a time when it should occur: exactly four months from today. This would allow time to get supplies stockpiled along the front.

Gorcey remained in high spirits for the remainder of the day. Not only would this assure that his name would be included in future lists of the great conquerors of the world, but the addition of new land would put an end to most of the petty domestic problems that daily consumed so much of his time. Once again, he unfolded his old roadmap of the United States and studied it closely, outlining the shape of each of the target states with his finger. Then, distastefully, he asked his secretary to summon the members of the Council. Even though it no longer had any governing power, he felt an obligation to inform its members of his plans and actions.

Increasingly, Gorcey had grown distrustful of the Council, and felt some of its members were capable of taking action to depose him from his seat of power. At their infrequent meetings, these members were overly silent, almost sullen. Unfortunately, because they were a visible carryover from the popular Poynter regime, Gorcey needed the presence of the Council to show publicly their unanimous support for actions he took. Each of his meetings with the Council was a public relations fete, complete with a battery of television cameras and carefully orchestrated questions to key Council members. Today would be no exception.

Gorcey wasn't prepared for the Council's reaction to his announcement of a planned invasion of the U.S.A. Not only did one member swear loudly when he outlined his plans, but several others tried to argue with him and one, a veteran of the Poynter days, loudly predicted disaster. "Our troops," he pointed out, "are untrained conscripts and no match for the professional forces of the U.S.A." This man had left the meeting angrily, not even bothering to remain for the traditional social hour that followed.

A bewildering variety of food and a huge bar serving almost any type of drink were standard fixtures at these Council events. For Gorcey, they were a diplomatic bone tossed to a collection of people he didn't want around but needed for public relations purposes. At the time when he seized power, Gorcey had disbanded the Council but soon found, to his dismay, their presence was needed if his regime was to have acceptance by the public. Without the Council being visible occasionally, his new government appeared too much like a dictatorship. So, with the adaptability that had allowed him to survive on the streets, Gorcey had found minor jobs for the Council and had restored them to their seats.

Their power today was limited to debating minor domestic matters and settling disputes between the states. However, to make them feel needed and to assure their support, or at least silence, on major issues he had adopted the policy of briefing them on decisions he had already made. Each time he did this, the announcement was followed by one of these social hours where the Council members were sent home eventually, filled with good food and plenty to drink. Later, this gave Gorcey the right to claim Council support for his actions and, if the venture failed, he could blame the Council for its failure.

Until today when the one veteran member had stalked angrily out of the Council session, all of its members had looked forward to these social sessions as a pleasant highlight to their governmental careers. It wasn't unusual for a few members to remain overnight in the White House after sampling too much of the liquor. This session, though, had been a disaster from the start, lacking the loud talk and boisterous laughter whose volume increased as the hours passed and the refreshment flowed. Tonight, the Council members stood around in small knots and just talked quietly to each other. Periodically, one Councilman would gesticulate angrily while making a point to others gathered around him.

After his guests had joined only halfheartedly in a toast to success in this new venture, Gorcey had become increasingly disturbed and then angry. This Council owed its existence to him, and it owed him allegiance in his efforts to make this nation into a major world power. He had brought its members back from the ash heap and restored them to their offices, so they owed him a debt of allegiance. Without him, they were nothing, no better than the hordes found on any street in any city. Finally, Gorcey disgustedly left the ballroom and went to his quarters in the Presidential suite, slamming the door behind him. *Let the hogs stay at the trough and root until nothing is left! Damn them!* He wouldn't need them much longer. As soon as his nation was expanded, he would get rid of them, all of them, and replace the Council with a small group of professional advisors.

By noon of the following day, sketchy details of Gorcey's invasion plan had reached the intelligence outposts maintained by the U.S.A. in Washington. Alarmed Council members had told friends.

These friends had told their friends, and eventually the news had reached these outposts and contained enough details for it to be taken seriously. By morning of the next day, these stories had been confirmed and a courier was ready to leave for the U.S.A. with his first stop in New Orleans, where a border crossing was relatively easy and simple.

The news confirming that an invasion was being planned by the A.S.R. was no surprise to President Knowlton. It did nothing but validate the scenario he had already formulated in his mind. In Gorcey's boots, he would probably do the same thing. Earlier reports from Washington had stressed repeatedly that major cracks were appearing in the social fabric of the A.S.R. Factory production was sluggish. Agricultural output was a yearly disaster. Meanwhile, consumer demand remained strong as a result of the guaranteed annual wage. Also, according to diplomatic reports, most other nations were beginning to question the stability of the yellowback dollar of the A.S.R., and whether or not the new nation could survive much longer.

Privately, Knowlton agreed with Gorcey in one respect. Invasion of an adjacent land mass was the only way the A.S.R. could create new wealth and simultaneously stimulate patriotic loyalty among its population. What Gorcey could not afford was a defeat, even a minor defeat that did nothing to decide the outcome of the war. The type of government Gorcey had created could hold the loyalty of its people only by victories, one after another. Any indication of failure, even by a minor military defeat, would cause the same people who put Poynter in the White House to turn against Gorcey. They wouldn't overthrow him but, instead, would just desert him and become a leaderless mob. Yes, Knowlton agreed, in Gorcey's position he would create a patriotic fever by invasion of a recognized enemy power, the U.S.A.. Now, how would he do it if he were Gorcey? And how could it be stopped as soon as it got underway?

At that moment, the coming invasion became a war between two men rather than one between nations. Knowlton knew he couldn't prevent an invasion from occurring, because he lacked the manpower needed to reinforce the border heavily enough to repel a determined assault by the forces the A.S.R. was able to muster. Because he couldn't afford to withdraw many units from the southwestern states, Knowlton must compensate for the lack of military force with a strategy that would cause the A.S.R. to abandon the invasion before any new territory was seized.

Immediately, he put himself in Gorcey's position and tried to think and plan like Gorcey. He gave top priority to the collection of intelligence about all aspects of the A.S.R., its government and especially its people. Every night he was in his office until almost midnight, studying every detail of the A.S.R., trying to pinpoint weaknesses and strengths. In all cases, he tried deliberately to put himself in Gorcey's position. What would he do about this? How would he react to that? What reaction could be expected from the populace from success or failure? Within a week, Knowlton was satisfied. The intelligence bulletins began reporting trends or actions he had already predicted. *By God, I've got him! I know how he thinks and how he'll do it when the time comes. Now I know what I have to do and where I have to do it.* The following day, Knowlton returned to his normal schedule.

Unaware his strategy had been deciphered, Gorcey continued to filter military units into the territory along the border separating the A.S.R. from the U.S.A. The engineering units worked feverishly to build rafts from logs and heavy planking. Amphibious tanks were secreted in villages and barns. One by one, the helicopter gunships were moved within easy flying range of the border. Each morning the military advisors huddled with Gorcey in the White House, remaining for more than an hour while their large staff cars remained parked on the circular driveway.

The guaranteed annual wage within the A.S.R. had caused street vendors and panhandlers to become almost extinct in the larger cities. There was no longer any reason for a person to sit on a street corner all day, selling newspapers or flowers as a way to create an income. With rental rates pegged at only five percent of this guaranteed income, there was no incentive for a person to spend an entire day on the street, regardless of weather, to earn a pitifully few dollars. Remaining at home, even in a furnished room, was much more pleasant than huddling on a street corner for ten or twelve hours each day.

This was why the appearance of a flower vendor on a corner across the street from the White House attracted attention. Beginning on the second morning when the military advisors began meeting daily with Gorcey, this aged woman with her folding camp chair and card table could be seen easily from the White House and every nearby building. By afternoon, her flowers were all sold and she folded her table and chair and then headed toward the bus stop in front of the venerable Willard Hotel, plodding painfully down the sidewalk.

Her hair was gray and wavy but somewhat unkempt and her face was deeply furrowed with the lines of age. Its features would disappear into a crinkle when she smiled, which she did whenever someone bought one of her flowers. She would drop the coins into a pocket in her billowing dress and then rearrange her wares to make them attractive to the next customer. Gorcey discovered her presence during her third morning, during a period when he was gazing out of a White House window as he tried to organize his thoughts for that day's session with the military advisors. He watched her absently for a few moments, then forgot about her when the meeting convened.

Later in the day, her presence was recalled when Gorcey's attention was drawn to a colorful bouquet on his secretary's desk. She told him she had bought the flowers that morning from "that poor old lady out on the street corner." When he looked outside a few minutes later, the flower vendor was still at her corner, but most of her flowers were gone. He watched, fascinated, as the shabby old woman gestured toward each pedestrian. When her last flower was gone, she folded her table and chair and hobbled away.

She remained in Gorcey's mind long after she had gone. He admired her industry. Visibly, she wasn't one of the millions who drew their monthly wage and then spent their time drunk, playing or simply doing nothing. This woman, despite her age, had ambition and wasn't afraid to work. Probably she grew the flowers herself, in a garden that required continued labor for it to produce the quality he had seen on his secretary's desk. If she bought the flowers and then re-sold them at a profit, she was an even better example of personal ambition.

It rained the next day, but the woman was at her corner with her flowers protected by a plastic shield. She remained huddled beneath an umbrella as the hours passed. Despite his busy schedule, Gorcey was drawn several times to his window. Each time he looked out, she was there despite the rain. She appeared to be so wet he felt pity for her so, after the session with his advisors ended, Gorcey sent a messenger to the corner with instructions to buy the woman's entire stock of flowers. He watched the transaction from his window. As soon as the messenger left, the woman folded her chair and table and hobbled away in the direction of the bus stop. Once she was gone, Gorcey returned to his busy routine.

The woman remained on the bus for only a mile, just far enough to be out of Washington's central district. She got off at a street corner near Georgetown, shuffling clumsily out of the narrow door with her folded table and chair, and remained standing on the corner until the bus was out of sight. Then she walked quickly to a parked car, pitched the table and chair behind the front seat and drove away. By the time she had reached the shabby second-floor office Henderson had visited, her frowzy wig had been discarded and her false teeth were back in her mouth, changing her appearance drastically.

Art and Jack were at their customary posts in the oyster brokerage, obviously awaiting her arrival. They scowled when she entered, uncomfortable with this assignment they had been handed by the Knowlton regime in Denver. Bootlegging refugees out of the A.S.R. was one thing, but providing an operations center for surveillance of the White House was another matter entirely. Each day the woman would come here when she left her corner and dictate a tape of the day's activities at the White House, with special emphasis on the daily sessions of the military advisors. This tape would go to Denver. A second tape went to field agents in Washington, to be used in gathering intelligence about the planned actions of the Gorcey regime.

Walking briskly instead of shuffling, the woman entered the office and headed for the restroom without a pause. When she finally emerged, her frowzy appearance was gone. Her hair had been combed and was no longer a rusty gray. Most of the wrinkles had vanished from her face as soon as her false teeth entered her mouth. Instead of a faded print dress, she was wearing one tailored to a body no longer padded to look lumpy and shapeless.

Only after she emerged from the restroom did the woman say anything to the other occupants of the office. By now, after several days she had spent selling flowers, they had learned to leave her alone until she shed her disguise.

"What a day!" she commented as she sank thankfully into a chair. "I feel like a sponge after sitting in that rain all day. Do you know who bought the flowers I had left this afternoon? The White House, no less! How did it go for you two today?"

"So-so," Jack replied. "No better and no worse than any other day in the fish business. Otherwise and except for the regulars like you, we didn't have any business at all."

"Better get your taping done, Edie," Art interrupted. "We've got a package about ready to go out and we need to get it on its way. Any film today?"

"One cartridge," she responded. "I'll get it out and give it to you with my tape."

Art slid a recorder across the desk and she moved into the other room and shut the door. For five minutes she dictated into the machine, her voice barely audible through the closed door. When she returned, Edie slid the recorder across his desk to Art and then opened her large, lumpy purse from which she withdrew a small, flat camera whose lens had fitted snugly into a ragged hole in the purse. She removed a tiny film pack from the camera, replaced it with a new one and handed the used cartridge to Art.

"See you tomorrow, boys," Edie commented as she headed for the door. "I can't afford to stay here too long or the neighbors will talk. It's all in your hands now and I'm headed for a nice, long bath."

Gingerly, as if it were hot, Art slid the tape and film into a small packet resembling a toilet case of the type carried by any traveler. The items fit snugly beneath a false bottom. Neither of the men spoke while Art added the usual personal things found in such a case. Then he slid the case across to Jack.

"Same place," he commented. "Same person." Sighing, Jack rose and left the office carrying the case casually by its loop that permitted it to swing freely by his side.

Two days later, this report and the film were in Denver and copies of the photographs were on President Knowlton's desk. The license numbers on each of the cars parked in the White House driveway identified the vehicles as those used by Gorcey's military advisors. A man shown emerging from another vehicle was identified as the commander of the Air Force. In one photo, Gorcey's face was seen framed in an upstairs White House window, gazing pensively toward the camera.

Knowlton studied the pictures, listened three times to the tapes and then slid them across his desk, where they joined similar reports from other locations within the A.S.R. There was one summarizing a long conversation overheard between a member of Gorcey's Council and another person, one itemizing the A.S.R. troop buildup along the Mississippi and a large but fuzzy photograph taken from an ancient, high-flying U-2 aircraft that depicted rows of helicopters parked in pastures identified as Illinois and eastern Louisiana.

"He's right on schedule," Knowlton commented to himself. "He's throwing everything he has into those two places, but he's still planning or those daily meetings wouldn't be going on. About two more weeks, maybe three, that's all we have! Then it all hits the fan! God help me, I hope I'm right—and if I'm wrong, God help all of us!"

# 11

A month passed with no major military activity along the border with the A.S.R. The raids that occurred were mostly hit-and-run affairs designed to create a continuing nuisance. A squad from the A.S.R. would paddle across the Mississippi, terrorize nearby farms or communities and then withdraw to the other bank of the river. One squad that penetrated almost twenty-five miles into Minnesota aboard armored vehicles was surrounded by National Guard troops and destroyed, with no survivors left to be interrogated.

At first this lingering delay bothered President Knowlton and caused him to doubt the accuracy of his reasoning. When the A.S.R. troop concentration began along the border, he had expected an invasion within a week or two. His study of Gorcey's behavior had led him to anticipate a sudden strike that Gorcey could use to consolidate his power. Every scrap of intelligence data indicated this to be the case. He had tried to put himself into Gorcey's position, facing the mounting economic problems of a nation in which no real loyalty or patriotism existed. The only lasting solution to these problems was annexation of new land to create new wealth.

Instead, days and now weeks passed and nothing happened. Knowlton spent sleepless nights analyzing this affair to find what he had overlooked in his reasoning. Eventually he found the answer, and it was ridiculously simple. Gorcey could not launch an invasion until he had stockpiled enough foodstuffs and ammunition to supply his troops throughout the early stages of the assault. Also, Gorcey had filled the frontier with raw, green troops who had to receive at least minimal training before being thrown into combat. This explained the rash of apparently pointless border raids. They were part of this training.

*I was right all along,* Knowlton told himself. *It was Gorcey who slipped, not me! He let his ambition run away with him and then had to back away at the last minute. Nothing is really changed. He's just playing it safe so he can win. Now, how long do I have? Another month or two, or will he make his move next week? All I can do is wait and watch, and then be ready when he does move.* With that final thought, Knowlton dropped off to the first sound sleep he had enjoyed in almost two weeks.

Through his military chiefs-of-staff, the President ordered increased surveillance along the border with special emphasis on Iowa, Missouri and Louisiana. And he ordered two warships to make protocol visits to Greenland, where they would be within easy range of Boston and New York. Until needed, they would remain in the waters around Greenland, conducting a routine exercise. With these preparations completed, Knowlton turned his attention to other matters and began spending more time in the residential quarters, where he and Lucy entertained a stream of guests. Their social life blossomed.

Congressman Pat Conway and his wife Bea were always included in these social affairs, partly because they were old friends of Michael and Lucy Knowlton and partly because this was a simple way for the President to remain informed about their daughter and grandchild who had escaped from the A.S.R. Since leaving Congress to become President, Knowlton had also grown to miss the legislative banter and the "Pat and Mike" jokes that always accompanied the introduction of a bill by Conway and Knowlton. Now, while there was still time, the President wanted to recreate as much of that atmosphere as possible.

As the days passed and the uneasy peace continued, informal social luncheons and dinners involving only the Knowltons and the Conways became almost commonplace. At these affairs, the talk was never of the coming invasion but instead was limited to social and personal comments. One evening, the President even prepared hamburgers in a charcoal grill on the patio. Another night they were entertained by a string quartet from the University of Denver.

At least twice a week, the lights burned late in the Presidential mansion and the music of an orchestra drifted across the lawn. Most of the guests at these affairs were old acquaintances of the Knowlton family, plus Cabinet officers and ambassadors from the diplomatic community in Denver. The war, if there was to be one, seemed far away during this period, an impossible nightmare that could never happen. News of these gatherings, of course, reached Washington and left Gorcey puzzled: *Could that stupid jackass in Denver really be that dumb? Doesn't he know by now that he's about finished? He has to be aware of the extra troops along his border and here he is just having fun instead of watching the store. Is he up to something? And if so, what?*

Every scrap of intelligence Gorcey had collected had indicated the U.S.A. was aware of a military force being gathered along its border. Why did it have to be so difficult to begin a military assault, and why must there be so many delays? Every day, Gorcey had pushed his military advisors unmercifully to try to hasten preparations for the invasion but, each day, another reason for delay had been presented in a lengthy, annoying manner with no minor details omitted. First it was the necessity of acquiring more troops in numbers large enough to keep all frontiers protected. Then the additional soldiers needed more supplies, which had to be moved to the border area. Most recently, the new troops required combat training beyond that provided in the recruit depots. Meanwhile, they were eating like horses and wasting thousands of rounds of ammunition in firing at stationary targets. Enough was enough! Why did a simple invasion have to be so difficult? In the life Gorcey had led, if you decided you wanted to eliminate a rival, you just did it. You didn't find daily reasons why you shouldn't do it.

He would continue pushing his military advisors unmercifully to get them to convert endless talk into action but, meanwhile, the actions of that bastard Knowlton disturbed him. With his endless rounds of social events, Knowlton must know something he, Gorcey, did not. But what? That endless round of parties made it appear that Knowlton either wasn't aware his nation was an invasion target, or else he was so confident of success that he wasn't worried about its outcome.

What Gorcey could not know was that, for President Knowlton, the colorful functions were a form of exorcism, a desperate clinging to a way of life that was vanishing. The music, the dancers whirling in colorful configurations on the ballroom floor and the murmur of polite conversation among his guests would remain implanted in Knowlton's memory as long as he lived. As the days and nights passed, he would frequently walk outdoors while a party was underway and stand quietly beneath a tree, listening intently to the muted sounds of the orchestra as they floated across the grounds of the mansion. In these moments, his mind was far away, in another time and place.

Except for the evenings, the routine of his days remained unchanged, beginning with his early morning trip to the kitchen for coffee, followed by his daily shower and his stop to awaken Lucy while en route to his office, where he studied overnight reports from each governmental agency and the bulletins from the Mississippi border. Then, he would listen intently as the general staff summarized the latest events along the border and in the southwestern states. As he had always done, Knowlton would make notes of items he considered to be especially important, and later request more data about them.

Lately he had reserved one hour to himself, beginning as soon as the general staff departed. During this period, Knowlton was not to be disturbed for any reason other than news of the start of the expected invasion. This was a time when, on the basis of the reports received that day, he attempted to put himself in Gorcey's position, to try to reach into Gorcey's mind and identify the actions he would take if he were Gorcey. Knowlton knew this was a dangerous game because he was not, and could never be, Gorcey. But by now he felt he knew the man like a brother. So far, there had been no surprises. Gorcey had done nothing that Knowlton had not predicted a day or so in advance.

When the hour was over and Knowlton emerged from his office, he would be exhausted, perspiring visibly. He would stroll through the outer office, making pleasantries to members of the staff, and then return to his private quarters. Afternoons were devoted to domestic matters and appointments with ambassadors or members of Congress. Just before he left at five o'clock, his secretary would bring the correspondence and other papers requiring his personal signature. Normally he would be sitting at his desk, awaiting her arrival.

She was disturbed one day when she found the President standing in front of one of the huge windows, muttering to himself. Obviously he hadn't heard her approach. When she neared him, she was able to understand the words he was muttering so softly. It was the Lord's Prayer. Careful to make no sound, she backed away and left the office. When she returned several minutes later, Knowlton was seated at his desk and chided her gently about being a few minutes late.

Several evenings later, Pat and Bea Conway were guests of the Knowltons at an informal dinner served on the mansion patio, where the lights had been dimmed to help repel the evening insects. The steaks had been delicious, thick and charbroiled to perfection. There were roasting ears of corn with plenty of butter, a selection of salads, and peach pie for dessert. It was an authentic ranch dinner impossible to serve at any formal function. A choice of coffee or tea was the final course, after which the domestic staff vanished.

For several minutes the Knowltons and the Conways at quietly in the deep patio chairs, saying nothing but listening absently to the songs of the night insects chirruping in foliage on the mansion lawn. In the background was the sound of a Viennese waltz, with the volume on the tape player turned so low the music created only an orchestral background to the night. The President turned toward Conway and began speaking.

"Did you ever read about that period in Vienna or Prague just before Hitler invaded their countries?" he asked. "The people in Austria and Czechoslovakia loved music like this. They danced every night, pretending that an invasion wasn't just around the corner. And all the time the Nazis were marching toward them.

"They had plenty of warning, but they just enjoyed themselves and danced away the time they had left. That was the last time the world had style and grace in everything it did. Now we're facing the same thing as Vienna and Prague and, by God, we're going to meet it with style and grace. But it isn't going to end like it did before. Not as long as I'm alive, it isn't."

Conway remained silent. He didn't know how to respond to a comment like this. For several minutes the only sound was the droning song of the insects and, faintly, that of the Viennese waltz. Then Knowlton spoke again.

"You know, of course, that we're going to be invaded just like those other countries," he continued. "It isn't far off, either. A few more weeks. That's all the time we have left. We can't afford a thousand-mile battle along the Mississippi. We don't have the manpower to protect a front that long—not even if we drafted everyone in the country over age ten. And not even if we pull every soldier out of the southwest and move them to the Mississippi."

Conway only nodded, not wanting to interrupt his friend. Despite the warm night, he was chilled by the tone of Knowlton's voice. It was that of a stranger, not the man he had known for so many years.

"We're not Vienna or Prague," the President almost whispered. "I know how it will begin and I know how to stop them. The invasion will fail. Oh, they'll get across the Mississippi and probably a few miles into Louisiana. We can't prevent that. But that's all.

"Do you know why I've been having so many big parties here in the mansion?" he remarked, changing the topic. "It's because I want this period to be remembered as one when a way of life went out with style and grace. That's why I play that Viennese music so much. It forces me to face what happened to Vienna and Prague when they were faced with a situation like this." Without warning, the President once again moved to another subject and shot a quick question at Conway.

"What's the most important thing we have?" he asked. "Is it things that have become almost sacred to us because they are symbols of our way of life, or is it the things that are in our minds as part of this way of life?"

The question caught Conway by surprise and he didn't know how to reply. He wasn't sure exactly what Knowlton had in mind or what type of answer he expected to receive. Of one thing, though, he was certain. The answer to this question was of vital importance to the President.

"I don't really know how to answer that," Conway replied. "I guess I'd say it was us, ourselves, and what is inside of us. The pioneers who settled this part of the country didn't have things, but they had themselves and that was enough. Everything that's here today came later, all but one thing: the land. It will always be here."

"That's the way I see it," Knowlton murmured softly. "It isn't what's here, not here or not in Vienna or Prague or anywhere else, but what we do with it that counts. I'm glad you said that. Maybe, now, I can have some peace of mind!"

They sat quietly for almost fifteen minutes, each wrapped in his own private thoughts while the Viennese music and the faint drone of insects in the trees provided a faraway symphony to the night. Occasionally the sound of a passing vehicle could be heard on the street in front of the mansion and, once, one of the security guards somewhere on the grounds coughed and cleared his throat. The indigo night sky was punctured by hundred of tiny stars winking like faraway fireflies. Finally, the silence was broken by a final comment from President Knowlton.

"Pat, when it comes, I want you to know that I had no choice," he murmured, punctuating each word carefully. "We just don't have enough men to oppose them and turn them back. And we can't surrender, because that would be worse than defeat on the battlefield. We wouldn't be just surrendering our land. We would be surrendering our minds and every generation in the future.

"Don't answer. Just remember that I had no choice, none at all. And may God help my soul, if there is one somewhere."

Conway was shocked. This wasn't his friend of so many years. It was not the man with whom he had joked in Congressional hallways, or the man who had been an overnight guest in his home and with whom he had shared more than one cold beer in his basement family room. This was a stranger who was facing an impossible problem and had reconciled himself to a solution he would have to live with for the rest of his days. It wasn't an abject surrender—of this, Conway was certain. Neither was it a battlefield defeat followed by a truce. Before his analysis could go any further, his thoughts were disrupted by the arrival of Bea and Lucy, both chattering happily and laughing about something.

"Are you two going to sit out there all night?" the President's wife asked brightly. "It's almost midnight!"

Going home, Conway drove very slowly and circled through the heart of Denver where lighted signs shimmered in front of restaurants and other nighttime businesses, and where people moved apparently aimlessly on the sidewalks or in the parking lots of the larger establishments. His eye was caught by a young woman in a tight red dress, being escorted by two equally young men in military uniform. When the young woman threw her head back in laughter, her long hair cascaded over her shoulders. On one street corner there were three workmen carrying lunch buckets, waiting for a bus to arrive to take them home. Near a seedy bar, a drunk sat dejectedly on the curb, his head in his hands.

These, and others of a similar nature, were new sights to Conway after the private talk with President Knowlton. Even though they had passed before him a thousand times in other trips through the heart of the city, he had never really seen them before. They had been just people and things seen in the glare of streetlights and signs. Now they suddenly had a new and important meaning to him. They weren't just random people—a girl going, probably, to a hotel with two soldiers, a group of factory workers headed home at the end of their shift, and a hopeless drunk wasting his life. Instead, they were the face of this country; and their individual actions were of far greater importance than anything he or Knowlton could do, because of one very simple thing that was so commonplace it was overlooked.

These weren't just individual people. They represented the entire nation because they were doing only what they chose to do and in the manner they chose to do it. That girl in the red dress was with those soldiers because she wanted to be with them and, above all, because she had a right to be with them whenever and however she chose. The drunk was killing himself gradually because he preferred that way of life to any other. It was his own decision, made freely.

Suddenly, Conway knew what Knowlton had meant when he said he had no choice. The knowledge sent an icy spear through his mind and he was silent until he and Bea were home once again.

Cynthia was idly watching a late movie on television, sitting curled on the sofa in the family room. Susan was upstairs, asleep. Conway had never felt closer to his family in his life than at that moment. Everything was so normal. That was the word, *normal.* He knew he was acting strange and could feel Bea watching him with an unspoken question in her eyes. She knew him too well. She could sense when his mind was groping to try to find the answer to something. This was one bit of knowledge he could not share with her. Just this once, she had to be locked outside, at least for a while. Her first effort to find out what was bothering him came later, when they were in their bedroom.

"What is it?" she asked softly. "What did he tell you tonight? Can you tell me?"

"Not this time," he replied tonelessly. "This time I can't, so please don't ask me."

It was almost dawn before exhaustion overcame him and he fell asleep. At committee meeting the next morning, he was unnaturally silent but listened intently to all of the comments made by the other members, and he cast his vote exactly as he had always done at earlier debates on this minor topic.

"I want you to take Cynthia and Susie and go home," he told Bea that evening. "Don't ask me why and don't try to talk me out of it. Just start getting ready and leave as soon as possible. Open up our old house and get it ready and, as soon as this is over, I'll join you there."

It was more of an ultimatum than a request and it shocked Bea. Her place as a wife was here, not in that small town they called home. She wouldn't leave without a struggle.

"How can I go just now?" she asked. "What about Cynthia and her new job? She can't just walk away from it without giving any notice. What about Susie? She still needs the care they're able to provide here in Denver. We can't just walk away and leave you here alone."

Conway was adamant. In the end, his wife agreed to pack only enough things for a week or so, and join the next highway convoy headed toward their home. Reluctantly, Cynthia decided to join her, but she had two jobs that needed doing first. She telephoned her employer and resigned her new job. With that done, she vanished upstairs to prepare Susie for the trip. Two mornings later, Conway's family started home, leaving him alone in that big house which felt utterly empty because of the silence. He was relieved when the telephone rang and he was told of their safe arrival.

In Washington, Gorcey's temper had improved. Plans for the invasion were finally going well and the Soviets had once again bolstered his currency. And with most of the young men conscripted into a uniform, the streets didn't appear to be quite so infested with idlers coming from nowhere and going nowhere. The continuing reports of stagnant industrial and agricultural output still upset him, but that was a problem which would be solved very soon. That new land and those new cities, all containing factories, which he would annex to the A.S.R. would solve that particular problem.

Yes, it would happen soon; very soon. In fact, he had already picked a date when it would occur. Unless those damned generals informed him they had fired all of their ammunition or eaten all their food, history would be made on the day he had chosen. Right now, all he could do was to try to relax and wait. At the last moment he would review all of the details with those generals and, unless a major botch emerged, that new land would be his in a matter of days, no more than a few weeks at worst.

He uncrossed his feet and dropped them from the Oval Office desk, then strolled unhurriedly to his favorite window in the White House, the one that gave a clear view of the tip of the Washington Monument and the flight path leading into Washington National air terminal. A speck of sunlight glittered from the monument and a silvery airliner floated past, making its descent to the airport runway. On the ground, a green-and-white bus lumbered slowly down the street, headed toward the Capitol Building. On the White House lawn, a gardener was giving the grassy carpet its daily manicure. The old flower vendor was at her customary post across the street, sitting behind her table filled with floral bouquets. Because he admired her industry, he had given orders to the White House staff to keep all vases filled daily with her flowers. *I'll bet I'm her best customer.*

Precisely on schedule, the military advisors arrived in their individual limousines and accompanied by their aides. As they did every day, they brought a variety of maps, statistical charts and other items telling the story of the troop concentration along the border with the U.S.A. Gorcey was back at his desk when they marched into the Oval Office and remained at attention until told to be seated. Their news was good this day. Everything was in place along the front and there was no reason to delay the assault. Even the weather forecasts were cooperating. The long-range prediction called for fair and dry conditions before, during and immediately after the date of the invasion.

Gorcey was so excited that he paced the room, slapping one fist into his other hand. He was so pleased he invited the generals and their aides to join him at lunch in the White House dining room. Lunch, of course, was preceded and followed by cocktails and the big limousines remained in the White House driveway until midafternoon. One general who had celebrated too well had to be helped into his vehicle by his aide, while Gorcey stood by smiling broadly. He remained in the circular driveway until the last limousine had departed, then returned to the White House with a spring in his walk.

All of this was captured on film by the flower vendor across the street. As soon as the last vehicle had departed, she chucked her remaining bouquets in a nearby sewer, folded her table and hurried away to catch her usual bus. Had Gorcey been watching, he would have seen that, today, she didn't hobble but instead walked with a long, pacing stride. A half-hour later, she burst into the office occupied by the oyster brokers and, without delaying to remove her wig and padding, grabbed the recorder and headed into the other room where, behind its closed door, she dictated her report. Emerging, she stripped the film cartridge from her hidden camera and pressed it and the tape into Art's hand with visible urgency.

"This is it!" she said. "They're going to do it! I'm so sure of this I put it in my report. They celebrated until one of the brass had to be poured into his car with brother Gorcey watching and grinning like he just ate the canary. This has got to get to Denver just as fast as possible."

Within minutes, the tape and film were in the false bottom of the toilet case and dispatched to Denver by courier. They would be there early the following morning.

In Denver at exactly the same time the Washington celebration was ending, an exasperated President Knowlton, accompanied by his executive chief-of-staff, was stalking along the sidewalk leading from the barracks to the mansion. He had just undergone an extremely unpleasant two hours with the minority leaders of both houses of Congress and the mayors of four of the largest cities in the southwestern states. The session had been arranged by Ron Knecht, his executive chief, and Knowlton had agreed to participate only because he felt it was unavoidable.

Normally, Knecht acted as go-between with the Cabinet departments and the executive agencies housed in the barracks. From his offices in the barracks, he made the daily operational decisions on the basis of policies established by the President; he tried to keep the press satisfied and he screened all of the requests for appointments with the President. This kept Knowlton insulated from the details of government operations, but the daily report from Knecht covered all actions taken. It was one of the first things the President read each morning. At some convenient time during the day, he met with Knecht and outlined his views and policies. Normally it was a good working relationship, but today Knowlton was annoyed with Knecht for persuading him to participate in this hearing with the mayors and those politicians from the opposing party.

The mayors had demanded this hearing to secure more federal assistance in handling the waves of illegal Mexican immigrants swarming by the thousands into their cities. Their earlier pleas, they felt, were being ignored by the federal government and, as a result, their cities were rapidly becoming war zones beyond the ability of local authorities to control. The small number of troops sent to augment local law enforcement agencies were unable to make a dent in the problem. Fifty desperate Mexican families arrived for every five captured and deported.

The frantic city governments turned to Congress for assistance and their plea was seized for political reasons by the minority party, who saw in it a chance to embarrass the administration. Election, after all, was only a year off and these cities represented several million voters. It was a fine opportunity to help these voters while, simultaneously, putting the majority party on the defensive. Knecht had faced a dilemma: if he refused to grant the hearing, the Knowlton Presidency would appear heartless; but if he did approve this forum, it was sure to become a political shooting gallery with the President as the target. Reluctantly, he and the President had agreed the hearing must occur despite its hazards. It became worse than either had anticipated.

It began politely with a lengthy summation of the problem and its impact upon the finances and people of the cities. Knowlton listened intently but heard nothing he hadn't already known. Then came individual pleas by the mayors, all telling similar stories. Each asked the President to station more troops in his city and to halt the flood of migrants by sealing the Mexican border with enough soldiers to create a human fence extending from Texas to California.

The session became bitter when the opposing politicians accused the Knowlton administration of wasting tax dollars by using the military draft to prevent unemployment. Knowlton then had reminded the politicians of the threat of invasion by the A.S.R. The continuing draft, he pointed out, had been supported at all times by them and their political party. The lowest point in the hearing occurred when the mayor of one of the largest cities used the forum to vent his helpless rage.

"What do you expect us to do, just give them our cities?" he shouted. "Have you been out there to see what has happened? Do you know I don't even have a city park left? They're all filled with shanties and tents filled with Mexican families! You can't get into a shopping mall because it's filled with them and they're squatting all over the parking lots. What in the hell do you expect us to do if you won't lift a finger to help us? If you can't even seal off that border, how can you expect to run a country?"

This outburst had generated a wave of protest from the other mayors and Knecht had hammered his palm on the podium to try to restore order to the hearing. A furious President had turned white as he resisted the desire to tell this mayor to go to hell and follow this with a full explanation of why additional troops were impossible to supply. The hearing had finally ended indecisively after order was restored and the mayor had apologized for his accusations. In return, the President promised to transfer more troops to the southwest as soon as possible, once the threat along the Mississippi was deflected. He felt safe in making this promise because, if the U.S.A. was successful in repelling the expected invasion, adequate military manpower would be available. If the invasion succeeded, it really didn't make any difference, one way or the other.

By the time he left the barracks and headed toward the mansion, his mind was already on other matters. But the desperate pleas of the harried city officials remained like a half-hidden photograph, one more dimension of the horrendous problem he was facing. Somehow, he had to squeeze some extra soldiers out of the mass of troops at the Mississippi front and move them into the southwest, concentrating them first in the cities until order was restored and then moving them to posts along the Mexican border. He had to do this. What good would it do to stop an invasion of the eastern states but then lose the western states to a peaceful invasion by millions of hungry families? The end result would be the same. The U.S.A. as he knew it would be destroyed forever!

The President was concentrating so deeply he barely noticed the twin row of armed Secret Service guards lining both sides of the walkway like twin fences. They were there whenever he had to cross this stretch of open ground between the mansion and the executive office building he called *the barracks.* They remained at their posts, facing outward toward any possible danger, until he vanished into the mansion. If necessary, they would give their lives to protect the President from a sniper or a suicide assault.

"Don't ever do that to me again," he told Ron with a smile after they were inside his office. "You know what we're facing. We don't need to get partisan sniping mixed up in it, not at this stage of the game. Seriously, though, I think it was unavoidable and necessary. It served an educational purpose for all sides. Did you see the faces of those mayors? They were at the end of their rope and didn't know where to turn."

Chafing from the time he had lost today in that hearing and with the afternoon shadows lengthening on the mansion grounds, the President very quickly scanned his incoming messages and reports, then rose and stood staring blindly out of the enormous window for almost fifteen minutes, his mind locked on the defensive dilemma he was facing. Sighing deeply, he returned to his desk and picked up the telephone, answered at once by his secretary in the outer office.

"Get me Navy," he said calmly. "Right now! Get him up here as fast as he can come."

The Navy commander, a man named Bradshaw, rushed into the office fifteen minutes later, an alarmed and questioning look in his eyes. He saluted, then abandoned it and settled into a chair when Knowlton pointed. He waited respectfully for the President to begin speaking.

"How many carriers do we have on the West Coast, or within fast sailing distance of the West Coast?" Knowlton asked without preamble or explanation.

"We have three at Los Angeles and San Francisco, and one docked in Texas," Bradshaw replied immediately. "The fifth is in Hawaii."

"How many planes are there aboard all of these carriers?" Knowlton shot back.

"About one hundred and sixty on the West Coast, minus any that might be down for major inspection, and another thirty-five or forty in Hawaii. That makes a total of about two hundred available now."

"How long before you can get them into the air?"

"Within one day we can have all of them flying. But I'd have to know where, because of fuel requirements. They have a fairly short range."

"Good!" Knowlton replied. "That should be enough. Get all of them on standby alert and ready to take off immediately when the order is given out of here. Get your transports ready to haul extra ammunition to keep them supplied for at least three or four days. Don't let those carriers leave the harbor, and bring that one back from Hawaii as fast as it can get here. Get its planes ready while it's enroute back so they can take off if necessary as soon as it lands."

"May I ask, sir, where these planes will be heading?"

"The Mississippi," the President retorted in a level voice. "Up and down the Mississippi, wherever an invasion army is likely to cross. They'll be stationed temporarily at any airport big enough to put some of them. Their firepower should be enough to give us the edge we need. You handle the airplanes and their ammunition, and let me handle the airports and fuel. Now go and get this thing started.

"That's a direct order," the President added, smiling broadly. The substitution of these planes for soldiers should give him the extra manpower he needed to protect the southwestern states against the peaceful invasion that was gradually devouring them.

# 12

There was absolutely nothing in Michael Knowlton's background to indicate he would one day become Chief Executive of this nation. Born the son of a less than prosperous merchant in the small Colorado town of Walsenburg, he had followed a somewhat aimless course through elementary and high school, never quite an honor student but always well above average when the report cards were distributed. Classmates from his elementary and high school days recalled young Michael more because of his insatiable curiosity and love of history than for any other visible trait of personality.

By the time he entered high school he had developed an overwhelming curiosity about almost everything that surrounded him, with extra emphasis on anything historical. At this point in his life, Michael gradually developed a competitive instinct in those areas of special interest to him at that particular moment. If he entered a contest, his intention was to win, not just become a participant. He was selective, though; if the reason for the contest didn't interest him, he wouldn't take part in it and had very little concern about its outcome.

The turning point in his young life came when he managed to acquire an old car that enabled him to explore the scenic countryside around Walsenburg, from the high plateau at Westcliff to the ancient mining remains around Trinidad. Once he even managed to reach Pueblo and Colorado Springs, where massive military installations were located. Something about the stark contrast between the past, as typified by the old mine dumps around Trinidad, and the future being unfolded at Colorado Springs captured the imagination of young Michael.

That was the same summer when he began to be seriously interested in girls. By the time classes convened again in September, from sampling the pack in random, meaningless dates he had discovered what type of girl appealed to him and what type he preferred to overlook. This knowledge, along with the rest he was acquiring, went into his mind and was firmly implanted. He graduated from high school in the upper third of his class and with a vision of his ideal girl buried in the background of his mind.

After four years of drudgery from the odd jobs he was forced to seek to finance his higher education, Michael graduated from college, where he had majored in business administration with a minor in American history. He attended college and graduated more from a stubborn acceptance of uncontrollable facts than for any other reason. Until he graduated from high school, Michael had expected college to be an automatic extension of his schooling. It was midsummer before he learned his parents could not afford to pay the tuition and other academic expenses. He sold the old car, paid his initial collegiate expenses and landed a job in a supermarket the same day classes began.

The education he received from the series of odd jobs proved to be as valuable as that offered in the classrooms because it forced him to mingle with all levels of society and compete fiercely for the rewards. His final year before graduation was spent as a case investigator in the field office of the local Congressman. Whenever a constituent had a problem, Michael was expected to make contact with the constituent, learn the facts and try to develop a solution. This was his first brush with governmental processes and he discovered he had a natural talent for this type of work. He remained with the Congressman after graduation.

His career became somewhat sidetracked two years later when he met Lucy Carter at a dinner where he was appearing on behalf of the absent Congressman, who had been forced to remain in Washington because of crucial debate over new trade legislation. The initial cracks in the U.S. economy were, at that time, just beginning to appear and this bill was being hailed as the permanent solution to these incipient problems. In the absence of the Congressman, young Mike Knowlton was expected to address this gathering. He was terrified but, after a painful beginning, he discovered he enjoyed making public appearances.

After the speech, he was surrounded by members of the audience but he saw only Lucy Carter—who resembled not in the slightest the vision he had carried in his mind but who, at first sight, replaced that vision. They were married three months later. The years since that day had passed pleasantly, marred only by the fact they had remained childless. When Mike Knowlton died, his family tree would come to an end. This bothered him but was kept forcibly locked in a far recess of his mind.

Unconsciously, he tried through the years to compensate for this fact by taking career steps that would implant his name in such a way that it remained long after he was in the grave. Indirectly, this is what led him into the Presidency.

Four years after his marriage, he had become a candidate for the House of Representatives and he and Lucy had stumped enthusiastically throughout the Congressional district. They planned privately for the day when they would move to Washington. In November they were defeated badly, but along the way Mike had learned the secrets of campaigning; he wouldn't make the same mistakes twice. Two years later, he was elected by a wide margin and remained in Congress until Washington fell and the breakup occurred.

When it happened, Mike and Lucy were in their home district, stranded and unable to return to Washington because of the virtual collapse of public transportation. Had they been in Washington, they probably would have vanished into detention camps, which was the fate of most members of Congress. The Knowltons had lost many good friends in this manner. As time passed, Representative Knowlton became a student of the A.S.R. and their tactics and was author of a variety of legislation designed to strengthen the new U.S.A. and, hopefully, to checkmate the ambitions of the A.S.R.

At the first formal election following the peace treaty, Representative Knowlton had become a candidate for the Presidency, winning by a wide margin. This election, he remained certain, probably was illegal and not binding upon history. The electoral rules had been written for a nation much larger than this fragment of geography and the tiny conventions of the two political parties were more like corporate annual meetings than formal nominating bodies. The number of votes cast in November were, to Knowlton, almost a sham and the Electoral College ratifying these votes was almost a farce because it was so small. But, legal or not, he had accepted the Presidency and now faced the worst crisis in this new nation's brief history.

From the day he entered office the Presidency had, for Michael Knowlton, been like walking through a series of minefields in which any mis-step would lead to explosive disaster. Because almost all records had been lost when the capital was moved from Washington to Denver, he could not rely on precedents for guidance. Even if they were available, their value would be questionable because there were no precedents for the types of problems he faced. So, for guidance, Knowlton began to rely more and more on the lessons of history, one of his favorite classes when he attended high school and college.

Deliberately, he began to adapt historical incidents to present-day circumstances. He became a student of military tactics and involved himself more and more in the role of Commander-in-Chief of the military arm of the U.S.A. Now, faced with an almost certain invasion on the eastern front by the A.S.R. and in the southwest by swarms of migrant Mexicans whose overwhelming presence posed a threat as great as the A.S.R., Knowlton had groped through history in search of a parallel. Finally, he found a series of actions that had been decided by the sudden appearance of a secret new weapon.

He discovered his new weapon by accident when, one night, he and Lucy were watching an ancient movie involving carrier warfare. He leaped from his chair when he saw the tiny, feeble airplanes of that earlier day landing and taking off from the deck of the carrier. The following day, he ordered all carrier-based planes in the U.S.A. fleet to be moved near the Mississippi front where their airborne firepower could be used against the invading armies of the A.S.R. These extra and mobile guns should give him an edge when hostilities erupted.

By placing these carrier-based planes in every airfield within close proximity to the front, they could appear suddenly like swarms of angry hornets and strafe the A.S.R. landing parties while they were crossing the Mississippi. They could strike ammunition and fuel stockpiles along the eastern shore and wreak havoc on convoys bound for the river. Because their pilots were accustomed to operating from the tiny airstrips of a carrier, landings and takeoffs from rural airstrips would present no problem. At best, though, these planes were nothing more than a holding action to delay the invasion for one or two days. By that time their ammunition and fuel stockpiles would be exhausted, with only enough fuel left to allow them to retreat to safety in the western states.

Knowlton's goal was to keep them active on the eastern front for two days—no more than that. On the third day, it would make no difference. They would have accomplished their purpose. Already, ammunition and fuel dumps were being established at all civilian airfields within easy range of the Mississippi and temporary kitchens were being created in the hangars or any other available building. Knecht, in cooperation with the military chiefs, was handling this phase of preparedness. Within a week, no more, all of the aircraft would be flown from the carriers to their assigned sites where they would be dispersed to become as invisible as possible. Then the period of waiting would begin.

There weren't enough troops to permit the Mississippi to be defended for more than perhaps a week, not even if the entire Army was transferred to the front. Invasion could be delayed, but not prevented. The population of the A.S.R. was so large the U.S.A. could be overwhelmed by sheer numbers. Once the carrier-based planes had been thrown into the battle, Knowlton would have committed his entire forces. All but one, the final chip to be played once the opposing forces had become engaged.

There were no more preparations to be made before the expected invasion was launched. The President could turn his time and attention to other matters and could, he hoped, spend more time with Lucy in the domestic quarters of the mansion. Several times lately, as the pressures mounted and he groped for solutions to problems where none were available, Knowlton had caught Lucy studying him with a worried frown. Neither of them were as young as they had been when they were part of the Washington social scene or even when the breakup had occurred. In this fortified mansion where she was little more than an honored prisoner, Lucy had little to do but watch over herself and her husband.

As the crisis drew nearer, she had seen her husband gradually withdraw into himself in a way that was frightening. He had become somewhat secretive and she had awakened in the middle of the night several times to find him standing in front of the window, gazing absently into the sky, completely unaware of her presence. Each time, she had crept back into bed and remained motionless but awake until she heard him return, slide under the covers and sigh wearily. From his irregular breathing, she knew he remained awake, once for more than an hour. The following morning she had mentioned the incident to him, concerned about his lack of sleep.

"Just ate too much last night, I guess," was his reply. Then he smiled and changed the subject.

As the days passed, her husband had also developed a deep interest in religion. The Knowltons were Methodists but had virtually abandoned church attendance after entering public life. By remaining at home on Sundays, they diplomatically avoided being put in a position where they would feel compelled to grant every favor requested by other members of the congregation. This way they could not be compromised. It was just one of the prices public figures must pay for their prominence.

Now, yesterday, Michael had spent almost an hour behind the closed door of his office in a discussion with the pastor of their home church in Walsenburg. Whatever was said in that meeting remained private. When Lucy commented later about the session, the President had only smiled and dismissed it as "a talk with an old friend." This, too, was unlike Michael. Until now, there had been no secrets between the two of them. The secrecy bothered Lucy.

Today, at her husband's suggestion, they were spending the evening at an informal dinner on the patio, with Conway as the sole guest. This pleased Lucy. She always found Conway to be pleasant and relaxing. He was an old friend, not an official guest. Also, Conway had been alone since Bea and the children had left and he was bound to be lonely. She hoped nothing would happen today that could ruin tonight's dinner. It was time the three of them just relaxed for a while and forgot the cares of the nation and the world!

The President spent most of the afternoon at home. He had delegated all of his routine duties to his staff. He wanted to relax while he could, before the next crisis erupted. It was like old times, before Knowlton was elected to this official fishbowl. He even substituted a pullover shirt for his customary suit and necktie, and insisted on building the fire in the charcoal grill on the patio. Before the charcoal was glowing to his satisfaction, the President had enlisted the aid of a nearby security guard assigned to protect him. For Lucy, it was like old times when they had the luxury of a private life.

At first the evening was lighthearted, with the usual banter passed back and forth across the circular patio table standing beneath its decorative umbrella. The three of them talked about everything and nothing, they laughed and they joked. The President was animated, especially when he described the scene when he appeared before the angry mayors, and how Knecht had banged the podium with his open palm until order was restored. But at some invisible point during the evening, a dark shadow gradually settled over the participants and spread like a blanket until it became dominant. The laughter and banter dwindled until it became strained, only an empty husk of what had existed earlier. Finally Lucy excused herself and went indoors where, behind her closed door, she wept silently.

The two men sat in silence for several minutes, listening absently to the tiny sounds of the night, of insects in the trees and the distant baying of a hound somewhere in the neighborhood. The mournful howling of this faraway hound was like an epitaph to the night and the era in which these people lived. After several minutes passed, Conway turned toward the President.

"How does it look?" he asked quietly, knowing the other man would understand the meaning of his question.

"Not good at all," the President replied. "We have only about two or three weeks left, that's all. That's all there is. There just isn't any more time left to us. Then our world comes to an end and a new one begins. I give it two weeks, give or take a day or two. It's too late now to stop it for any of us, here or over there. Too late!"

"Are we ready? Can we stop them?"

"We're as ready as we can ever be," the President responded thoughtfully. "Stop them? No! We can't stop them, no matter how ready we are. There are just too many of them and not enough of us, even if we sacrifice those southwestern states and move every serviceman to the Mississippi.

"Did you hear that old hound, howling away into the night like a voice out of the tomb? He was howling at the moon. They do that on clear nights. He has about as much chance of reaching the moon as we do of stopping that mob!"

"What are we going to do about it?" Conway asked. "Can you tell me or is that too classified?"

"Did you ever read that old fairy tale about killing a dragon?" the President mused. "It's worth reading. The moral of that old fable is that the only way you can kill a dragon is by cutting off its head!"

Before Conway could reply he stood up, walked to the edge of the patio and remained there, gazing into the night sky, for several minutes. Conway sat and waited silently, aware that Knowlton didn't intend to provide any details which might explain his final remark. Once again the distant hound howled at the night, ending with a long, mournful wavering note that sounded as eerie as if it came from an open grave. Sighing, the President returned to the table and sprawled in his chair.

Neither spoke for more than fifteen minutes. They just sat there, each wrapped in his own individual thoughts and only partially aware of the countless small sounds of the night. At regular intervals, the old hound continued to bay at the full moon. There was nothing more to be said because of the artificial barrier created by the Presidency and its accompanying secrecy. Conway rose silently and entered the mansion. Lucy was upstairs, so he left quietly and returned to his home. Almost an hour later, Knowlton wearily climbed the stairs to the second floor and slumped into bed. When she felt his presence beside her, Lucy moved against him and slipped an arm around his body. Neither moved until morning.

The recorded message and the enlarged photographs from Washington were on his desk when the President entered his office. The message was almost brutal in its frankness. The woman who recorded it had absolutely no doubt that a date for the invasion had been decided in the White House by Gorcey and his military advisors. In her mind, this could be the only reason for the drunken party that had followed the daily briefing. One of the photographs depicted a smiling Gorcey standing beside a limousine into which a portly military officer was being poured. The man was giving the traditional "thumbs up" signal that denoted success.

The day's intelligence summaries from other sources confirmed the views of the woman whose voice was on the tape. Unless the weather interfered, the invasion would be launched in massive force within no more than two weeks, probably in seven to ten days from today. This meant Knowlton had to accelerate the movement of the carrier-borne planes to airfields along the front and move the additional troops to the southwest almost immediately.

*So now we know,* the President said to himself. *We know the day when everything that has gone before will come to an end and a new page in the history of this land will be written. How could we let it come to this, but how could we prevent it once all of the pieces were in motion? It's like a monstrous comedy of errors that had its beginning not long after I was born. Maybe those people back then who wanted to keep everything like it was despite changes that came almost every day were no different than we are today. We're doing the same thing. We're trying to keep change from occurring so everything can remain exactly like we remember it from the time when all of us were younger.*

*What about those poor Mexicans who are flooding into the southwest to try to find a home and adequate food? They're one of the changes that are taking place. What right do we have to deny them the same opportunities we've always enjoyed? They want only the same things we want, and didn't we do the same thing to the Indians that they're doing now to us? I can understand and sympathize, also, with the position Gorcey and the A.S.R. finds itself in today. They tried to rewrite history and make too many changes come too fast, and now they're paying the price of their ignorance. Or was it only a form of innocence on their part? No matter! They're ready to make their move and my responsibility is to stop them.* Becoming disgusted with himself for allowing his mind to wander into this analysis, Knowlton sighed deeply and turned to other matters on his desk.

Within an hour he had gained a clear mental picture of the status of the nation, had initialled several reports, and now was ready to begin a vital step in his plans to halt the impending invasion almost before it began.

The first move was to summon Knecht to his office for a thorough briefing on the developing crisis, with orders that for now the information must remain confidential, on a need-to-know basis. Next would be signing of an emergency executive order transferring two thousand troops from the front, and into the southwestern states to be distributed according to a formula Knecht could develop. This would be followed by another executive order commandeering whatever public transportation would be needed to move aviation fuel and foodstuffs to airfields that would be used by planes from the carriers. Finally, an undated executive order would be prepared and signed—one that declared an immediate state of emergency throughout the nation. This order would be held until released personally by the President.

Ron Knecht was appalled by the news he received from the President. Even though almost everyone in the federal government knew an invasion was likely to occur at almost any time, this probability had now become a certainty. He huddled in his chair, forgetting to take notes of the jobs he had been assigned. They could be transcribed later from the tape of this meeting. What horrified Knecht more than the news he received was the President's behavior. He had been so calm, almost apologetic. Instead of pacing the large office, or fidgeting in his chair, the President had appeared almost relaxed, leaning forward with both arms resting on the desk and itemizing the orders without reference to notes, as if they had been memorized in advance. His expression hadn't changed until the sequence was completed.

After the final order had been given, Knowlton rose from behind his desk and strolled across the office. For almost a minute, he gazed out of the big window, absently studying the faraway mountain skyline that never changed except by the passage of the sun or when the peaks were hidden by a gathering thunderstorm. Finally the President returned to his desk and lowered himself with a sigh into the leather chair. He turned toward Knecht.

"There's one final job I want you to do for me, and it must remain completely confidential," Knowlton said. "Get the commander at Colorado Springs up here this afternoon and tell him to bring two of his best, most reliable electronic technicians.

"Make sure he understands this trip doesn't exist. It didn't occur and there must be no record of it. For him and his technicians, the entire thing is on an ultra-top-secret basis and nobody, repeat nobody, is to know about it."

Knecht returned to the barracks in a daze. As well as he knew Knowlton, he had never seen the President behave as he had today. It wasn't natural. Anyone facing invasion by a hostile power with overwhelming force should at least be excited. Why wasn't the man excited or at least angry about this news? *Thank God I'm not in his shoes. I'd be so terrified I'd be climbing the walls.* By the time he reached the barracks and was putting the orders into motion, Knecht had reached the conclusion that Knowlton hadn't told the entire story. He had an ace up his sleeve that he wasn't yet ready to reveal. Knecht felt better now. Maybe everything wasn't lost after all.

The team from Colorado Springs arrived at mid-afternoon and were shown immediately into the Presidential office. They spent almost an hour with Knowlton, with the private meeting interrupted only once—by the delivery of unlimited passes to the trio from Colorado Springs. This gave them full access to the mansion at any time, day or night. No record of these passes existed anywhere, except in the personal Presidential accounts. As soon as the team left, Knowlton announced he was "going home," and immediately headed for the living quarters on the upper floor of the mansion.

Lucy was absently reading a book when he entered, surprising her by his sudden appearance during the afternoon. He was shedding his coat and necktie as he crossed the long room. She leaped up from the sofa where she had been curled and turned toward him with a question in her eyes. He vanished into their bedroom, then immediately reappeared without his coat and tie. He was smiling in a way she hadn't seen since this latest crisis began.

"Babe," he asked with a lilt in his voice, "how would you like some good, old-fashioned fries and hamburgers this evening, and maybe a cold beer or two, instead of the usual stuff we're served? A regular old burger and fries like we used to get in Washington! I could send out for some."

Uncertain about how to reply to this unexpected behavior, she chuckled to buy time to analyze her husband, who happened to be also the elected leader of this country. Lately, he had been so grim; but now he was acting more like the man who had courted her so many years earlier. "I suppose we could," she replied, smiling. "It's been a long time since we did just what we wanted to do."

Stepping over to the tape player, Knowlton selected a cassette, inserted it in the machine and started it playing. The lilting notes of a Viennese waltz filled the room. He reduced the volume slightly, then wrapped Lucy in his arms and they began to dance, whirling across the floor in time with the music, the President with a faraway look in his eyes and his wife with her head resting on his shoulder. When the tape ended, both of them settled onto the sofa, laughing intimately at their behavior in this public building during the afternoon hours.

Once again, they were young and had most of their lives ahead of them. They were young, in love with each other, and didn't live in the shadow of one crisis after another. The music and the dancing had caused Lucy to capture the carefree spirit of her husband on this afternoon stolen from the endless cares of high public office. When the golden glow of a setting sun began painting the mountain peaks visible through the large window, her husband called the head housekeeper and ordered burgers, fries and a half-keg of beer delivered to their quarters.

They ate in the kitchen, leaving the dining room untouched. They washed down the burgers and fries with mugs of draught beer, sitting like youngsters around the kitchen worktable. In the background, the music from Vienna during a long-ago age wrapped itself around them, drifting into the kitchen from the other part of their quarters. This was just a man and his woman, enjoying themselves during a very special evening, a night that had meaning only to them. The mood was broken when the red light on the intercom panel began blinking. Lucy saw it first and nudged her husband, who froze and then headed for the small desk he kept in the living quarters. When Knowlton answered, the voice on the other end was that of the chief of domestic staff.

"I thought you should know, sir," the caller said. "There are two men in white coveralls working, doing something in the conference room. What shall I do about them? They have proper passes, but I thought you should know."

"They're fine," the President responded. "It's just a job I needed completed today, so don't worry about them. And you did exactly right in calling me. It could have been something serious."

The connection was broken and the call ended. This was proof the crew from Colorado Springs were already at work. They should be finished before morning and the room could return to its customary use by the time the office staff arrived. If anyone noticed the new cabinet that had been installed, its presence could be explained easily. The President privately doubted if anyone would even mention it.

With this call, the mood of the night was broken. Once again, it was not just a man and a woman but was the President and the first lady of the land. Something had died when Lucy spotted the tiny red light glowing on the intercom panel. The glow had forcibly brought the present back into this room and with it all of the uncertainties and terrors that were a part of this unstable era. Dejected, Lucy sank onto her favorite sofa and stared at her husband, who still stood by the little desk with the telephone in one hand and a faraway expression in his eyes—a remoteness that told Lucy he was no longer with her but instead was on another plane beyond her reach, one which she could never penetrate.

The rest of the evening was a failure. Despite their best efforts, the earlier mood could not be recaptured. The lilting strains of the music became more like a dirge than a waltz. Unusually early, they abandoned the pretense of gaiety and went to bed, using this as an escape from what was outside.

Throughout the night, the messages were arriving in Denver at one or another of the agencies attached to the executive branch of government. The armies of the A.S.R. were definitely on the move, being consolidated along the Mississippi front. No great effort was being made to hide them from watchers across the river. Near Baton Rouge, several aged tanks had been spotted crawling along the riverfront highways. In Washington, the lights in the White House had remained burning throughout the night. The circular driveway had been virtually clogged by staff cars and limousines which came and departed until after midnight.

On the other side of the continent, special chartered trains and semi-trailer trucks were moving fuel, repair parts and ammunition from storage depots to every airport, large or small, within easy flying range of the river. Orders had been sent to the carriers specifying the airfields to which their planes would be flown. Already, the troops to be moved to the southwestern states had been selected and notified. They would be flown to their new stations tomorrow morning.

A special briefing with both majority and minority leaders in Congress had been scheduled for early afternoon. Commanders of the various branches of the military would be present to answer questions by the Congressmen.

All of this was on Knowlton's desk when he entered his office shortly after eight o'clock. As he did each morning, he had left without awakening Lucy. The memory of the previous night, how it had begun so brightly but ended like a beautiful flower suddenly wilted, remained in his mind as he entered his office and began to organize the pile of communications put there by Knecht. Taking a deep breath to steady himself, he began to read.

By noon, he had studied each item and dictated responses or actions he saw as needed. All domestic matters, those involving queries from states or inter-agency disputes, were assigned to Knecht for disposition. If there were to be any chance of saving the nation, Knowlton had to confine himself to guiding its defense and making the decisions that were a part of his role as Commander-in-Chief. After a quick lunch at his desk, he was ready to face the four Congressional leaders and outline to them in blunt terms the danger faced by their nation.

First to arrive were the military commanders, who arranged themselves in chairs on either side of the podium. They were barely seated before Ron Knecht hurried into the room carrying a file folder containing the agenda and a yellow notepad. The Congressional leaders all arrived together, sharing one limousine. Once inside the mansion, they separated into party factions. They remained separated when they seated themselves around the long conference table. Knowlton would not enter the room until every invited guest had arrived and was seated. As soon as he was introduced by Knecht, he would deliver his loosely prepared statement, after which the Congressional leaders could respond, argue or pledge support.

When he stepped behind the podium, the President didn't mince words or try to be polite. He spoke for less than five minutes, then seated himself to the right of the podium.

"Gentlemen," he began, "I've called you together to get your support on a non-partisan basis. We have concrete proof that, in no more than two weeks, this country will be invaded by forces from the A.S.R. that outnumber us by a ratio of two and maybe three to one. I am today issuing a proclamation placing this country in a state of national emergency, under martial law if you will.

"I do not plan to make this proclamation public, not yet, not until or unless it serves a necessary purpose. Right now I would much rather have your voluntary support and cooperation while we prepare to meet this crisis that could destroy our nation forever. I see by the way you've seated yourselves that normal partisan separations are being maintained, with the majority on one end of the table and the minority on the other. We simply cannot afford these divisions in the crisis that is coming. Let me emphasize one thing to you: If we lose this war, your party affiliation will have no meaning whatsoever because there won't be any political parties!

"You have one chance, just one chance and no more, to put any divisions aside and join together and with me in meeting this crisis. This is not a matter that can be debated until a compromise is reached. If we do not walk out of here together as a single entity with party politics left behind, I will immediately use the emergency powers that have been in place from the time when the capital moved from Washington to Denver and I will issue that proclamation before this day ends, placing all forms of decision making within this office.

"Do not reply just yet. Hear what we have to say and examine the photos we will pass around the table, and then make your decision."

Knowlton turned away and sat down in the nearest vacant chair. He was succeeded at the podium by Knecht, who called each of the military commanders, one after another, to present their analysis of the situation. After the last one concluded, tapes made in Washington were played for the Congressmen and photos taken in Washington and from a satellite were distributed around the table. Until then, the President had sat quietly. Now he rose and returned to the podium where he stood for a moment, looking from one shocked face to another. Then he began to speak.

"Now, gentlemen, you have seen the evidence," he said. "So what's your decision? Do we do this together or go our separate ways?"

For several seconds the room was so silent that traffic on the nearby street could be heard. A chair creaked audibly when someone changed position. Then Senator Clark exploded. As Minority Leader of the Senate, he felt it his duty to have his views included in the record of this meeting.

"That's blackmail!" he shouted. "I'll concede we're facing a crisis and that we must put differences aside, but I resent having that emergency proclamation held over us like a blackjack. I'll go along with you because we don't have any real choice, and I'll do everything I can to support you in this, but I want my opposition to that proclamation entered as part of the record."

Turning away, he resumed his seat without waiting for a rebuttal from Knowlton. One by one, the others around the table nodded their heads in agreement. Without rising, the Majority Leader of the Senate spoke for all of them.

"We're with you all the way," he said softly. "Just keep us informed about what you need. Now let's go win that war."

# 13

There is nothing as beautiful as the early hours of morning in Kansas, a brief period when the shadows are long, the perpetual wind hasn't yet begun to cause trees and growing plants to dance, and the air is so calm that distant sounds appear to be nearby. For a short while, until the sun establishes itself as the monarch of the sky, the cool of the night remains and the day is at peace with itself. It is a time when people in the cities and towns care for their lawns or gardens and enjoy the outdoors.

Not really caring whether or not he finished today, Dwight Davis pushed his hand mower around the yard in ever-smaller circles, his favorite way to cut his grass. He preferred circles to parallel cuts because, with circles, there was no necessity to stop, turn the mower around and then retrace the same path across the yard. Also, each circle was smaller than the one before it. When nothing was left but a tiny rectangle in the middle of the yard, Dwight would make a few frantic cuts and the rectangle would vanish. By that time the sun was high enough in the sky to cause Dwight to begin sweating so, with the lawn finished, he would wheel his mower to the garage, brush the clippings from its blades and prop it against an inside wall until time for the next mowing.

This morning, he reached the small rectangle just as the sun's rays began to be uncomfortable. He was thirsty and, because he had plenty of time, Dwight propped the mower against the house and strolled into the kitchen. He would clean the mower later, after a cup of coffee and a few minutes of relaxation. Hearing him enter, Ellen called from the front of the house where she had been idly watching television. Carrying his coffee, Dwight walked carefully into the living room and dropped gently into a chair, careful to avoid spilling any of the contents of his cup.

The game show originating in Los Angeles was one Ellen watched every morning. Dwight considered the show to be silly and a way of exploiting the participants. Without removing her eyes from the screen, Ellen began to speak.

"I'm glad you're done," she began. "There's supposed to be a news special right after this program is done. I don't know what it is but

I thought you might want to watch it. I'll call you when it comes on if you're still in the kitchen. You are done with the lawn, aren't you?"

Dwight returned to the kitchen, rinsed his hands in the sink and dried them on a nearby hand towel, then seated himself at the small breakfast table they had owned for so many years. Because both of their children had grown up around this table, he and Ellen had kept it even though much of their other earlier furniture had been replaced through the years. This little table was special.

While he sat there with his mind virtually idle, once again the visions of Allen and Anne as young children could be seen as they gobbled their breakfast before heading for school. It had been so long, so many years ago. Their mother would scold Allen sharply whenever he tried to bolt his food and run out of the house to meet some classmate. Now Allen was gone forever and Anne had her own home. As the years passed, he and Ellen would watch Anne grow older and more mature but, in their minds, Allen would always remain young and vital. There was nothing left of Allen but a gravestone in the local cemetery, a gravestone beneath which nobody rested. This had never ceased to bother Dwight and Ellen, for whom a family burial plot was the final resting place for generations of the Davis family.

They hadn't been able to reconcile themselves to Allen's anonymous burial somewhere around St. Louis after he had been killed while serving his mandatory time in the Army. By now, Allen had been gone long enough that the Davis family--all but Ellen--had accepted his death; but they hadn't been able to accept fully that gravestone standing guard over an empty piece of land. Placing flowers on this plot seemed to Dwight almost like a form of blasphemy despite the way the action had been explained by the preacher. Their pastor had, many times, told them the act was honoring the soul of the departed, not the body lying in the ground. This comforted Ellen but to Dwight, somehow, the explanation seemed inadequate.

The pastor was right about one thing, though. Allen would now never grow old. Throughout the passage of time, he would always remain as young in their minds as he was when he left home to serve his country. He would never become ill, or acquire wrinkles, or have to face a tragedy in the family he would never have. For Allen, the limitations of advancing age would never occur. On that night in St. Louis, he had become ageless, a son who existed only in memory.

Dwight's idle musings were ended with a call from the living room, from Ellen notifying him the news special was about to begin. Sighing, Dwight arose and returned to Ellen, arriving just as the broadcast began.

"We bring you this special bulletin," the familiar anchorman said in his ringing voice. "A bipartisan committee of both houses of Congress has just ratified action that would permit President Knowlton to take emergency steps to prepare for a possible outbreak of hostilities with the A.S.R. We have learned from confidential sources that all available military forces are being rushed to positions along the Mississippi River as a precaution against a surprise attack."

The broadcast continued, but Dwight barely heard it. His mind was back on that day similar to this, the day when the cyclists arrived at this house to notify him of his son's death along the Mississippi. The universal military draft that made every town a community filled with old people was supposed to prevent an invasion from happening or else stop it before any enemy troops managed to cross the river. What good was the draft if it couldn't prevent an invasion? Apparently one was about to take place, if this network announcer was to be believed. *And what if we can't stop them and they get across the river and begin marching west, toward Denver? Will we be safe in this town and this house, or will we be right in their line of march? What happens to Anne and her husband when they reach Colorado?*

Dwight's mind returned to the broadcast in time to hear a concluding comment by the newscaster. "According to his spokesman, President Knowlton remains confident about the outcome of the hostilities, if they occur. Any attempt at invasion, this spokesman said, will be stopped before any territory has been seized. We'll bring you other bulletins as this breaking story develops. Now, we return you to your regular programming."

Dwight wasn't overly disturbed about this broadcast because the networks did this with regularity to try to capture viewers. The key to whether a special bulletin was factual or just educated guesswork was an appearance by a high public official to confirm the incident. This made it factual rather than supposition by the network newscaster. Lately, there had been many of these special bulletins, all warning of a possible invasion that never seemed to materialize. This one was probably no different than the others. Dwight lost interest and returned to the yard to clean his mower and pull weeds from Ellen's flowers.

The bulletin and his initial reaction to it continued to bother Dwight, though. This one had been more definitive and had included a comment by the President, who hadn't appeared in person but had obviously authorized a staff member to make a statement. Something could be brewing, and Dwight was old enough to recall vividly the period just before Washington fell and the United States almost overnight became involved in a paralyzing civil conflict. There had been terse bulletins like this one during that confusing period just before the collapse. The President then had said everything was under control and the people, at least those living out here, had believed him. Then everything had collapsed and suddenly there was a new capital in Denver, operating initially from a hotel, with the President secreted at Colorado Springs.

For almost a week there had been a virtual news blackout for people in this part of the country, not because the news had been suppressed but because most of the reporters had found themselves trapped in Washington or New York when the nation fell apart. Matters hadn't improved until the news agencies were able to create new headquarters in Los Angeles and San Francisco, with some of their hastily recruited reporters stationed in Denver to cover the governmental news. *But that was then, and times are different today. We are two nations today and, if war comes, it will be a conventional war where two armies face each other. But what if neither side can win and the war drags on for several years like that situation in the last century when the old United States got itself involved in that Asiatic nation called Vietnam?* But then, Dwight reminded himself, *that was Asia and this is here. We're just climbing out from the mess left by the War of Division that almost paralyzed little towns like this which depended upon the cities for almost everything sold in the stores.*

Dwight had completed his weeding, so he seated himself on the steps of the back porch to analyze the questions his mind had raised as a result of this news bulletin. Maybe there was something behind it. Maybe, once more, everything was going to hell in a handbasket and he had better prepare for it. He decided to waste enough gasoline in his car to drive downtown and stock up on enough food and other household necessities to last him and Ellen for a month or so. If worse came to worst, they could huddle in this house until the matter had been decided, one way or another.

Two hours away, the same thing was happening in a much larger town where the family of Representative Pat Conway was unpacking in their formerly empty home that was kept locked while they were in Denver. The trip here by convoy had been slow but uneventful, with a stop at almost every town to permit a few cars to leave the convoy and be replaced with others. The speed of the convoy had been that of the slowest vehicle in the procession. By the time they reached here, Bea was exhausted from gripping the steering wheel and staring fixedly at the rear end of the vehicle they were following, trying to maintain the required fifty-foot interval that was standard in all highway convoys. According to the regulations read aloud by the convoy commander, this prevented stragglers from separating one part of the convoy from the remainder of the vehicles.

For the first few hours, until they reached the almost flat prairie of Kansas, Susan had watched the passing countryside until she became drowsy and rested her head on one arm, her eyes shut. In the front seat beside Bea, Cynthia was silent, lost in thought as this familiar panorama flowed past the moving vehicles. Eventually they reached home, dropping out of the convoy at the city limits and stopping at a downtown restaurant before facing the silent, empty house. The truck with the heavy luggage and other items from Denver hadn't arrived until the following day.

By now Bea had the house ready for her husband, if and when he could pull himself away from Congress long enough to return home. She and Cynthia had dusted the entire house, laundered and put away the sheets covering the furniture, and made minor alterations in furniture placement. At first Cynthia had felt uncomfortable in the upstairs room that held so many memories of her childhood and adolescence. Everything had been kept exactly as she had remembered it; that was part of the problem. The place was haunted by too many ghostly memories of her years in high school, when the most important things in her life were graduation and the latest boy she was dating.

Those were good years! The world had been rose colored then, hers for the asking. She had such high hopes, plans and dreams. There wasn't anything she couldn't do if she really wanted it, and there was a man out there somewhere, just waiting for her. She knew exactly how he would look! She might meet him in Washington when the family went there during the summer months, or after graduation when they could stay as long as they pleased, even an entire year. Washington was where she had met and married Rich Sheldon and had surrendered this girlhood room, trading it for the house she and Rich had bought.

Now here she was, back here in this room that held so many memories of an earlier, carefree life; and she had brought with her the child she and Rich had conceived, but he was gone forever, only a ghost from the past. For some troubling reason, Cynthia felt the loss of Richard worse here than in the house they had owned in Arlington, probably because it had ceased to be their home before he was lost to her. He had been miserable after their home was confiscated and they were consigned to only a pair of rooms on the ground floor. As the days and weeks passed, Rich had become morose and always angry. He had stopped grooming himself, not caring how he looked when he left the building on some errand, or even to sit on the porch when a spot was available—which wasn't often because of the other occupants of the building, who spent most of their time there.

Rich was gone. He wasn't a part of this new life she must make for herself, here or in Denver. As quickly as possible, Cynthia planned to remove the traces of her own girlhood from this room and then allow it to become Susan's domain. But that could wait a while. For now, she and Susan would share the room and she could show Susan all the odds and ends left from her time here, including that old formal gown still hanging in the closet.

By chance, because they were both in the living room at the same time, Bea and Cynthia both heard the special television news bulletin warning of an invasion by forces of the A.S.R. Because of their status as wife and daughter of a Congressman, and especially one with personal access to the President, they didn't dismiss it as lightly as Dwight Davis did. It was Bea who commented that it was probably a planted leak designed to, simultaneously, alert this nation and also put a possible damper on any A.S.R. invasion plans. Bea knew now why her husband had been so insistent about their returning home instead of remaining in Denver.

If there were an invasion, it might have air support and this could include bombing attacks upon Denver. Pat couldn't leave but he didn't want his family to face this possible danger, so he had sent them home to a place that couldn't possibly become a military target. Unable to keep this knowledge to herself, Bea turned to Cynthia. By the time she had finished outlining her fears, Cynthia had become pale, her eyes large and staring, and one hand covered her mouth. She drew Susan to her and held her tightly, as if to shield her from this knowledge.

"Where will it all end?" Cynthia asked in an unnatural, strangled voice. "Wasn't it enough before, when you couldn't get back to Washington and when we lost our house to that mob, and then Rich was lost, and that awful trip back here when we had to hide in that little town and listen all night to that bombing? Wasn't that enough? And now it all starts all over again. What will happen to Daddy if they bomb Denver? Will it be like Rich, where he just disappears? How much do we have to lose before it's over?"

Bea had no answers because these were the same questions she was asking to herself. She wished Pat could be here with her, but he had an obligation to remain in Denver as long as he was needed and as long as Congress lasted this time. He had been saved once before because he was out here, instead of in Washington, when that city fell and Congress collapsed. Now here it was, all starting up once again and this time he was trapped in the heart of it. *Oh Pat, Pat, why can't you be here with us, now of all times.*

But there was nothing she could do about it and there were practical things that must be done if a war was about to begin. They must get this house filled with food and everything else a family would need in the weeks ahead, a supply that would last for about a month. Toilet paper—she must not forget to add that to her list. And soap, and a tank of gasoline in her car—she must not forget these. What about the daily newspaper? She must begin having it delivered, because they couldn't afford to be without the details of the news which it would provide. And she might as well get a supply of garbage bags and a couple of extra light bulbs. They might prove useful.

By the time they reached the supermarket, it was already filled with an excited, clawing mob purchasing huge volumes of almost everything on the shelves. After Bea was jostled several times, Cynthia took the lead and made use of her experience in Arlington, where she had been forced to compete with a mass of humanity similar to the excited people in this store. With Bea and Susan trailing behind her, Cynthia used the shopping cart as a battering ram, forcing her way down the aisles and grabbing items from shelves even if it meant shoving someone else out of the way. Bea was shocked. This wasn't the daughter she had raised so gently. This was a predatory stranger using tactics completely alien to her and her way of life.

After they had bulldozed their way through the checkstand and the bags were piled in the car, Cynthia sent the shopping cart rolling away from the car and climbed into the front seat. Bea was already behind the wheel with Susan in the rear seat.

"Go!" Cynthia ordered. "Get out of here as fast as you can."

This behavior gave Bea a better insight into the type of life Cynthia had led after Washington had fallen and she was trapped in only two rooms of the large house she and Rich had owned. In this supermarket, Cynthia had become no better than a predatory beast fighting off others of its kind to capture its prey. *No wonder Susan was like a frightened little animal when they arrived. She wasn't old enough yet to learn what was needed in the type of world where she lived. How could they have lived like that? But they did, and they survived, and that's the important thing.*

There was a long line at the service station and they waited almost a half-hour before getting the car's gasoline tank filled. As they left the station, Cynthia looked back down the street. The line of waiting vehicles was even longer than when they had arrived. At this rate, the station's supply of fuel would be exhausted long before nightfall.

Most of the evening television newscast was devoted to the crisis in Denver and steps being taken to prepare the nation for a possible war. The President, in a brief and unusual interview, called for calm and patience by the people of this nation. War, he said, still could be averted despite the movement of additional A.S.R. troops to areas along the Mississippi, combined with an increase in the number of hostile raids across the river. Then, appearing more stern, he announced immediate federalization of all forms of public transportation. Of course, he added, chuckling lightly, that did not include street buses or taxicabs.

"We need to move food and supplies to our troops," the President explained. "We have moved so many extra men to the area and they will be hungry if we aren't able to feed them, and there are the usual support items that soldiers need anywhere. That's why we need all of those railroad cars and trucks. Now I'd like to add a final word to every citizen in this country.

"There is no cause for panic and no reason for hoarding of food or just about anything else. We aren't at war, and I hope we won't be; but the choice isn't mine to make. The steps my administration has taken, moving extra troops to the border and requisitioning vehicles to keep them supplied, are for peace and not war. Go about your normal daily affairs as if nothing has happened--because it hasn't, at least not yet. We're doing everything we can to maintain the peace so, let me repeat, there is no cause for panic by the people of this country."

He was replaced on the screen by the newscaster and a series of scenes along the Mississippi front, all of them showing massive amounts of troops in fortified positions overlooking the river. When the newscast turned to brief items about other happenings of the day, Bea turned the knob and the television screen became black and empty. The newscast had left her empty, more chilled inside than before when she had seen the clawing mob in the supermarket and the endless line of vehicles at the gasoline station. The newscast, she realized, was a masterpiece of double-talk aimed at viewers in the A.S.R.

From the evenings she and Pat had spent with the Knowltons, she had grown to know Mike Knowlton very well. He was a planner able to execute the plans he conceived. If the stakes were high enough, he was not above having those television cameramen hauled to specially selected spots along the front where large numbers of troops were stationed and then using the resulting television footage to illustrate why so many trains and trucks, allegedly hauling food and supplies, were needed. That newscast tonight had been a bunch of hokum. It wasn't what he or the anchorman said. It was what they didn't say or show that was the real story that wasn't told.

*We're just as good as at war,* she thought. *Right now he's just bluffing, trying to buy time for something he has in mind, like a multinational shell game where the other country is put into the position of trying to guess which shell covers the jackpot.* She smiled to herself despite the gravity of the situation. *Where did I learn those terms like shell game and jackpot? They aren't words a real lady would use, ever!* She surprised herself not only by this choice of words but also by her analysis of the situation. *I guess,* she admitted, *I've been a Congressman's wife too long until now I'm able to think like a Congressman!*

Pat Conway shared his wife's analysis of the newscast, but from a vastly different perspective. He knew the President's words were only an illusion created for a purpose whose details were known only by Knowlton and possibly a few of his advisors. That interview with the President had been taped much earlier, during the afternoon, but was embargoed until the evening newscasts. It wasn't, as the anchormen insinuated, a live appearance.

Shortly after the taping, Conway had received a telephone call from the mansion asking if he could "drop over" for a private dinner this evening. There were, Knowlton said, several things he wanted to discuss. The evening began socially with polite inquiries about his family. Routine domestic issues in Congress were touched upon very lightly, then dismissed when Knowlton walked to a television set and flipped the knob, turned toward Conway and grinned.

"I thought you might want to see a preview of what will be on the news this evening," he commented. "As soon as it's over, I want to get your reactions, not as a legislator but as a person. I had Ron set this up with the boys this afternoon because I wanted to get this message out as fast as possible."

The screen flickered as the tape began moving and then the interview with the President, uncut and not yet edited, flashed onto the screen. Conway watched intently, trying to identify any hidden meanings behind the comments. He studied Knowlton's face on the screen. It remained sober and serious throughout the interview, even during the joking comment about buses and taxicabs. His mouth smiled, but his eyes did not. Alert viewers might notice this. Overall, the entire message was reassuring but didn't really say or mean anything specific, except that a state of war didn't exist today. Obviously this was a message intended for the A.S.R. and the average citizen in this country. To Conway, it also appeared to contain a warning against mounting an invasion, whose price tag could be higher than the A.S.R. was willing to pay. And what about all of those railroad cars and highway trucks that were being commandeered? Why were they suddenly needed?

"Well?" the President asked when the tape concluded and the screen became blank. "What do you think of it?"

"This isn't an impartial opinion but I think you're up to something," Conway responded, smiling. "I think the average citizen will feel better after hearing this but I think if I were across the river I'd be asking myself a lot of questions, like what does he have that I don't have! You may get some thorny questions out of Congress because of this, especially on a partisan basis."

"No I won't!" Knowlton said sharply. "I've already taken care of that. There won't be any problems out of Congress. Now for the rest of it, a lot of what I said was deliberately aimed at Gorcey and the A.S.R. to try to make them think twice before they go too far. Maybe it'll work and maybe it won't. We'll see by what happens in a week or so, but at least I tried!"

"What about those trains and trucks?" Conway asked. "There's no way that much food and supplies can be needed by an army along the river, even with the new draftees."

Knowlton walked slowly across the room, stared for a few seconds out of the large window and then returned to where Conway was seated. To remove the sting from the words, he smiled as he made a terse reply.

"Frankly—and please don't take offense—it isn't any of your business," the President said. "If anybody asks, you can just say I told you it's food and supplies!"

From that point on, the evening was devoted to informal social talk, the kind that always occurs when old friends get together. Conway left early, with the unanswered questions nagging at the back of his mind. That man had some kind of ace up his sleeve and perhaps more than one. Somehow, he hadn't been the same tonight, part of his mind elsewhere on another plane beyond Conway's reach. That tape from the newscast which had been seen earlier that evening throughout the nation had seemed to be very important to the President. Conway felt it was a final warning to the A.S.R. rather than a reassuring message to the people of this country. Knowlton had seemed to brighten when the Congressman had interpreted it that way. *Maybe the bluff will work,* he thought, *but I'd bet that it won't. War is just around the corner.*

He reached home just in time for the late newscast, in which the President's message was repeated. More footage showing the results of A.S.R. raids into cities across the border was included, as well as interviews with state officials and retired military officers. All were agreed that a full-blown invasion could occur at any time. One segment of the newscast was devoted to scenes of alarmed shoppers clawing through supermarkets in the Denver area. An operator of a string of service stations predicted a gasoline shortage would develop if additional supplies were not received quickly. This was followed by a quick view of a line of vehicles awaiting their turn at a pair of gasoline pumps.

*Mike, you may have been too late,* Conway said to himself. *You may need to do more than just try to reassure the people, because they've lived with this threat for too long. War has been just around the corner ever since this country began and everybody knows it, whether they talk about it or not. The absence of young men on the streets because they've all been drafted keeps the topic visible to everyone at all times. They're reminded of it every time they go from one town to another and have to join one of those highway convoys to have protection against terrorist raids. I hope you know what you're doing, because you're playing a dangerous game and the odds are against us.*

The President's message, taped from a newscast by a St. Louis station, was watched by Gorcey on the following morning. Overnight, the contents of the tape had been transmitted to Washington and a duplicate was lying on Gorcey's desk when he arrived that morning. This action was unusual. It was routine for all newscasts within range of the border to be monitored and taped, but most were of no value to anyone but the military planners. These didn't find their way to his desk, but this one must contain something special. He inserted it into the machine and flipped the knob. President Knowlton's face filled the screen and Gorcey listened intently to his measured words. He did this three times, rewinding the tape back to the beginning. Portions of the message disturbed him. Reaching for his telephone, he summoned his three top military advisors.

"Listen," he said when they arrived several minutes later. "See what you can pick up from this. Listen carefully, particularly to that part about federalizing trucks and trains to haul stuff to those extra troops. What troops? You know because you've brought it to me that there are no extra troops, not in big enough numbers to need every truck and train to haul supplies!

"You even told me that bastard seemed to be moving troops away from the border, not to it. Either you're full of crap or downing too much of that free booze, or else he knows something we don't. You find out which it is and you find out fast or you'll find yourselves out on your butts. You just don't haul more supplies for fewer soldiers, not here and not there and not anywhere. I don't care how you do it, but you find out what's going on and you do it damned fast. We don't have any time to waste!"

Once again, staring intently at the small screen, Gorcey watched the face of President Michael Knowlton and listened to the words he spoke. Unless it was just a smoke screen to pacify the population, this message made no sense whatsoever. Watching it again, Gorcey began to analyze it, separating it into its various segments. First came an admission that he knew war was about to begin. Then came news of additional troop movements to the border, combined with a hope that war could be prevented. After that was the announcement of federalization of public transportation, supposedly to haul food and supplies to these troops. It ended with another plea for peace.

Gorcey almost recoiled from the screen after completing his analysis of Knowlton's remarks. *Good God, he wasn't talking to his people. He was talking to me. That was his way of reaching me, man to man, and telling me to back off. That son-of-a-bitch knew I would see this tape and that's why he made it and then made certain it would reach me. He did everything but carry it here and drop it in my lap.*

*He's daring me to make a move and he's telling me he has something I don't know about. That poker-faced son-of-a-bitch. It won't work. We'll go ahead just like we planned. In fact, we'll move even faster if we can, just in case he does have something up his sleeve!*

# 14

Almost two weeks had passed since President Knowlton had appeared on the evening newscast and issued his veiled warning to the A.S.R. The weather throughout most of the nation had remained calm and beautiful, and farmers were starting to harvest their winter wheat crops throughout the plains states. Forecasters had predicted that this year's harvest would be much larger than those of the previous years.

Schools throughout the nation were closed, their pupils released for the summer months. That lazy time of year when the young foliage on trees and shrubs is heavy and green, and when the outdoors beckons to a people weary of the cold of winter and the bluster of spring, was covering the entire nation—all but the desert southwest, where summer had already arrived with its arid, blistering heat. In Denver, the last of the snow had melted from the highest peaks of the Rocky Mountains, leaving only a white tip on the tallest cone.

In cities and towns throughout the land, the supermarket shelves were filled once again, and the panic buying by the population had dwindled away until it vanished. The days had passed and there had been no attempted invasion so, as is always the case, panic had been replaced by normalcy and the possibility of war had been filed away in dark corners of everyone's minds. Of course, the news each day contained items about raids across the border and isolated military actions in which fierce, tiny battles occurred, but there had been no invasion. It was early summer, time for vacations and picnics in the park or along the bank of a sparkling stream, a time for outdoor recreation of any type, the traditional time of year when weddings and honeymoons occurred. It was not a time when wars began and young people by the hundreds died on a battlefield.

Michael Knowlton, like the rest of his countrymen, felt the lazy pleasure of this early summer season. He had been tempted many times to walk out of this office, get into his personal car, and drive far away into the foothills of the Rockies, somewhere around the Spanish Peaks, and just vanish until this crisis had departed. Instead, he must remain behind his desk and monitor each individual action as these two nations probed each other for weaknesses. For the past week, the border raids by A.S.R. military squads had been increasing in numbers and strength. The most recent one had involved several hundred men on each side and casualties had been heavy. Thirty-four parents in this land were being notified today of the loss of their son.

Another nine had been lost when a plane carrying troops from the front to the southwestern states had crashed in west Texas. This had been the only tragic incident to mar the transfer of this contingent and, by now, they were scattered from Corpus Christi to San Diego. The flood of illegal immigrants had been slowed but not halted, but it was a small victory because the tide had been reduced from thousands each day to only a few hundred. And this troop transfer appeared to have been accomplished without the A.S.R. becoming aware of the withdrawal from along the Mississippi front.

The last of the carrier-based planes had been ferried to small airfields along the Mississippi, far enough away from the border to be hidden from watchers on the east bank, and the carriers had been ordered out of port to prevent any possibility of an A.S.R. agent reporting the total absence of airplanes on their decks. The carriers would remain a few miles offshore until this affair was over, one way or the other.

It had been relatively simple to transfer supplies of ammunition and fuel to storage sites near these airfields and now everything was in place. When the A.S.R. launched its assault, its troops would be strafed unmercifully while they were crossing the river. Simultaneously, those on the other bank waiting to cross would also become targets for the low-flying aircraft from the carriers. Loss of life, Knowlton knew, would be terrifying because the invaders wouldn't be prepared to protect themselves from this type of defense. A part of his mind, that part containing his conscience, had to be kept closed at all times because of the carnage he would create in this action.

The new communications room in the mansion was completed and had been tested repeatedly. Equipment installed in this room would permit him, at any time, to monitor actions along the front on television screens fed from cameras on the ground and others mounted in a communications satellite used normally by the networks. Using his emergency powers, the President had commandeered this satellite but, until action began, the television networks could continue to use it. For what he had in mind, access to this satellite was vital. When hostilities began, most of his time would be spent in that communications room, watching each of the screens fixedly, hoping forlornly that his troops, alone, would be able to repel the assault.

Each day for Knowlton was a duplicate of the one before it. He would arise very early and have his usual coffee downstairs, after which he rushed through his morning shower and shave to permit him to arrive at his office well before seven o'clock. After a quick glance at the night's bulletins to see if any new crisis had erupted, he would spend most of the next hour with Ron Knecht, organizing and coordinating the routine domestic duties of the Presidency. All of these were being handled by Knecht in the name of the President. This freed Knowlton from all but the crisis the nation was about to face.

Knecht was hardly out of the door each morning before the President began checking the television scanners and studying the reports from along the Mississippi. To save time, he often abandoned his customary notes and instead used a tape recorder for his comments. By the time this task was completed, it was almost nine o'clock, the time when his military commanders arrived each day. They were led by General Rupert Rogers, an Arkansas native and former commander of the mid-continent sector that included Missouri and Arkansas. Rogers also was a specialist in guerrilla warfare and house-to-house combat. He had been promoted by Knowlton to act as his liaison officer with the military departments. This temporary appointment would end when the crisis was resolved, one way or another. Until then, he had become an extension of the Presidential office, running vital errands and providing expert advice.

The daily session devoted to strategy and examination of reports from the front seldom concluded earlier than eleven o'clock and then it was time for a similar session with Congressional leaders, this one devoted to conditions in the beleaguered southwestern states and to the domestic economy of the nation. At all costs, the internal strength of the U.S.A. had to be maintained and the twin ghouls of panic and despondency had to be prevented from gnawing at the populace. A military victory would be meaningless if it was accompanied by a crumbling of the nation's internal structure. Knowlton's policy was to maintain an appearance of complete normalcy until the last possible moment. To accomplish this, he had to rely upon the voluntary support of both houses of Congress.

At these daily meetings he had to exude an air of total and complete confidence, hiding beneath a perfect camouflage the fact that, inside, he was quaking with uncertainty about his ability to manage this crisis. He was neither a military tactician nor a spellbinder able to sell ice cubes in the frozen Arctic. He was only a man who had been moderately successful in Congress and then, probably because it was such a fearsome job, had been elected President.

After a hurried lunch at his desk, the President then would devote an hour or more to an intensive study of the scanners, flipping from one sector along the front to another, meanwhile jotting notes on the yellow pad he always carried with him. When the afternoon shadows began creeping down from the mountain peaks came another, private conference with General Rogers, this one devoted to analysis of the scanner tapes and the points Knowlton had jotted on his pad. The positions and relative strengths of known forces were plotted on a large map of the area along the Mississippi, using colored pins with numerals on their heads. Each numeral referred to a brief typewritten text prepared on the basis of Knowlton's notes and comments by Rogers. This map was kept in the room containing the scanners, away from the view of anyone entering the President's office or conference room. A new map was prepared each day and the previous maps were hung where they were readily available. It was a crude system, but it satisfied the President.

Darkness was enveloping Denver when Michael Knowlton and Lucy sat down to dinner, always until now a leisurely period of the day, one that was devoted to private talk and jokes. During this period each day, the office of President was forgotten and it wasn't uncommon for Knowlton to dine in his shirtsleeves, his necktie discarded for the rest of the day. Once, he had appeared at this table wearing comfortable bedroom slippers. It was a time when he and Lucy became nothing but a man and his wife enjoying a family dinner alone. No more.

From the time when this crisis had begun building toward an inevitable climax, the President had become increasingly silent, absorbed in thoughts that excluded Lucy. When she tried to tell him about her day, or make a joke about some insignificant incident, her husband might or might not respond. Several times, he hadn't even seemed to hear her. He would gobble his food, sit impatiently for a few silent moments and then vanish in the direction of his office and the scanner room.

He seldom returned until almost midnight, leaving Lucy alone in the spacious living quarters of the mansion. One night she had heard a flurry of activity below, the sound of running feet. Looking out of the window, she had spotted her husband on the lawn, gazing absently at the sky and surrounded by panting security guards summoned from throughout the mansion.

As the days passed with each one exactly like its predecessor, Lucy became more and more worried about her husband. This was a stranger, not the man she had married so many years ago. This man was living in another world, one from which she was all but excluded.

Each night since this began she had lain quietly, pretending sleep, until she felt Michael drop with a deep sigh into the bed beside her. Several nights, Lucy had been awakened by his tossing and turning and incoherent muttering from a troubled sleep. Each morning she was awakened when her husband left the bed in response to the clock alarm and, rather than his accustomed stretch, would just plod into the bathroom and then shuffle downstairs to the kitchen.

Over and over, Lucy asked herself the same unanswerable question. *What can I do?* She felt that somehow she was failing Michael. He was carrying this horrifying load of uncertainties and there should be something she could do, some action she could take, to remove part of his burden. Whatever that action was, she couldn't find it. All she could do was wait while the days passed, one by one, and watch her husband destroy himself by his unending tension. *Oh God, let us get out of this alive, whether the nation survives or not, and let us go back home where we belong and forget all about this mansion, this title of President, and about government. Let us just be ourselves, just once more, and not be puppets jumping at the ends of the strings of one crisis after another.*

The days passed, one after another. There were big raids and little raids along the front, and each took its toll on Michael Knowlton. Each one was met by fierce resistance from the defending troops of the U.S.A. and, each time, the invading forces withdrew across the river.

After the fourth day, a definite pattern was detected by Knowlton and General Rogers during their analysis of activity along the front. The invaders were testing their men and equipment in these forays into enemy territory. The raids, which always resulted in heavy losses, were a way to whip their troops into a vengeful frame of mind, eager to stamp out the defending forces who had resulted in the death of their countrymen.

"Primitive tribes used to do this," Rogers explained to Knowlton. "They would send a group of their warriors into a battle they knew would be lost. When the few survivors returned home they would be furious and eager for revenge. By the time they were through, they had the rest of the tribe whipped up into a frenzy and that's when the real attack took place, usually with no enemy survivors."

As a result of this assumption, Knowlton ordered that detailed reports of every action were to be sent to his office immediately, beginning at the time of the assault and including a description of the tactics used. Did the invaders use boats or rafts? Was it a daylight raid or did they slip across during the dark of night? Were the raiders supported by artillery or did they carry portable rocket-launchers? Finally, did they attack a specific target or just raise hell and then withdraw?

A definite, identifiable pattern developed rapidly. The raids were coming with increasing frequency and ferocity, but so far they were still confined to rural areas and into small communities along the river. The Louisiana front remained suspiciously quiet and this worried both the President and Rogers. It was too quiet. Were the raids farther north a ruse to cause the U.S.A. to withdraw troops from Louisiana and assign them to protect Missouri and Arkansas? This question was one of the reasons why the President spent sleepless nights. He would fall asleep almost as soon as his head hit the pillow, a habit that had been with him his entire life. An hour or so later, he now would awaken with a start, leaping almost upright in bed, his mind haunted with visions of armed soldiers pillaging a small midwestern town and leaving its inhabitants dead or maimed. In this dream image, the defenders of the town always were too few and too lightly armed to repel the invaders. When his mind cleared and this ghastly vision evaporated into nothingness, Knowlton would find himself bathed in a cold sweat, sitting there in bed and shaking uncontrollably.

*I'm not cut out to be a soldier,* the President thought to himself after one of these incidents. *How can someone like Rogers remain so calm and look at these attacks as if they were nothing more than games? He doesn't see them as dead civilians guilty only of being in the wrong place at the wrong time, or of mass killing by men who probably never wore a uniform before in their lives. To Rogers, this is like a game of baseball or football where you win or lose according to the strategy you employ and the skill you're able to use. But then, he's a soldier and I'm not. Maybe that's what separates us and makes us different. But I'm learning! For what's ahead, I'd better learn fast, damned fast. How I'd like to just walk away and have all of this disappear like that dream. Fool! It won't disappear and you can't make it disappear, so you'd better learn to live with it. You know what you have to do and when that time comes, you won't have any time for second thoughts or regrets.*

Sighing, he lowered his head back onto the pillow and eventually drifted into a troubled sleep peopled with savage warriors and their victims.

Eventually the probing raids stopped and there came a day in which a serene peace existed all along the front, from Louisiana northward to Wisconsin. Coincidentally, this was also a perfect early summer day with a shimmering sun riding high in the sky and gentle breezes tempering the radiated heat from the land. It was a day when, in more normal times, everyone would have been outdoors or else dozing in the shade of an overhanging porch, doing nothing but taking advantage of this perfect weather. In the towns, people stopped to visit with their neighbors in front of a local store and in the cities, everyone escaped from the dark upstairs apartment or the confines of a suburban home. In Denver, a gentle breeze from New Mexico blew lightly along the foothills of the frontal range of mountains, making the air in Denver light and sweet.

This weather pattern continued for a second day and, once again, there were no raids across the border. The Mississippi could have been a placid giant of a stream lapping its way southward until it emptied into the Gulf of Mexico south of New Orleans. The only sign of the presence of an army was when a brownish-green vehicle could be seen scooting down a highway visible from the western bank of the river. The Knowltons decided to take advantage of this perfect weather and the lull in hostilities by inviting Pat Conway to an informal dinner on the mansion patio. They felt sorry for Conway. They had each other but his wife and family had gone home, where they would remain until this crisis was over.

Michael and Lucy Knowlton were already on the patio when Conway arrived. The President, by his attire, could have been any suburban accountant or storekeeper who wore jeans and a pullover shirt while at home. Lucy was attired in a loose skirt and flowered blouse, the type seen at any picnic or in any park. She was sipping a cold drink while her husband tended the charcoal grill, poking the coals to create a uniform heat. Three large steaks, glistening from the sauce with which they had been brushed, lay on a small metal table beside the grill. It was a scene that could have been duplicated at any suburban home throughout the land.

There was even a musical background. It came from a portable tape player whose speakers gave full orchestral depth to the sounds of the Viennese waltz, the same one Knowlton had played another night when this group tried to relax awhile, a night when this present crisis was new and unknown and could hopefully become only a false alarm creating unfounded temporary fears.

Smiling broadly at the scene, Conway stripped off his coat and tie and sank into one of the metal chairs, accepting an icy drink from Lucy. With the fire burning to his satisfaction, Knowlton plopped the three steaks on the grill, moving them about until they were placed to his satisfaction. Immediately they began to simmer in the radiated heat. Pulling another chair near the grill, the President sank into it and sipped a cold drink Lucy handed to him.

"This is nice," he said, to himself as much as to the others. "It's a hell of a lot better than that job I have. We should do this a lot more than we do."

"There's only one reason why we can't," a smiling Conway retorted. "You're the President and I'm not. If I started spending too much time over here, people would begin to talk."

The evening was an oasis for the three of them, a pleasant haven from which all dimensions of the probable coming invasion were excluded as if it were nothing but a bad dream or an unfounded rumor. They basked in the gentle night breeze floating down from the mountains and their laughter and bantering comments were no different from those heard in any suburban neighborhood in any land able to enjoy peace and prosperity. This was a night none of them would forget for the rest of their lives. It was the beginning of the end of an era, the twilight of the uneasy peace that had prevailed over this divided land mass.

When the steaks had become nothing more than gnawed bones, when the potato salad was gone and the embers in the grill were darkening into dead ashes, the three of them sat slumped comfortably in the heavily padded patio chairs, drowsy from the huge meal and the warm and lazy summer night, whose silence was broken by the faint sounds of insects in the trees and grass and by the soaring majesty of the music from a Vienna as it existed almost a century earlier. On a night like this, it seemed almost sacrilegious to ruffle the peace by loud talk and laughter. When they spoke, it was in low tones audible only among themselves and not loud enough to shatter this very special and peaceful night.

The spell was broken when Knowlton became restless and finally arose after muttering that it was time he checked the communications room. Lucy watched him as he vanished indoors, heading toward the room containing the scanners. She was rigid, her eyes very large and staring at some faraway mental image. Conway remained silent. There was nothing he could do until Lucy returned from her fearful world. Eventually, she sighed and turned desperately toward him. When she began speaking, her voice was strained, each word separated sharply from the others before and after it. She sat rigidly, her hands clasping and kneading themselves desperately in her lap.

"Pat, it's killing him," she almost whispered. "He doesn't know it and he'd never admit it, but it's killing him. A little bit more of him dies every day and there's nothing I can do to help him or stop it. Why did this have to happen to him right now of all times? It's just eating him up, day and night. I've never seen him like this and I don't know what to do to make it better. Pat, what can I do? Is there anything I can do?"

Conway didn't reply immediately. This was a question for which there were no real answers. Throughout history, there had been women like this who had been forced to sit helplessly on the sidelines while their men were consumed by some national or even global catastrophe in which hundreds or thousands or possibly millions of people would die as the direct result of the decisions he made. He recalled reading that in the faraway past, an American president named Lyndon Johnson had lived in agony as the result of a minor war in Asia, an anguish that eventually caused him to forfeit the office he held. What could he tell Lucy, and what could he say? This was a highly personal matter and he was an outsider. Choosing his words very carefully, Conway began to speak.

"You can and you must continue doing exactly what you are doing," he began. "Give him your support and hear him when he wants to speak about it. Don't just listen, but actually hear him and what he's saying. He needs that worse than anything else in this world. You can't ever be a part of what he has to do, or of that part of his life; but what you can do is every bit as important.

"I'm convinced there's going to be a war, and it may get nasty before it's over. He's just like you are. He's never faced this type of situation before and he is feeling his way through it, step by step, and it frightens him just as much as it does you. Give him your support and be there when he needs you, but don't interfere with what he's doing or criticize it—because he doesn't have any choice in the matter. None at all! That's the price of this office he holds. That's about all I can tell you," Conway concluded with an embarrassed chuckle. "So much for the sermon, but I'm always available to you any time you may need me. You and Mike both know that."

Lucy didn't reply at once. They sat there wrapped in the whispering silence of the summer night listening to the tiny voices of the insects and the faint, distant sounds of a city in which people like them were living their everyday lives, going to work each morning and then returning home in the late afternoon hours and now, as the midnight period approached, were preparing to consign this day to their own personal past. She turned toward Conway.

"Thank you," she murmured. "I'll never forget what you said to me, not ever."

The moment was disturbed by the return of the President, who appeared to be hurrying. Reaching the table, he lowered himself into the vacant chair and turned toward Conway. There was a tiny tremor in his voice when he began speaking.

"They're moving," President Knowlton said in a low and private voice. "Our units have picked up signs of movement over there on the other side of the river. It's mainly in Missouri but there's movement at other spots along the border. It looks like something is about to happen within the next day or two. I've put all of our units on alert and Rogers will meet me here early tomorrow morning.

"I had hoped we could avoid this. That's why I've stalled along and tried everything I knew to postpone it, maybe long enough for someone with reason to prevail. Now I guess they've decided to do it after all!"

Neither Conway nor Lucy replied. There was nothing that could be said. This might be the last night of peace any of them would ever see and be able to enjoy. Wars, Conway thought idly, probably always began just like this with a period of stalling and probing, followed by a sudden assault upon the opposing power. At this point, just before the spark ignited, both sides always were confident of victory and the dismal truth wouldn't be revealed until it was too late for any retreat to sanity. By then there would be a winner and a loser, and there would also be casualties—always too many casualties, with most of them innocent men who never knew they were only pawns sacrificed on the altar of a victory that might never materialize.

Excusing himself, Conway departed from the ruined celebration and left Knowlton and Lucy alone on the deserted patio. They were just standing there, unmoving figures on the patio, outlined in the faint light from the darkening grill and the soft bulbs hanging from nearby trees. They never heard the door close behind him when Conway entered the mansion and continued through it, eventually reaching his car and returning to his dark and empty house.

The initial probes across the Mississippi were cautious affairs to learn the extent of resistance by the defenders, little more than raids by assault troops in flatboats powered by outboard motors and upon which one or more rocket launchers had been installed. Rays of the morning sun were barely touching the tips of trees on the western bank when the first squads headed across the river. This was the same type of raid that had been occurring for the past two weeks, but with one major difference. All of the earlier assaults had been isolated, hit-and-run incidents—whereas today's raids were occurring simultaneously from southern Arkansas to Iowa.

President Knowlton, General Rogers and three military aides had been in the scanner and communications room since four o'clock that morning, called there by the President as a result of the earlier warning messages received while he was on the patio with Lucy and Conway. These communications from along the front hadn't contained any startling facts but their tone had made Knowlton suspicious. Activity had continued on the eastern bank well after nightfall. That in itself was unusual. The hooded flashlights of scouting parties had been observed near the water's edge; Knowlton thought these A.S.R. units might be looking for obstructions that could prevent the launching of invasion rafts or boats. After darkness had covered the land, watchers on the western bank had reported mechanical sounds from across the river, sounds that could have been made by tractors hauling boats to the riverside.

Even though he felt somewhat foolish doing it, the President had ordered a full alert and called a meeting of his executive defense council for early the following morning. Rogers and aides were ordered to bring shaving gear and be prepared for an extended stay in the executive quarters. Beds had been made ready in a dormitory room within the barracks. In taking these unusual steps the President had been acting on nothing more than a hunch, because there was really nothing in the overnight communications which would indicate conclusively that an invasion was being launched. Now he was glad he had made this decision.

Throughout the morning, the probing assaults continued along the border. In each case, they were met by heavy gunfire from the defenders hunkering in rifle pits previously dug on high ground that provided an unobstructed view of the riverfront. Losses by the invaders were very heavy. Most of the bodies lying along the bank were as lifeless as rags, while others tried painfully to drag themselves to shelter or back to their landing craft. It was almost noon before the first assaults began in Louisiana, beginning with half-hearted probes near Baton Rouge and below New Orleans and then expanding to include attempted landings throughout the length of the state.

At noon, the group in the communications room ate sandwiches prepared in the mansion kitchen and drank coffee from the constantly-replenished electric pot in one corner of their room. Their eyes alternated between the scanner screens and messages received on the facsimile machine. Seated at a small desk in full view of the screens, General Rogers kept the white telephone held to his ear and issued quiet, continuous orders to the troops in the field. Other than the droning monotone of his voice, the room was unnaturally quiet. The sound of President Knowlton's heels as he paced from one location to another made staccato reports that ricocheted across the silence. At some point during the morning, the President had shed his necktie.

As the afternoon hours passed with an infuriating slowness, the ferocity of the invasion raids dwindled and, by the time the shadows were starting to lengthen on the trees, the invaders began withdrawing across the river, back to the eastern bank. Here and there, a few dug-in squads remained on the western side of the river, hunkering within a beachhead they had established. During the coming night, parties of the defending troops would eliminate them and leave no survivors. By now, Knowlton and his military aides had been inside the communications room for more than twelve hours. For all practical purposes, the routine duties of governing this nation had been handled by Ron Knecht, the executive aide.

Shadows were creeping down the slopes of the mountains west of Denver before all sectors along the Mississippi front reported an end to the day's activities and carnage. Rogers arose from behind his little desk, stretched and headed for the restroom. Knowlton felt there would be time for a quick trip into the mansion to let Lucy know the nation still survived, and also that he planned to spend the night in the communications center. Something about this abortive invasion bothered him. Each assault began exactly as he pictured a beachhead to be, complete with supporting fire from heavy guns on the eastern shore, but no effort was made to penetrate beyond the riverbank. All the invaders did was land, charge inland until they drew fire from the dug-in defenders and then, during the late afternoon, they paddled back across the river. This, he thought, was a hell of a way to run a war.

Rogers agreed, but his analysis was more grim. Today's activities were, he explained, nothing more than a testing of the defenses and the degree of defensive firepower that could be directed toward the riverfront. He called today's action a "red herring," a costly prelude to the real effort that would occur, very likely, within the next two days. He predicted that it would begin with massive movements of troops across the river during the darkest hours of the night, followed by a smashing blow inland at dawn.

"That's how I'd do it," he explained to the President. "If this was my invasion, I'd try to secure a foothold at night and be ready to roll inland as soon as the sun appeared. I'd pick the places easiest to cross and capture and then dig in there until I had my heavy artillery and my wheels across, and then I'd hit my target with everything I had."

That made sense to the President. He was glad now he had resisted the almost overpowering urge to order strafing attacks by the carrier-based aircraft secreted on country airstrips along the river. Rogers had agreed. It would amount to overkill and also alert the enemy to the existence of an additional weapon. Knowlton was appalled at the loss of life in today's little assaults. He had watched the casualty reports as they arrived on the facsimile machines. As the hours passed, it became obvious the military leaders of the A.S.R. had utterly no regard for the lives of their troops. Entire landing squads had been slaughtered along the bank of the river.

This thought was in his mind as the President made his way to the living quarters in the mansion. By now he was haggard and unshaven, and his walk had slowed to the pace of an elderly man. Lucy stared at him as he entered and sank gratefully into a soft, overstuffed chair. He looked up at her and smiled, but it wasn't his normal smile. To Lucy, it resembled the brave grimace that accompanies pain. Because she needed to know, she asked the question that had been bothering her as the hours passed, one after the other.

"What happened today?" she asked in a tiny, hushed voice. "Are we at war? Are we being invaded?"

"Not yet," her husband responded after a deep sigh. "There were raids all up and down the river but now they've withdrawn, back onto the other side. Rogers and I believe this was just a dress rehearsal and the real thing will happen tomorrow or the next day. I just don't know! God, how I'd like to know what's going to happen so maybe I could do something—anything—to stop it. You didn't see all of those dead bodies today on the screens. Thousands of them! And there's nothing I can do to stop it. Not one damned thing! Whatever I do, it's going to happen. I feel so useless, so damned useless. I didn't run for this damned office to watch people die. I ran so I might be able to keep it from happening.

"Now I feel like a mass murderer, because I gave the orders. I gave the orders that caused all of those people to die. And there will be others, too many others. How can I possibly live with that on my conscience for the rest of my life? How can I?"

Sighing, he rose and headed for the bedroom for a quick shower and a change of clothing. When he emerged later, the dark mood had vanished and, freshly shaved and dressed in clean slacks and shirt, Knowlton greeted Lucy with his familiar smile. Hugging her to him almost desperately, he kissed her and headed back toward the communications room.

Throughout the evening and into the night they did nothing but wait. As darkness silently shrouded the countryside, in Denver and along the Mississippi, the group in the communications room waited impatiently for something to happen along the front, which remained quiet, almost as if no military action had occurred or was imminent. At first General Rogers prowled the room like a caged bear, studying the scanners suspiciously, making endless trips to and from the facsimile machines and scowling at the telephone which failed to ring for other than scheduled routine reports.

The military aides repeatedly studied the day's reports from the field, debating each question raised by some action somewhere along the river. As the hours passed maddeningly, an unnatural quiet settled like a fog over the room. After ten o'clock had come and gone, Rogers made his professional judgment about this absence of any movement anywhere along the front.

"It will come tomorrow morning," he said flatly. "I may be wrong, and I hope I am, but I'm just as certain about this as anything in my life. This is the stage when everything you have is moved up to the jump-off point. They've made their commitment and now they're ready. They'll hit us with everything they've got tomorrow morning. What are your orders, Mr. President?"

"You know what must be done," Knowlton responded in a voice he barely recognized as his own. "This part is in your hands now, so give your orders and let's pray it will be adequate."

Not waiting for a reply because Rogers knew exactly what must be done, the President left the room and headed for his private quarters down the long hallway. Before trying to fall asleep in this strange bed, he had one final chore to handle. He telephoned Ron Knecht and ordered him to take immediate action to invoke the emergency proclamation, the one placing the entire nation into a state of national emergency. With this accomplished, a weary President Knowlton removed his shoes and shirt and sank onto the unfamiliar bed in this sterile and cheerless room only a few feet away from the communications center. Eventually he slept, but his unconscious mind remained peopled with faceless visions of the thousands who had died this day in pointless little battles along the Mississippi.

# 15

They came at dawn, tens of thousands of them crouched down in a polyglot assortment of boats, powered barges and rafts of all descriptions. They came when the first rays of morning sunlight first brushed the tops of trees along the western bank of the Mississippi, all the way down the river from Iowa to Missouri, Arkansas and Louisiana.

When they pushed away from the eastern shoreline, they were silent, nothing more than dark shapes huddled in or upon the boats or barges. The placid silence of this sunny morning was broken by the continuous sputter of outboard engines, a raucous noise that triggered sharp outcries from awakening birds in the trees along both banks of the river.

The supporting artillery fire did not begin until this monstrous floating mass approached the western shoreline. Then, like an unending sheet of flame, it erupted with a continuous roar from heavy guns located several miles inland, away from the riverfront. The first shells of this barrage raked the western shoreline in a sheet of explosions from which uprooted trees, debris and shattered bodies of the defenders erupted.

Ponderously, the shellfire moved inland, away from the waterfront. The armada of small boats and rafts nudged the western bank immediately afterward, disgorging their cargoes of armed assault troops. They leapfrogged ashore, each wave providing covering fire for the units following them. Within minutes a beachhead had been secured in almost a dozen spots along the river, from southern Iowa to Louisiana. Defending forces had been manhandled back away from the riverfront and now were regrouping on higher ground.

President Knowlton had been awakened from his agonized and restless sleep more than an hour earlier. By the time the invasion was launched, he and General Rogers were at their customary locations in the room, where they could watch the scanners and have access to telephones and the facsimile machines. After drowsy morning greetings had been exchanged, they had sat silently drinking coffee and waiting for reports to begin arriving from the front. The aides were at their posts but, like the President and Rogers, had nothing to do but organize themselves for what could be another long and tiring day, waiting in dread for something to happen.

Because it was still dark outside, the scanners were able to provide only shadowy images, a winking light here or the glimmer of moonlight there on the river, caused by reflection from its wavelets. Whenever the facsimile machine chattered to indicate arrival of a routine hourly report from somewhere along the front, the group in this room were momentarily startled. These reports uniformly indicated the unnatural silence still prevailed, all the way from Iowa to Louisiana. Motioning for an aide to take his place in front of the scanners, Rogers headed for the restroom and remained gone for almost fifteen minutes. The President alternated between sitting in his chair and pacing the room impatiently. Doubts were beginning to gnaw at his mind, doubts about his wisdom in placing the nation in a state of emergency. If nothing actually happened, he would look like an excitable fool.

Every man in the room jumped reflexively when every instrument in the room came to life at almost the same moment. The President spilled part of his coffee and absently brushed the puddle from the arm of his chair with his unoccupied hand. Rogers grabbed a telephone with one hand while he ripped facsimile copies from the machine with the other. He motioned to the aides, each of whom was assigned to one sector along the front. Smoothly, they began receiving reports by telephone and making additions or deletions on maps spread before them. While the situation was being clarified militarily, the President was ignored. Involuntarily he looked down at the coffee cup in his hand. The slight, persistent tremor that caused the coffee to jiggle in the cup registered itself in his mind.

*My God,* he said to himself, *it's really happened and where will it all end? According to those screens, even if the light is still faint, the entire length of the river is being crossed and invaded and they're getting the job done. How many young men will die today? A thousand or maybe a million? How many families will be grieving when they get this news, or will they ever get it if we lose this war? We can't lose it. We don't dare lose it or our form of civilization will be lost, maybe for a thousand years. What will happen to Lucy and to me if we lose this? We're not as young as we were once and I don't care about me—not after this—but Lucy must be protected, somehow, against the consequences. She can't have her face pushed into the mud, and that's what will happen if we lose.*

He was jerked back to reality by Rogers, who was motioning for him. Leaping from his chair, the President rushed across the room and began to read the latest reports handed to him by Rogers. They showed a decided lull in activity in Iowa and most of Arkansas. In Missouri and Louisiana the ferocity had, if anything, intensified. At one point in rural Louisiana the invaders had managed to seize an entire town which had barges tied at its docks. The barges were being used now to ferry mobile equipment across the river, mainly trucks and small tanks.

Most of downtown St. Louis was aflame from the artillery barrage to which it had been subjected. Columns of tanks were crossing the bridge from East St. Louis. Steadily, inch by inch, the defending forces were being driven backward by the overpowering weight of this invasion. This was the last facsimile able to be transmitted from St. Louis. In his concluding comments, the operator announced that his machine was being shut down and he was joining the retreat to safer ground in the west.

Without warning, Ron Knecht rushed into the room and motioned to the President. Feeling actually ill, Knowlton crossed the room to where Knecht waited. As soon as the President came near, Knecht began babbling excitedly, the words almost running together in his haste.

"I don't know how much longer I can handle things," he said, almost pleadingly. "The Congress is in an uproar and the telephone lines are all jammed with calls from city officials everywhere in the country. And the news people are about to break down my door for anything I can give them."

Before Knowlton could reply, General Rogers beckoned to him and the President rushed back to the screens. In his brief absence, the scene had changed drastically. Rogers had waited without emotion until Gorcey had committed his entire forces to the river crossing, and then had called the waiting carrier planes into action. Now they were strafing the invaders unmercifully, hitting them with a hail of bullets and rockets. The carnage left from this assault was beyond belief. Bodies floated like leaves in the river and lay strewn across both banks. Several tanks that had been landed on the western shore were aflame. The planes were still zigzagging up and down the channel, firing at anything seen moving.

Knowlton was horrified, both at the results of this aerial assault and at the coldblooded way in which Rogers had waited patiently until the A.S.R. had committed its entire forces before ordering this air strike. If this type of engagement continued for a few more days, thousands of lives would be lost each day it occurred. At least, though, the invasion had been halted for today—but probably not permanently. There would be time now for him to return to his normal chores and remove some of the pressure from Ron Knecht. Rogers could handle things here.

Lucy stared at him when he walked into their living quarters. He was unshaven, rumpled and obviously had slept without undressing. She was so happy to see him, though, that she would have welcomed him if he wore only a barrel. Running to him, Lucy threw her arms around her husband and almost wept with joy. They were safe now. The invasion must have failed or he would not be here now, in his home and obviously in no rush to return to the war room in the office wing. They stood there, just inside the door, with their arms around each other, for several seconds. Neither spoke. Words weren't needed for this moment. Leaning backward in his arms, Lucy asked the question gnawing at her mind.

"Is it over?" she whispered. "They've given it up. I just know they have."

"It isn't over," her husband replied sadly. "It's just over, at least the worst of it, for today. We haven't won and maybe we can't win on the battlefield; but even if we do, the cost will be so high it will ruin this country, maybe for a century or longer. They'll hit us again tomorrow and we'll try to stop them again and it can go on and on like that until we don't have anything or anybody left to stop them.

"I'm just back here this afternoon to meet with the Congressional leaders and make a few appearances so everyone will know I'm still alive and haven't run for cover. That's all. Tonight I have to go back to the war."

The afternoon went swiftly, far too swiftly for a President who had left part of his mind back in that communications room where the fate of the nation was being decided. He briefed the Congressional leaders about the status of the war. He answered questions from reporters for fifteen minutes and he reviewed and approved actions taken during his absence by Knecht, who appreciated the confidence his boss placed in him and his ability to make decisions. Then it was back to the communications center, where Knowlton received a thorough briefing on the day's activities along the front. It had remained virtually quiet but nobody in the room felt it would remain that way. The A.S.R. had made its commitment and now could not afford to back away regardless of the cost in lives and materiel.

The river exploded into flame again the next morning in exactly the same manner as on the previous day. Wave after wave of soldiers crossed the river in boats of every description and they were supported by a continuous bombardment from heavy artillery. Wave after wave of them kept paddling across the river, so many of them the heavy losses seemed insignificant. Overhead, the planes from the carriers screamed and dived upon the human carpet, shredding it with gunfire and missiles. This scene of horror went on and on and on as the invaders kept throwing men and weapons at the river regardless of losses. Several rafts containing ammunition exploded after direct hits from missiles fired by the screaming carrier planes. When this happened, bodies—some of them afire—were thrown in all directions.

Gradually the invaders began to overwhelm the defending forces by sheer numbers. The turning point came when, one by one, the planes abandoned combat and flew away because their ammunition was exhausted. Finally only one plane was left. Using everything it had, the pilot scored a direct hit on a large munitions barge and then flew away after wagging the plane's wings at the defenders as a final salute.

Ashore, the invading armies had begun moving inland away from the river, rushing along the highways in the trucks ferried across the Mississippi and terrorizing small communities as they passed.

The President watched in horror as his armies were overwhelmed by the limitless numbers of invaders, who obviously cared nothing about the number of lives lost. He watched Rogers while the man tried vainly to stop this massive assault that consumed everything in its path. An icy chill replaced the horror the President had felt. Finally the moment he had dreaded arrived. General Rogers turned to Knowlton and, in a tightly controlled monotone, made the announcement the President had hoped would never come.

"There's nothing more we can do," Rogers said. "There are just too many of them for us to hold back. There's only one thing left to do. It's time now to do it."

Knowlton hesitated, not replying. This wasn't the way he had pictured it. He felt an overpowering urge to run from this room and hide, either in the living quarters of the mansion or somewhere in the Rockies, some isolated pocket where he could never be found and where the scenes of these past days would be erased gradually from his mind. He felt dirty, chilled and somehow to blame for this disaster. How many had died in these last few days because of him and the decisions or actions for which he was responsible?

The general's words repeated themselves dismally in his mind. *It's time! It's time! It's time!* How easy it would be to pretend he wasn't here today but instead was with Lucy on a beach somewhere, or in a room that was private to them alone, or anywhere but in this grubby and cluttered room where scanner screens mocked the viewers and where only dismal news spewed from the facsimile machines.

The President arose and stood immobile for a moment. He took a deep breath, held it for several seconds and then exhaled with a prolonged hiss. He walked across the room stiffly, like an automaton. When he reached the cabinet installed days ago as a precaution, he unlocked its door and the entire front swung aside to come to rest against the wall. Inside was an extremely large video screen and a small keyboard with one key hidden beneath a red cover punctuated by two keyholes. A small stool stood beneath the keyboard.

After a moment's hesitation, Knowlton reached forward and flipped a switch on the keyboard. As images started to form on the massive screen he withdrew another key from his pocket, this one painted red to match the red cover, and inserted it into one of the keyholes. Then he paused, glancing at Rogers. Before moving, the general studied the scanners and minutely read each bulletin from the facsimile machine. He glanced from one aide to another as they sat immobile, looking from the President to General Rogers. One by one, each nodded his head and then looked away as if ashamed of the action.

Slowly, very slowly, Rogers rose from his chair and walked forward to join Knowlton at the cabinet. From a pocket, he produced a red key similar to the President's and inserted it into the other keyhole in the red cover on the keyboard. Holding it gingerly as if it were filled with explosive, the general turned his key to match the other and then stepped backward, leaving the President standing alone in front of the keyboard and the huge video screen which, by now, had produced a clear, sparkling image.

It was a view of Washington, D.C., produced by a camera mounted on a satellite floating far away in the sky above the capital city and magnified many dimensions, magnified so much that individual cars could be seen scooting down the streets and knots of pedestrians were sharp and clear in the heart of the city. A light summer breeze was blowing in Washington. The foliage on the many trees shimmered as it tossed gently back and forth. There were small boats on the Potomac and an airliner was seen landing at Washington National. The dome of the old Capitol Building glistened with a coppery sheen and a long black shadow was being cast by the

Washington Monument. Early summer was the time of year when Washington was at its best, even in this era of despotic government where people were made to live like animals because of the repeated errors made by eager but ignorant previous generations of bureaucrats and governments. Today, in this screen image, Washington was at its best, like a painting that has been animated.

Standing before the keyboard and this image, President Knowlton turned to Rogers and spoke so faintly his words were barely audible.

"One final check," he murmured. "Give it one final check."

Rogers returned to his scanners and the facsimile machine and studied each image and message carefully, then turned back to the President and shook his head slowly from side to side. His face was grave and he stood at attention, waiting patiently with resignation.

The President reached to one side of the keyboard and produced a worn Bible in which one passage had been marked by a scrap of paper inserted between two pages. The President leaned forward and began reading this passage to himself, his lips moving silently as one finger crept forward until it rested on the red key that had been hidden beneath the locked red cover. His finger continued resting on this key until he had finished reading the passage in the Bible. Then, as if afraid to hesitate, his finger stabbed downward on the key. He turned to the others in the room.

"May God have mercy on our souls," the President said softly as every eye in the room turned upward toward the huge video screen inside the cabinet.

Ashen faced, the President joined the others in watching as the Potomac shoreline, the gleaming Capitol dome, the Washington Monument and the crowds on the streets all vanished in a hideous sheen, a blinding glare that billowed across the screen, a silvery glare containing suggestions of red and orange. Simultaneously, everyone in the room sucked in his breath with a faint hiss, the only sound breaking the absolute silence of this cubicle. And then the glare evaporated and the picture returned to the screen.

Where Washington had stood, where the domed outline of the Capitol had been visible and where the airliner had been seen floating into Washington National Airport, there was nothing. All of it was gone, the monuments, the governmental buildings, the people on the streets, and everyone who had been guiding the A.S.R. juggernaut to victory over the U.S.A., all of them were gone forever.

Where they had stood, walked, laughed and made plans, there now was nothing, absolutely nothing but a barren gray plane from which tendrils of smoke or possibly ash dust arose and drifted away in the light summer breeze that until now had made this a perfect day in Washington, a day for anyone to be outdoors enjoying the sunny breeze or simply being alive, the type of day that comes only in early summer to Washington. But Washington no longer existed. Instead of flowers and lawns like carpets, there was only ash from which whispers of dust arose in the soft breeze. The war was over.